D0855540

Executive Compensation
Best Practices

Executive
Compensation
Best Practices

FREDERICK D. LIPMAN
STEVEN E. HALL

WILEY

John Wiley & Sons, Inc.

HD
4965.2
.L57
2008

This book is printed on acid-free paper. ∞

Copyright © 2008 by Frederick D. Lipman and Steven E. Hall. All rights reserved.
Published by John Wiley & Sons, Inc., Hoboken, New Jersey.
Published simultaneously in Canada.

No part of this publication may be reproduced, stored in a retrieval system, or transmitted in any form
or by any means, electronic, mechanical, photocopying, recording, scanning, or otherwise, except as
permitted under Section 107 or 108 of the 1976 United States Copyright Act, without either the prior
written permission of the Publisher, or authorization through payment of the appropriate per-copy fee to
the Copyright Clearance Center, Inc., 222 Rosewood Drive, Danvers, MA 01923, 978-750-8400, fax
978-646-8600, or on the web at www.copyright.com. Requests to the Publisher for permission should
be addressed to the Permissions Department, John Wiley & Sons, Inc., 111 River Street, Hoboken, NJ
07030, 201-748-6011, fax 201-748-6008, or online at http://www.wiley.com/go/permissions.

Limit of Liability/Disclaimer of Warranty: While the publisher and author have used their best efforts
in preparing this book, they make no representations or warranties with respect to the accuracy or
completeness of the contents of this book and specifically disclaim any implied warranties of merchant-
ability or fitness for a particular purpose. No warranty may be created or extended by sales representatives or written sales materials. The advice and strategies contained herein may not be suitable for your
situation. You should consult with a professional where appropriate. Neither the publisher nor author
shall be liable for any loss of profit or any other commercial damages, including but not limited to
special, incidental, consequential, or other damages.

For general information on our other products and services, or technical support, please contact our
Customer Care Department within the United States at 800-762-2974, outside the United States at
317-572-3993 or fax 317-572-4002.

Wiley also publishes its books in a variety of electronic formats. Some content that appears in print may
not be available in electronic books.

For more information about Wiley products, visit our Web site at http://www.wiley.com.

Library of Congress Cataloging-in-Publication Data:

Lipman, Frederick D.
     Executive compensation best practices / Frederick D. Lipman, Steven E. Hall.
       p. cm.
  Includes index.
     ISBN 978-0-470-22379-6 (cloth)
       1. Executives—Salaries, etc. 2. Compensation management. I. Hall, Steven E. II. Title.
  HD4965.2.L57   2008
  658.4'072—dc22

                                        2007045581

Printed in the United States of America

10 9 8 7 6 5 4 3 2 1

To
Jordan Sienna Lipman

University Libraries
Carnegie Mellon University
Pittsburgh, PA 15213-3890

Contents

Preface

There are many conscientious members of the compensation committee of the board of directors of public companies. This book is written for them as well as for executives who want to use best practices in negotiating their own compensation packages. The best practices suggested in this book are, in many cases, also applicable to not-for-profit organizations and private companies.

Best practices do not necessarily lead to lowering executive compensation. In fact, as discussed in Chapter 4 of this book, they may require an increase in executive compensation in order to compete with private equity funds. Indeed, the recent wave of private equity fund acquisitions of public companies is partly due to the failure or unwillingness of compensation committees to provide equity compensation to senior management that is competitive with private equity funds. A stingy compensation committee can be as harmful to the organization as an overly generous one.

Executive compensation practices are under enormous scrutiny from activist shareholders, corporate governance rating groups, the media, and lawmakers. Outrage has been repeatedly expressed by both the media and the public over allegedly excessive executive compensation. Corporate governance groups have accused boards of directors and their compensation committees of mass giveaways of shareholder wealth to greedy CEOs. As of April 1, 2007, investors had made 266 proposals related to executive pay for insertion in public company proxy statements, about twice as many as in 2006 according to Institutional Shareholders Services. A bill has been introduced in the U.S. Congress to require an "advisory" vote by shareholders on CEO compensation and one state (North Dakota) adopted such a law.

Equally important is the view of corporate governance rating agencies who are judging the quality of the board decision-making process by the disclosures required to be made concerning executive compensation. For example, Moody's Investors Services, Inc. has stated that they will analyze executive compensation arrangements with a view to "assess how favorable the terms are compared to peers and consider what this suggests regarding the quality of the board decision-making process."[1] Institutional investors may well refuse to support the reelection of directors whose decision-making on executive compensation has been criticized.

The public controversy over executive pay has resulted from the failure of compensation committees to use "best practices" in establishing CEO compensation and in the failure to adequately explain to shareholders both the methodology used and the growing competition for executive talent with private equity funds. The Securities and Exchange Commission (SEC) attempted to remedy the full disclosure problem by requiring a very comprehensive discussion in public filings of the executive compensation methodology practiced by public companies in a section of these documents called "Compensation Committee Discussion and Analysis." However, it is not enough to make full disclosure of the methodology unless the compensation committee also uses best practices.

Best practices will vary with each public company or other organization. However, this book attempts to explain what should be considered universal best practices for all public companies. In addition, many of the best practices recommended for public companies are equally applicable to not-for-profit organizations and private companies.

WHAT ARE BEST PRACTICES?

Best executive compensation practices are those that align the rewards to the executive with what is critical for the company to succeed in both the short-term and long-term and to accomplish its strategic plan. Best practices should create conditions in which executives feel a strong commitment to the results. However, best practices can vary between industries and between companies in the same industry. Therefore, the best

---

[1] "A User's Guide to the SEC's New Rules for Reporting Executive Pay," April 2007, p. 4.

executive compensation practices discussed in this book must be tempered by the particular facts and circumstances of each company and of each executive within the company.

This book provides a list of best practices for the compensation committee of the board of directors. It is understood, however, that the compensation committee may delegate some of its duties to management, so long as it provides effective oversight over management and retains full responsibility for these best practices.

ORGANIZATION OF BOOK

Chapter 1, entitled "Introduction," is devoted primarily to a discussion of whether a CEO should be rewarded or punished for events beyond the CEO's control (as to which there is no best practice) and two conflicting theories for the rise in CEO compensation. We also quote Warren Buffett's theories on executive compensation, compare CEO exit packages with the compensation of sports and entertainment celebrities, and review the benefits of following good corporate governance.

Chapter 2, entitled "Motivating Executive Performance," explains the necessity of establishing goals and objectives for executives before performance, and of tying executive officer goals into the strategic plan of the company as well as the year-to-year budget. This chapter also deals with motivating executive performance through use of both long-term and short-term incentives and minimum equity requirements and discusses some of the unintended adverse consequences of misdirected executive compensation programs.

One method of establishing competitive compensation is through using peer groups and benchmarking. Chapter 3, entitled "Peer Groups and Benchmarking," reviews the best practices in establishing peer groups and benchmarking, the use of which will help avoid "headline risk" for the company.

Chapter 4, entitled "Competing With Private Equity Funds," discusses the competition with private equity groups for executive talent. We advance the theory that the significant number of private equity transactions to acquire public companies is partly the result of the unwillingness or inability of the compensation committee to provide sufficient equity incentives to management to remain part of a public company.

Despite the ebbs and flows in private equity acquisitions of public companies, which tend to vary with the ability to obtain debt leverage, the lead author believes that private equity competition for executive talent will become a permanent fixture in the future in establishing executive compensation.

Properly explaining executive compensation decisions to shareholders is crucial to maintaining good shareholder relationships. Chapter 5, entitled "Explaining Executive Compensation to Shareholders," contains illustrations of some of the best practices by major companies in describing to shareholders executive compensation goals and objectives. In this chapter we suggest that alternative Summary Compensation Tables may be necessary to adequately explain executive compensation if the SEC's official Summary Compensation Table is misleading.

Compensation committees must understand the full accounting, cash and tax effect of their executive compensation decisions and should use tally sheets. Chapter 6, entitled "Compensation Committee Ordinary Operations" reviews the best practices in the routine operations of compensation committees and should be read in conjunction with Chapters 7 and 8.

One of the major functions of the compensation committee is to negotiate executive employment and severance agreements, with both new and existing executives. Chapter 7, entitled "Negotiating Executive Employment and Severance Agreements," discusses strategies that can be used by compensation committees to obtain reasonable compensation levels from newly hired executives as well as negotiating executive employment and severance agreements with existing executives. Advanced planning by the compensation committee of the desired compensation range of potential new CEOs helps to prevent overpaying for executive talent.

Since the structure of the compensation committee and the processes followed by that committee must, by SEC rules, be disclosed to investors, it is important that the compensation committee adhere to best practices. Chapter 8, entitled "Compensation Committee Structure and Process," explains the best practices in the procedures followed by the compensation committee. In this chapter, we discuss different views as to what are the best practices, including whether or not two consultants should always be used (one for the board and one for management) and periodically changed, practices that we do not necessarily endorse.

Chapter 9, entitled "Equity Incentive Choices," explains various equity incentive choices available to the compensation committee, including the advantages and disadvantages of each choice.

According to an academic paper entitled "Lucky CEOs,"[2] there can be as many as 720 public companies that have option backdating problems. Chapter 10, entitled "Option Granting Practices" reviews the best practices in granting stock options and other equity incentive alternatives.

Independent directors should establish compensation for the members of the board of directors. Chapter 11, entitled "Director Compensation," deals with the delicate subject of director compensation and best practices to avoid charges of conflict of interest.

Executives should fully understand the best practices in negotiating their own compensation packages. Chapter 12, entitled "Negotiating for the Executive," presents best practices which should be followed by CEOs and other executives in negotiating their own employment and severance agreements. This chapter is written from the viewpoint of the executive rather than from the viewpoint of the company.

Compensation committees and executives should fully understand the federal income tax implications of their compensation decisions. Chapter 13, entitled "Executive Compensation and Section 409A of the Internal Revenue Code" deals with complicated provisions of new Section 409A of the Internal Revenue Code.

Appendix A of the book provides a model compensation committee charter for a public company. Appendix B summarizes the SEC's executive compensation disclosure rules which were adopted in 2006. Appendix C provides an example of an employment agreement that is favorable to the executive. Appendix D provides an example of a broad-based flexible public company equity incentive plan. Appendix E is for companies that may have trouble with the SEC because of past option granting practices. It gives an example of search terms required by the SEC enforcement staff in situations in which there may be option backdating problems. The breath of the SEC subpoena should serve as a wake-up call to compensation committees who have not yet reviewed their past option granting practices. Appendix F contains a simplified explanation for executives and other employees of stock options.

---

[2]"Lucky CEOs," Professor Bebchuk, Harvard Law School Program on Corporate Governance, November 16, 2006.

Acknowledgments

The authors wish to acknowledge the assistance of the following attorneys at Blank Rome LLP in preparing this book: Daniel R. Blickman, Esq.; Joseph T. Gulant, Esq.; Wilhelm L. Gruszecki, Esq.; Barry L. Klein, Esq.; David M. Kuchinos, Esq. and Jane K. Storero, Esq. The authors also acknowledge Michael Gevaryahu, a summer clerk at Blank Rome LLP, who assisted in proofreading the book.

Barbara Helverson, the excellent secretary to Frederick D. Lipman, served as the main editor and showed great patience in typing, retyping, and further retyping the manuscript for this book.

CHAPTER 1

Introduction

SHOULD THE CEO BE REWARDED OR PUNISHED FOR EVENTS BEYOND THE CEO'S CONTROL?

BEST PRACTICE

Companies should be prepared to articulate a consistent and defensible executive compensation policy when called upon by shareholders or the media.

Many investors are shocked by the size of CEO compensation, particularly in situations in which the CEO was seemingly the beneficiary of good luck. In the case of Exxon, the good luck was the increase in worldwide oil prices, which the media presumed was not the result of CEO efforts.

It was reported that Lee Raymond, the retired Chairman of Exxon, was paid $51.1 million in 2005, the equivalent of $141,000 a day, nearly $6,000 an hour. It was also reported that Exxon gave Lee Raymond one of the most generous retirement packages in history, nearly $400 million, including pension, stock options, and other perks, such as a $1 million consulting contract, two years of home security, personal security, a car and driver, and use of an Exxon corporate jet for professional purposes. Exxon defended Raymond's compensation, noting that during the twelve years that he ran the company, Exxon became the world's largest oil company and its stock price went up 500% (as of April 2006).

Given the time pressures and other constraints media reporters placed on Exxon's public relations personnel, this may have been as good a response as possible under the circumstances. However, the Exxon defense was unconvincing to skeptics because it failed to articulate an acceptable CEO compensation theory. For example, Exxon could have stated, if true, that Lee Raymond developed a strategy to expand the company's oil production and reserves, thereby positioning Exxon to benefit from the rise in oil prices, or that Mr. Raymond's compensation was developed after an extensive competitive analysis. Merely stating that the Exxon shareholders also benefited from the rise in oil prices was not a completely satisfactory explanation for the large amounts paid to Mr. Raymond. Moreover, given what happened to former CEO of Home Depot Mr. Robert Nardelli, it is possible that Mr. Raymond would have been fired had the stock price fallen during his tenure, even though due to events also beyond his control.

Those who believe that good luck should not be the basis for increasing CEO compensation should ask themselves whether bad luck should also be ignored. If a CEO is to be rewarded for events beyond the CEO's control that increase the profits and stock price of the company, then, arguably, the CEO should likewise be punished for events beyond the CEO's control that adversely affect the profits and stock price of the company. If it is not feasible to punish the CEO for events beyond his or her control, then, arguably, the CEO should not be paid more than what is competitively required to retain the CEO even if very favorable events occur over which the CEO had no control, which increase the company's profits and stock price.

The counter-argument is that CEOs are being held responsible for increasing the price of the stock and are being punished for failing to do so even if their operational performance was beyond reproach. According to a Booz Allen Hamilton study[1], almost 1 in 3 CEOs were forced out of office in 2006, compared to 1 in 8 in 1995. One example would be Robert Nardelli of Home Depot who was terminated based upon the failure of the Home Depot stock to appreciate, even though he was successful

---

[1]Lucier, Weeler and Habbel, "The Era of the Inclusive Leader," (May 22, 2007) contained on the Booz Allen Hamilton website: www.boozeallen.com

in significantly increasing the profits of Home Depot. See "CEO Forced Exit Packages" later in this chapter.

Professors Bebchuk and Fried[2] make a similar argument with regard to stock option and other equity-based compensation. They argue that executives should not be rewarded for increases in stock prices that are no greater than indexes for the market in general and, therefore, stock options and other equity grants should only reward the executive for increases in value over and above increases in these stock market indexes.[3] By rewarding executives only for stock price increases that are arguably due to their effort, the executive does not profit from events beyond his or her control.

WARREN E. BUFFETT ON EXECUTIVE COMPENSATION

The concept of rewarding or punishing CEOs for events beyond their control has caught the attention of Warren E. Buffett. The following are excerpts of Mr. Buffett's engaging views on executive compensation (including compensation of directors)[4]:

> "In selecting a new director, we were guided by our long-standing criteria, which are that board members be owner-oriented, business-savvy, interested, and truly independent. I say 'truly' because many directors who are now deemed independent by various authorities and observers are far from that, relying heavily as they do on directors' fees to maintain their standard of living. These payments, which come in many forms, often range between $150,000 and $250,000 annually, compensation that may approach or even exceed all other income of the 'independent' director. And – surprise, surprise – director compensation has soared in recent years, pushed up by recommendations from corporate America's favorite consultant, Ratchet, Ratchet and Bingo. (The name may be phony, but the action it conveys is not.) . . .

---

[2]"Pay Without Performance," Harvard University Press, 2004.

[3]A similar argument for indexing stock option exercise prices was made by Alfred Rappaport in an article entitled "New Thinking on How to Link Executive Pay with Performance," which appears in the Harvard Business Review on Compensation (2001).

[4]2006 Annual Report of Berkshire Hathaway, Inc.

"When we use [CEO] incentives – and these can be large – they are always tied to the operating results for which a given CEO has authority. We issue no lottery tickets that carry payoffs unrelated to business performance. *If a CEO bats .300, he gets paid for being a .300 hitter, even if circumstances outside of his control cause Berkshire to perform poorly. And if he bats .150, he doesn't get a payoff just because the successes of others have enabled Berkshire to prosper mightily.* An example: We now own $61 billion of equities at Berkshire, whose value can easily rise or fall by 10% in a given year. Why in the world should the pay of our operating executives be affected by such $6 billion swings, however important the gain or loss may be for shareholders? . . . [Emphasis Supplied]

"CEO perks at one company are quickly copied elsewhere. 'All the other kids have one' may seem a thought too juvenile to use as a rationale in the boardroom. But consultants employ precisely this argument, phrased more elegantly of course, when they make recommendations to comp committees.

"Irrational and excessive comp practices will not be materially changed by disclosure or by 'independent' comp committee members. Indeed, I think it's likely that the reason I was rejected for service on so many comp committees was that I was regarded as *too* independent. Compensation reform will only occur if the largest institutional shareholders – it would only take a few – demand a *fresh* look at the whole system. The consultants' present drill of deftly selecting 'peer' companies to compare with their clients will only perpetuate present excesses."

CEO COMPENSATION THEORIES

There are two rival theories for the rise in CEO compensation. The first theory blames lax corporate governance by directors of public companies, many of whom are selected by and beholden to the CEO. This is the Warren Buffett theory.

The second theory ascribes the increase to economic factors, including globalization and technology and other macroeconomic factors that have increased the productivity of a select few superstars. For example, a paper by Professors Xavier Gabaix, (Massachusetts Institute of Technology) and Agustin Landier, (New York University) dated May 8, 2006 entitled "Why Has CEO Pay Increased So Much?" states that a "large part of the rise in CEO compensation in the U.S. economy is explained without assuming managerial entrenchment, mishandling of options, or theft."[5]

> "Historically, in the U.S. at least, the rise of CEO compensation coincided with an increase in market capitalization of the largest firms. Between 1980 and 2000, the average asset value of the largest 500 firms increased by a factor of 6 (i.e. a 500% increase). The model predicts that CEO pay should increase by a factor of 6. The result is driven by the scarcity of CEOs, competitive forces, and the six-fold increase in stock market valuations. Incentive concerns or managerial entrenchment play strictly no role in this model of CEO compensation. In our view, the rise in CEO compensation is a simple mirror of the rise in the value of large US companies since the 1980s."

In 1981, Professor Sherwin Rosen of the University of Chicago wrote a paper entitled "The Economics of Superstars" which he characterized as follows: "The phenomenon of Superstars, wherein relatively small numbers of people earn enormous amounts of money and dominate the activities in which they engage, seems to be increasingly important in the modern world."[6]

Professor Rosen cites examples of a small number of popular comedians who can earn extraordinary sums as a result of the capacity of television to reach popular masses. He found two common elements in all of the so-called Superstars: "First, a close connection between personal reward and a size of one's own market; and second, a strong tendency for both market size and reward to be skewed toward the most talented people in the activity."

Professor David H. Author (Massachusetts Institute of Technology) cites advances in communications technology, including the Internet, for the proposition that there are "winner take all markets," (i.e., allowing individuals with extraordinary talent to serve substantial markets almost single-handedly) and that communications technologies may displace

---

[5]Gabaix, Xavier and Landier, Augustin, "Why Has CEO Pay Increased so Much?" (May 8, 2006). MIT Department of Economics Working Paper No. 06-13

[6]Prof Sherwin Rosen, "Economics of Superstars," The American Scholar, Volume 52, Number 4, Autumn 1983.

lesser talents, redistributing a larger share of the rewards to a smaller number of superstars.[7]

A January 9, 2007 blog by Stephen Kaplan of the University of Chicago[8] entitled "Are CEOs of U.S. Public Companies Really Overpaid?" makes some of the following points in defense of CEO compensation:

- The CEO job at large public companies is less secure today than it has been over the last 35 years, with CEO turnover at Fortune 500 companies running at over 16% per year since 1998 versus 10% per year in the 1970s, with CEO job retention of an average of six years today versus ten years in the 1970s.
- CEO turnover and pay at Fortune 500 companies is strongly linked to stock performance relative to the industry, citing the public dismissals of Hank McKinnell of Pfizer and Robert Nardelli of Home Depot, each of whom served over six years and presided over poor stock performance relative to their industries, and the fact that CEOs in the top compensation decile were with firms that outperformed their industries over the previous three years by more than 50%, while CEOs in the bottom compensation decile were with firms that underperformed their industries by more than 25%.

This book proceeds on the assumption that there are elements of truth in each of the rival theories. The dramatic increases in CEO compensation are both the result of economic factors, such as globalization which creates potential "superstar markets," and a failure of compensation committees of boards of directors to consistently use "best practices" in formulating and approving CEO compensation.

CEO FORCED EXIT PACKAGES

The following is a chart of the forced exit packages of some prominent executives that have stirred tremendous public controversy over the last ten years.[9]

---

[7]"Wiring the Labor Market," Journal of Economics Perspectives, Vol. 15, No. 1 (Winter 2001).

[8]The Harvard Law School Corporate Governance Blog.

[9]The Wall Street Journal, January 4, 2007.

Executive/Title	Company	Exit Package in Millions
Robert Nardelli Chairman, CEO	Home Depot	$210
Henry McKinnell Chairman, CEO	Pfizer	$200
Tom Freston CEO	Viacom	$59
Philip J. Purcell Chairman, CEO	Morgan Stanley	$62
Carly Florina Chairman, CEO	Hewlett Packard	$21
Jill Barad CEO	Mattel	$50
Michael Ovitz President	Walt Disney	$140

Many of these exit packages include items earned over many years, such as supplemental pension payments and stock option profits. Accordingly, some of these numbers may well be misleading.

According to the January 4, 2007 issue of *The Wall Street Journal,* Robert Nardelli, the former CEO of Home Depot, walked away with an exit package of $210 million, as noted in the CEO forced exit packages chart, a figure that was calculated before the announcement of his resignation boosted the potential value of his stock options.

Mr. Nardelli's exit package stirred up a hornet's nest of criticism of excessive CEO compensation. The Home Depot's share price had fallen 9% since Mr. Nardelli joined the company in December 2000. In contrast, the share price of Lowe's, its competitor, had risen 188% in the past six years. Mr. Nardelli defended his record by pointing out that Home Depot had posted earnings per share growth in excess of 20% per year for four consecutive years, only one of two companies in the Dow Jones Industrial Average to do so.

It has been suggested that the ousting of Robert Nardelli sent exactly the wrong message to CEOs, namely "manage the stock, not the company."[10] It used to be conventional wisdom that the CEO should run the company and the stock market would determine the share price.

Those shareholder activists who believe that the CEO should be responsible for the stock price have a short memory. Overemphasizing

[10]"Blame Home Depot's Board, Not Nardelli," V. Katsenelson, January 4, 2007, Contrarian Edge blog, http://contrarianedge.com/2007/01/04/blame-home-depots-board-not-nardelli/

the importance of the stock price is exactly how Enron got into trouble. Enron created a "numbers driven" culture in order to maintain the market price of its stock and this culture ultimately resulted in a major financial fraud and Enron's subsequent bankruptcy.

Moreover, the increasing pressure on CEOs to be responsible for share prices is an important factor in causing public companies to be purchased by private equity groups (see Chapter 4).[11]

PRIVATE EQUITY COMPENSATION

The compensation received by CEOs from private equity investors is instructive as to whether CEO compensation is driven primarily by passive directors or by macroeconomic factors. In Chapter 4, there is a discussion on David Calhoun, a 50 year-old former Vice Chairman of General Electric, who was offered a compensation package worth more than $100 million by VNU, a $4.3 million media company, controlled by a consortium of private equity firms. This provides at least anecdotal evidence that there is some merit to the macro theory of executive compensation.

Other "star" CEOs have also found a home with private equity funds, presumably with large compensation packages. According to *The Wall Street Journal* of May 16, 2007, "Kenneth W. Freeman, former CEO of Quest Diagnostics Inc., is now CEO at KKR-backed door-maker Masonite and Executive Chairman of medical-device firm Accellent. Firms have lured even bigger names as special partners or advisers, including former GE CEO Jack Welch as Partner at Clayton, Dubilier & Rice, and former International Business Machines Corp. CEO Louis V. Gerstner Jr., now Chairman of Carlyle Group."

ENTERTAINMENT AND SPORTS CELEBRITIES

Economists have noted that there is a substantial difference between the market for CEOs and the market for entertainment and sports celebrities. However, it is instructive to review the "reported" compensation of these celebrities since their compensation is clearly not determined by passive boards of directors beholden to the celebrity. Thus, the compensation

---

[11]See, "Is Shareholder Democracy Encouraging Private Buyouts of Public Firms?" L. Stout, The Harvard Law School Corporate Governance Blog, May 15, 2007.

levels described below are of some relevance in determining what an arms-length market value is of celebrities who achieved superstar status.

Entertainment and sports celebrities are reported to have received the following yearly compensation according to Forbes.com, although these figures are suspect and may reflect equity ownership returns as well as multiyear returns:

- Steven Spielberg $332 million
- Oprah Winfrey $223 million
- Jerry Seinfeld $98 million
- Tiger Woods $88 million
- Michael Jordan $32 million
- Shaquille O'Neal $30 million
- Barry Bonds $20 million
- Katie Couric $15 million

The reported compensation of these celebrities gives some credence to the superstar theory of the academic studies previously described.

BENEFITS OF GOOD CORPORATE GOVERNANCE

Are there any benefits of using best corporate governance practices?

Corporate governance rating groups maintain that companies with a reputation for good corporate behavior have stocks that sell at a premium, and investors agree.[12] Some argue that these corporate governance rating groups receive payments from the companies which they rate and, consequently, may not always be considered independent. However, it is clear that these corporate governance rating groups do have significant influence with many institutional investors and their ratings cannot be ignored.

Good corporate governance enhances the image of a company and there is at least anecdotal evidence that image and reputation can increase the company's stock price. In the case of United Technologies Corp., one study found a 27% increase in market value as a result of the company's excellent image and reputation.[13]

---

[12]P. Dvorak, "Finding the Best Measure of Corporate Citizenship," *The Wall Street Journal,* July 2, 2007.

[13]"What Price Reputation?" *BusinessWeek,* July 9, 2007.

A survey was conducted by a management consulting firm between April and May 2002 in cooperation with the Global Corporate Governance Forum. The survey covered the opinions of over 200 institutional investors collectively responsible for $2 trillion of assets under management. The survey found that institutional investors placed corporate governance on par with financial indicators when they evaluated investment decisions.

An overwhelming majority of investors stated that they were prepared to pay a premium for companies exhibiting high governance standards. Premiums averaged:

- 30% in Eastern Europe and Africa
- 22% in Asia and Latin America
- 14% in North America and Western Europe
- 13% in North America

The following table lists all the countries that were surveyed by the research and shows the premiums that investors are willing to pay for shares in a well-governed company in the respective countries.

Country	Premium (%)
Morocco	41
Egypt	39
Russia	38
Turkey	27
Indonesia	25
China	25
Argentina	24
Venezuela	24
Brazil	24
Poland	23
India	23
Malaysia	22
Philippines	22
S. Africa	22
Japan	21
Singapore	21
Colombia	21
S. Korea	20

Thailand	20
Mexico	19
Taiwan	19
Chile	18
Italy	16
Switzerland	15
U.S.	14
Spain	14
Germany	13
France	13
Sweden	13
UK	12
Canada	11

The survey emphasized that companies not only needed to be well governed but also needed to be *perceived* in the market as being well governed. However, care should be taken when determining what the results actually prove, since the research did not provide any evidence that the institutional investors actually acted on their opinions.[14]

There is some evidence that good corporate governance produces direct economic benefit to the organization. One study, conducted at Georgia State University and published in December 2004, found that public companies with independent boards of directors have higher returns on equity, higher profit margins, larger dividend yields, and larger stock repurchases.[15] This study was consistent with another study of 250 companies by the MIT Sloan School of Management which concluded that, on average, businesses with superior IT governance practices generate 25% greater profits than firms with poor governance given the same strategic objectives.[16]

The next chapter deals with methods of motivating executive performance.

---

[14]See also Deutsche Bank Study (2001–2002) and The Black, Jang and Kim Research in Korea (2003).

[15]Brown, et al, *Corporate Governance and Firm Performance* Georgia State University (December 7, 2004), http://papers.ssrn.com/sol3/papers.cfm?abstract_id=586423

[16]Weill, *IT Governance: How Top Performers Manage IT Decision Rights for Superior Results.* (Harvard Business School Press, 2004).

CHAPTER 2

Motivating Executive Performance

There is a universal consensus that the majority of executive pay should only be based upon "performance." The most difficult task of the compensation committee is to devise metrics for measuring performance. These metrics should motivate both short-term and long-term behavior, should preferably be ones that are not susceptible to being "gamed," and should not have unintended consequences.

This is easier said than done. Whatever metrics are devised by the compensation committee will have to be periodically reviewed to determine if they are in fact motivating the executive performance intended.

BEST PRACTICE

The compensation committee must establish goals and objectives for the CEO and other executive officers in advance of the performance period.

The Pfizer proxy statement, dated March 16, 2006, contained the following seven goals and objectives for Dr. Hank McKinnell, the Pfizer CEO:

1. Achieve specific revenue, EPS, operating cash flow per share, and merger-related synergy goals.
2. Effectively communicate strategy and financial results to increase shareholder value.

3. Deliver more new medicines more quickly to patients, through industry-leading R&D productivity and significant in-licensing activity.
4. Adapting to Scale.
5. Promote new directions in health and wellness.
6. Shape a positive environment for better healthcare.
7. Developing People, Talent, and the Organization.

The Pfizer proxy statement then analyzed each of these CEO goals and objectives and came up with the following conclusions, which resulted in a 22% decrease in the overall compensation of Dr. McKinnell (who was subsequently terminated):

"Overall, the financial targets, which reflected a significant stretch for the organization given the dynamic business environment and the loss of exclusivity for certain key products, were exceeded. However, given the performance of the Company's stock price in 2005 when compared to prior years, the Committee felt that the goal of effectively communicating strategy and financial results to increase shareholder value was not met. . .

"Based on its overall assessment, the Committee decided to maintain Dr. McKinnell's current base salary ($2,270,500) for 2005, and award an annual incentive of $3,700,000 for 2005 performance, which is a decrease of 7.2% from last year's annual incentive award. The total of all compensation for 2005 – including salary, bonus, other annual compensation, present value of stock options, present value of performance-share grant, and other compensation – decreased by 22% compared to the total of the same compensation awarded in 2004."

Not surprisingly, Pfizer abruptly replaced Dr. McKinnell on July 28, 2006, nineteen months before he was scheduled to step down. Apparently, the board acted in response to investors angered about his retirement package and a drop of as much as 40% in the company's stock price during his five years in charge. Dr. McKinnell's retirement package allegedly totaled more than $180 million, including an estimated $82.3 million in pension benefits, $77.9 million in deferred compensation, and cash and stock totaling more than $20.7 million. At Pfizer's 2006 annual meeting, a plane flew overhead trailing a banner that said "Give it back, Hank!"

TYING PERFORMANCE TO THE STRATEGIC PLAN

BEST PRACTICE

Each company should have a year-to-year budget and a long-term strategic plan, and reward the executive for accomplishing the goals of both.

Any good CEO compensation package must provide incentives to satisfy both its year-to-year budget and its long-term strategic plan. Most companies have a budget and reward the CEO for achieving or exceeding the budget or punish the CEO for missing that budget. However, many companies do not have a long-term strategic plan.

It is difficult to establish goals for the CEO in the absence of a clear and well articulated long-term strategic plan. Indeed, the CEO compensation package must, in part, tie into the strategic plan as well as the annual budget.

For example, assume that a multilocation retailer has an annual budget that contemplates an increase in revenues of 10% per year and an increase in profits of 12% per year. The long-term strategic plan of this retailer may contemplate doubling the number of retail stores over the next five years. Assume that in a given year, the CEO meets the year-to-year budget but fails to open any new stores. In this situation, the CEO should receive a bonus for achieving the annual budget, but no bonus based upon the strategic plan goal in the absence of compelling reasons why no progress was made in achieving the long-term strategic plan.

Although the Pfizer proxy statement clearly sets out the goals for the CEO, it is not clear how these goals mesh with the strategic plan of the company. Executive performance goals cannot be created in isolation. Every company should have a strategic plan and be certain that the articulated goals for the CEO assist in the accomplishment of the goals of that plan.

For example, if the strategic plan contemplates a significant increase in the market share of the company, as compared to its industry competitors, over a five-year period, executive compensation must in part be based upon the accomplishment of an increase in market share. If the articulated goal communicated to the executive is merely to increase earnings from year-to-year, this goal could be accomplished by the executive without ever increasing market share. Under these circumstances, the executive could be well rewarded for increasing earnings even though the market share of the company was flat or decreased.

BEST PRACTICE

Clearly explain performance-based compensation to executives and avoid overly complex formulas.

Executives must be able to easily understand how their efforts can affect their compensation. Complex formulas, which may be satisfactory in theory, are not necessarily the best methods of motivating individual executives. The proxy statement of Eli Lilly and Company makes it clear that they disfavor "elegant" performance-based formulas that are difficult to understand. For a performance-based plan to be effective in motivating executives, each executive must have a clear understanding of exactly how their day-to-day performance or the company's performance ties into their compensation package.[1]

UNINTENDED CONSEQUENCES

Unintended consequences are the bane of the law, contractual provisions, and financial metrics. For example, the lead author of this book has for years recommended the use of arbitration clauses to resolve contractual disputes. Arbitration was intended to avoid costly court battles, endless appeals and make the dispute resolution mechanism more cost efficient and quicker.

The lead author noticed that some arbitrations were not any quicker than judicial trials and in some cases took longer. Arbitrators, unlike judges, are generally paid on a per hearing basis, whereas judges are paid on a fixed salary, regardless of the number of hearings they hold. The lead author's

---

[1]Eli Lilly and Company Schedule 14A, filed March 5, 2007, p. 23.

use of an arbitration clause without a limit of a number of hearings or the arbitrator's fees had the unintended consequence of actually *lengthening* the dispute resolution process. As a result, the lead author now provides that no payment will be made to an arbitrator for hearings held more than six months to one year after the appointment of the arbitrator.

Compensation metrics are also subject to unintended consequences and gaming and in many cases reward or punish the executive for events over which the executive has no control. For example, a performance metric keyed to earnings per share is subject to each of the following problems:

- Earnings per share may rise or fall because of changes in worldwide commodity prices for raw materials (see Exxon example in Chapter 1), thereby making this metric unsuitable as a measurement of executive performance.
- Earnings per share may increase because management reduces its research and development expenditures, or, alternatively, earnings per share fall because the company must engage in needed research and development for long-term strategic reasons.
- Changes in accounting principles or their application cause earnings per share to decrease or, alternatively, cause earnings per share to increase.

Significant management bonuses based upon earnings per share have caused management to "cook the books." For example, according to a Securities and Exchange Commission (SEC) complaint, the senior management of Huntington Bancshares, Inc., in order to achieve earnings per share targets that determined bonuses and to meet Wall Street expectations, allegedly engaged in a number of misstatements. The misstatements included up-front recognition of loan and lease origination fees that were required by accounting rules to be deferred and amortized over the term of the loan or lease; improper capitalization of commission expenses and deferral of pension costs that were required to be recognized in the period incurred; misstated reserves; improper deferral of income; and misclassification of nonoperating income as operating income. As a result, Huntington Bancshares, Inc. paid a penalty of $7.5 million and suffered public embarrassment.[2]

---

[2]U.S. Securities and Exchange Commission, Litigation Rel. No. 19243 (June 2005), www.sec.gov/litigation/litreleases/lr19243.htm. Click on SEC Complaint in this matter; Securities Exchange Act Release No. 51781 (June 2, 2005).

BEST PRACTICE

Compensation committees should request the audit committee to order a more intensive audit prior to paying significant management bonuses based on financial results.

The motivation to "game" financial metrics where a significant management bonus is at stake should cause compensation committees to take greater care prior to authorizing payment of such a bonus.

The compensation committee should, in appropriate cases, request the audit committee to conduct a more intensive audit prior to such payment.

Recognizing these and other problems with performance metrics, many companies have developed nonmetric "formulas" to judge executive performance or have combined metric with nonmetric factors. For example, the Pfizer CEO compensation system (previously described) appears to be entirely nonmetric.

Dell Inc. combines metric and nonmetric factors under The Dell Short-Term Incentive Plan; the compensation committee establishes a specific annual performance target for each executive officer. "The performance target is represented as a specific percentage of consolidated net income and may not exceed 0.5%. The compensation committee has the discretion to reduce (but not increase) an executive officer's incentive amount from the amount that would otherwise be payable under the established performance target. Although the plan does not specify factors the Compensation committee will evaluate, the committee evaluates, among other things, overall company and business segment financial performance, as well as nonfinancial company performance, such as customer satisfaction in determining the appropriate final incentive bonus payout for each executive officer."[3]

---

[3]Dell Inc. Schedule 14A filed on June 5, 2006.

FIRM EXPANSION AND CEO PAY

Revenue size is often viewed as an indication of the complexity of an organization and this is a major factor in establishing the market for CEO compensation. The significance of revenue size differs from industry to industry. Some believe that revenue growth, which is one of the financial statement measurements less subject to manipulation, is a good metric to use in establishing executive compensation.

However, even revenue growth is subject to manipulation, as we have seen from the so-called "channel-stuffing" cases in which large amounts of inventory are shipped at the end of a quarter to enhance revenue even though there is no requirement to pay for it. Revenue growth can also be affected by mergers and acquisitions and thus revenue can become distorted as a performance metric.

The following is an abstract from a paper by Professors Bebchuk and Grinstein, November 2005, in which they ascribe significant CEO compensation growth to firm size (presumably revenue growth or market capitalization):

> "We study the extent to which decisions to expand firm size are associated with increases in subsequent CEO compensation. Controlling for past stock performance, we find a positive correlation between CEO compensation and the CEO's past decisions to increase firm size. This correlation is economically meaningful; for example, other things being equal, CEO's who in the preceding three years were in the top quartile in terms of expanding by increasing the number of shares outstanding receive compensation that is higher by one-third than the compensation of CEOs belonging to the bottom quartile. The correlation between firms' expansion and CEO pay remains significant and economically meaningful even when firms making large acquisitions are excluded, indicating that expansion through other means is also followed by pay increases. We find an asymmetry between size increases and decreases: while size increases are followed by higher CEO pay, size decreases are not followed by a pay reduction. Finally, stock returns are correlated with subsequent CEO pay only to the extent that they contribute to expanding firm size; only the component of past stock returns not distributed as dividends is correlated with subsequent CEO pay. *The association we find between expansion decisions and subsequent*

CEO pay could provide CEOs with incentives to expand firm size." [Emphasis Supplied]

EQUITY-BASED COMPENSATION

BEST PRACTICE

The percentage of equity-based compensation to the executive's total compensation package should not be so large as to cause the executive to unduly focus on the price of the company's stock, but should be large enough to compete on a risk-adjusted basis with compensation packages potentially offered by private equity funds.

In establishing the percentage of equity compensation of the CEO and other senior executives, public companies should take into account the potential competition from all areas, including private equity funds for talented management groups, as discussed more fully in Chapter 4.

It is appropriate for the compensation committee to try to align the interests of the executive with the interests of shareholders by providing stock options, stock appreciation rights, stock grants, and other forms of equity compensation. However, if the percentage of the total compensation package represented by such equity compensation becomes overly large, the executive may tend to focus more on increasing the stock price than on improving operational performance. Despite this potential disadvantage of a large percentage of equity compensation, the percentage of equity compensation should always be competitive with other opportunities available to the management group. The compensation committee should at least consider the equity incentives that may be provided by private equity funds which may wish to recruit the management team, possibly as part of an acquisition of the company.

Although there is no fixed percentage limit that equity compensation should bear to the total compensation package, each compensation committee must, through individual analysis, determine the right mix of equity and cash compensation to properly motivate and retain the executive.

A New Role for CEOs

The corporate governance movement has created new demands on CEOs and placed them in the role of politicians as well as managers. During the twentieth century, CEOs were judged primarily upon their operating results and lesser emphasis was given to stock price performance and adherence to high corporate governance standards. In the post-Enron era, CEOs must pay attention not only to operating performance, but also to stock price performance, to satisfying the demands of other constituencies including employees, customers, and the communities in which they operate, and to practicing good corporate governance. Today's CEO must be able to convincingly explain to securities analysts the company's long-term strategy and is being held responsible for increasing stock prices over which they may have only little control.

Boards of directors must be sensitive to these new pressures on CEOs in establishing compensation strategies. Direction must be provided by the board to the CEO as to the emphasis that should be given to stockholder demands for increasing stock prices, particularly short-term stock price trends. As noted later in this book, the board must decide how much emphasis to place on long-term performance, as opposed to short-term performance, in the compensation packages of CEOs.

BEST PRACTICE

Compensation committees must properly balance the total compensation package of executives between short-term and long-term performance goals, with a greater percentage being applied to long-term goals.

Moody's Investors Service, Inc. is particularly sensitive to the degree of emphasis on long-term performance goals. They have stated as follows: "In evaluating executive pay, we differentiate between short-term (base salary, annual bonuses and other annual pay) from long-term pay

(LTIPs and equity-based pay) so as to determine how pay encourages long-term decision-making."[4]

The Exxon Mobil Corporation has a unique annual stock bonus plan which attempts to combine both short-term and long-term objectives. Only half of the annual bonus award is paid in the year of grant. Payment of the balance of the annual bonus is delayed until a specified level of cumulative earnings per share is achieved. If the cumulative earnings per share do not reach the specified dollar requirement within three years, the delayed portion of the bonus is correspondingly reduced.

SATISFYING INVESTOR EXPECTATIONS

BEST PRACTICE

Although investor expectations should be considered in establishing executive goals, such goals should not be based upon the short-term expectations of investors and instead should be based upon the strategic plan of the company.

Today the average mutual fund turns over 100% of its portfolio in 11 months. Day-traders have an even shorter horizon, typically a few days or less.

The compensation committee cannot establish executive goals based upon the short-term objectives of some shareholders, whether they be institutional shareholders or day-traders. It is foolish to attempt to satisfy this segment of shareholders who are only looking for immediate gain to satisfy their own objectives.

A company should normally be managed to satisfy the objectives of long-term shareholders who have a horizon three to five years or more. Accordingly, goals that tie the executive's compensation to the interest of longer-term shareholders should be established. If the Board of Directors adopts this longer term philosophy, the CEO and CFO should have as

---

[4]A User's Guide to the SEC's New Rules for Reporting Executive Pay, April 2007, p. 4.

one of the goals the articulation of this longer-term philosophy to the stock market.

It is foolish to place too much emphasis on short-term stock performance. Wal-Mart places a heavy emphasis on performance-based compensation, and a substantial majority of each executive's total annual pay is tied not only to financial performance but also to the enhancement of shareholder value. Wal-Mart claimed in its proxy statement filed April 19, 2007 that less than 15% of the total direct compensation of its executives is base salary. During Wal-Mart's fiscal year ending January 31, 2007, the company determined that the compensation realized by certain executive officers was not competitive to the company's peer groups, even though the company had a strong financial performance. Presumably, this was due to the failure of the stock price to rise during the 2007 fiscal year. As a result of basing so much of the compensation on the short-term increases in stock prices, realized compensation of these executives became noncompetitive and the compensation system had to be revised.[5]

MINIMUM EQUITY OWNERSHIP REQUIREMENTS

BEST PRACTICE

Companies should establish minimum equity ownership requirements for their senior executives.

Many large public companies have adopted minimum equity ownership requirements for their senior executives, including the CEO. The purpose of these minimum equity ownership requirements is to further align the interest of these executives with the interest of shareholders.

For example, FedEx Corporation requires the CEO to own at least 100,000 shares of FedEx common stock and each of the other executive officers to own at least 30,000 shares of FedEx common stock. The stock

---

[5]Wal-Mart Stores, Inc. Schedule 14A filed on April 19, 2007.

ownership goal requires these levels to be reached within four years after the executive has been appointed to his or her position.[6]

Bank of America Corporation requires the CEO to hold at least 500,000 shares of its common stock and its other executive officers at least 150,000 shares. For this purpose, unexercised stock options (whether vested or unvested) are disregarded.[7]

Any minimum equity requirements imposed by the company should be subject to a prohibition on hedging transactions, which have the effect of mitigating the equity risk in holding company securities. Although SEC rules generally prohibit such hedging transactions, it is preferable to impose a separate antihedging rule on executives because of exceptions to such rules and to avoid undermining the very purpose of minimum equity requirements.

Establishing competitive executive compensation is a major task for the compensation committee and this task is described in the next two chapters.

---

[6]FedEx Schedule 14A filed on August 14, 2006, p. 36.
[7]Bank of America Corporation Schedule 14A filed on March 19, 2007.

CHAPTER 3

Peer Groups and Benchmarking

BEST PRACTICE

Any peer groups used in executive performance metrics must be of the same size and complexity and, if the company competes for executive talent with other companies outside of the same industry, should include or consider other such companies.

The selection of a peer group for performance comparisons is an important function of the compensation committee. It is typical to use peer groups in executive performance metrics. Any peer groups chosen to establish pay levels must be of the same size and complexity as the company. However, performance comparators do not necessarily have to be the same size and complexity.

Many companies fail to recognize that there is competition for their executive officers outside their immediate industry. For example, according to their 2006 shareholders report, the peer group of AstraZeneca P.L.C. included 12 other pharmaceutical companies and no companies outside of their industry.

If the company competes outside of its industry for executive talent, the peer group should include companies outside of the same industry. It is not unusual for very large companies to include companies outside of their industry as the comparators for peer group purposes.

For example, The Coca-Cola Company uses a very large peer group consisting of 32 companies including 3M Company, Abbott Laboratories, and Citigroup, Inc. The justification for this large and diverse peer group is to provide competitive information on potential employers of executives of The Coca-Cola Company.

A similarly large group of nonindustry companies is used by United-Health Group Incorporated. That company made the following statement in its 2007 proxy statement[1]:

> "Since 2003, in addition to survey data, we have most commonly used a group of 30 companies for compensation benchmarking. This group of companies was originally selected and is modified from time to time by management after consultation with Hewitt, on the basis of annual revenue, cash flow return on average equity, and total shareholder return over three- and five-year periods. The intent of the Compensation Committee and our management is to generate and maintain a group of companies representing multiple industries and have generally strong financial performance and median revenue similar to, or smaller than, that of our Company and to supplement the information regarding these companies by survey data. *This approach reflects the view that our Company competes for senior executive talent with successful companies across industry boundaries.*" [Emphasis Supplied]

In selecting peer groups, it should be noted that the most senior executive positions in Fortune 500 companies are generally not sensitive to geographic differences. A possible exception is if a product or service is concentrated in a given market, for example, investment banking in New York City. Smaller firms may have differences in pay, including cash compensation, based upon geographical supply and demand for executives and cost of living differentials. In assembling a peer group, it is useful to look at what securities analysts consider to be peers of the company.[2]

Although competition for executive talent may exist outside of the normal peer group, compensation committees should not necessarily compete with industries paying incredibly high compensation levels, such as investment banking and hedge funds. On June 7, 2007, it was reported

---

[1]UnitedHealth Group Incorporated, Schedule 14A, filed May 22, 2007.
[2]M. Davis and J. Edge "Executive Compensation," Windsor Professional Information (2004), p. 53.

that AstraZeneca's Chief Financial Officer, Jon Symonds, who helped create the company by overseeing the 1999 merger between Astra AB, Sweden, and Zeneca P.L.C., Britain, resigned to join the Goldman Sachs Group, Inc., a company that was not part of their peer group.[3] The compensation committee may have failed to recognize that there was competition for their executive talent outside their immediate industry. However, even if they had known that there was competition from the investment banking industry, they could have decided that they did not want to benchmark the CFO against the extraordinarily higher incomes available in that industry.

The use of inappropriate peer groups has been criticized by the media. In some cases this may be due to the failure to clearly articulate the reason for inclusion of nonindustry companies. The following excerpt, which appeared in *The New York Times* (November 25, 2006), reflects the potential for the gaming of peer groups:

Apples to Apples?

In setting executive pay levels, corporations choose companies they deem their "peers" for comparison purposes. But such peer groups often include companies that are very different, in terms of their size and the complexity of their operations. For example, Eli Lilly chose Johnson & Johnson, a much bigger and more diverse company, as a peer in several years, including 2005. How the two companies actually stacked up:

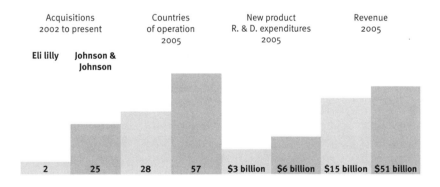

Acquisitions 2002 to present		Countries of operation 2005		New product R. & D. expenditures 2005		Revenue 2005	
Eli lilly	Johnson & Johnson						
2	25	28	57	$3 billion	$6 billion	$15 billion	$51 billion

---

[3]*The Philadelphia Inquirer*, June 7, 2007, p. C3.

ADJUSTING THE PEER GROUP

BEST PRACTICE

Compensation of peer group executives must be adjusted for the size and scope of the operation of the peer group company. Compensation committees must fully understand any so-called "regression analysis" performed by compensation consultants.

If the company has $1 billion of revenue, and the peer group company is twice the size, adjustments must be made in the compensation of the peer group executive to take this difference in size and responsibility into account. Compensation consultants call this a "regression analysis." Compensation committees should request the compensation consultant to explain exactly how such a regression analysis operates in order to determine whether it was properly applied.

An important part of using a regression analysis is understanding the statistical correlations, and the compensation committee should question the compensation consultant on these correlations. For example, a bad regression analysis would commonly exist where the correlation coefficient (called the "r squared value") in the regression analysis is low, indicating that it may be statistically invalid and unreliable. The closer the r squared value is to 1, the more valid the analysis. The lower that number, the less valid the answer. Regressions that rely upon correlations of .25 or less should be disregarded.

Another illustration of a bad regression is where the factor on which the regression relies does not really have a cause and effect relationship to compensation. In other words, does a particular financial metric really drive pay?

BEST PRACTICE

Consider using different peer groups depending upon the purpose for the peer group analysis.

Different peer groups may be relevant for comparison depending upon the purpose of the peer group analysis. For example, for purposes of establishing a measurement of long-term performance of a utility, the performance of other utilities is relevant since these other utilities compete for the same investors. However, for purposes of designing features such as the mix of compensation components and short-term incentives, a broader group of companies may be chosen that are outside of the utility industry but are relevant from a business viewpoint.

Although peer groups for the purpose of determining executive compensation levels generally include companies of comparable size based upon revenues (typically 50% to 2 times the company's revenues), other factors may also be used to select a peer group if they are relevant from a business viewpoint. These other factors may include the number of employees, asset size, units of production, operating complexity, geographic consideration, growth attributes and market capitalization.

BEST PRACTICE

Peer groups should be carefully chosen to avoid charges of "cherry-picking" those companies that will provide the highest executive compensation levels.

The company will have to explain to shareholders in the compensation committee discussion and analysis section of the proxy statement (or Form 10-K Report) the reason for picking a particular peer group. Therefore, the peer group should be chosen with an eye to the justification for the inclusion and exclusion of certain companies from the peer group and the ability to convincingly explain to shareholders the final peer group selection.

BEST PRACTICE

Avoid selecting outliers and unique situations for the peer group.

It is important to examine any proposed peer group for outliers and unique situations. A founder CEO, or one with a large ownership position, may be paid very differently (higher or lower) than other comparators. Other factors may include the scope of responsibility, perceived competence, experience, and ability. "How are these people similar to our executives?" is an important question to consider.

Peer Groups for Different Levels of Executives

BEST PRACTICE

Peer groups should be customized for the differences in responsibilities and authorities of different executives.

The proper peer group for the CEO may not necessarily be the proper peer group for lower level executives. Excellence in performance against the CEO's peer group may not effectively measure the performance of these lower-level executives since these executives have different authority and responsibility than the CEO. For example, Wal-Mart Stores, Inc. benchmarks against multiple peer groups and for associates who are not named executive officers, but who hold key positions, they review the total compensation provided to individuals in comparable positions in certain select peer groups.[4]

The peer group for lower-level executives may be much smaller than the peer group for the CEO or CFO position. For example, there may be 12 companies in the peer group for the CEO or CFO position, but only four companies in the peer group for the senior vice president position. Since only the highest paid senior vice presidents will be listed in this smaller peer group, this peer group may be unduly skewed toward a higher pay level. Consequently, care must be taken in using small peer groups for lower-level executives.

---

[4]Wal-Mart Stores, Inc. Schedule 14A filed on April 16, 2007, p. 22.

BENCHMARKING[5]

BEST PRACTICE

Compensation committees should benchmark against different percentiles of the peer group compensation practices to gain a better understanding of what is competitive compensation.

The compensation committee of The Coca-Cola Company benchmarks against the 50th, 60th, and 75th percentiles of its peer group's pay practices to gain a better understanding of what is competitive. For 2006, the company chose the 60th percentile as a reference point with respect to base salary and annual incentive compensation. However, a named executive officer's base salary may be higher or lower than the reference point based upon personal performance, skills, and experience. The actual range for total direct compensation in 2006 was the median of the peer group to the 75th percentile. The purpose of this range was to recognize the influence and impact of each executive on the entire Coca-Cola system, which is comprised primarily of independent bottlers and is substantially larger and more complex than The Coca-Cola Company alone.

BEST PRACTICE

The compensation committee should have access to all available sources for each executive position that is to be benchmarked.

The members of the compensation committee should be afforded access to all available data sources for each executive position to be benchmarked and have an understanding as to why such data was used or not used by the compensation consultant. The compensation committee should also

---

[5]See also Reda, Reifler and Thatcher, *Compensation Committee Handbook, Second Edition*, John Wiley & Sons, Inc. (2005), p. 26 et sec.

have an understanding of the relative weighting given to various data sources in developing the consensus for each executive position. For example, the cause and effect relationship between the data source or metric and competitive executive compensation should be carefully examined by the compensation committee.

BEST PRACTICE

Although internal pay equity is not a key consideration in establishing the CEO compensation package, the compensation committee must at least consider this issue as a benchmarking tool.

Internal pay equity is a benchmarking tool that has many different meanings depending upon who is advocating internal pay equity. Initially, when corporate governance activists and unions were advocating internal pay equity, it referred to the relationship of the CEO compensation package to the overall work force or, in some cases, the lowest paid worker. Intel compares the compensation of its executive officers with other Intel employees for internal pay equity purposes.[6] Some corporate governance activists had urged compensation committees to consider internal pay equity in establishing the CEO's compensation, citing studies that demonstrate that the ratio of the highest paid to the lowest paid over the last decade or so had significantly increased. This comparison makes little sense in a world in which the compensation committee must offer the CEO a competitive compensation package in order to attract and retain qualified candidates.

However, the meaning of internal pay equity has now evolved into an analysis of the historical relationship between the CEO's pay and those of one or more layers of the company's executives. DuPont measures the relationship between the CEO's pay and that of other

---

[6]Intel Corp. Schedule 14A filed on April 2, 2007, pps. 21 and 22.

executive officers.[7] This comparison makes more sense than the prior meaning of internal pay equity, since it is important to view management as a team and to create incentives on that basis. This view has been advocated by Jeffrey R. Immelt, the CEO of General Electric, although there is no reference to internal pay equity in the General Electric proxy statement.

The purpose for these comparisons is to determine if the CEO's compensation has gotten off-track from the rest of the management team.

Regardless of the results of the internal pay equity comparisons, CEO compensation must be competitive to attract and retain the CEO. If this requires that there be a distortion of the ratio of the highest paid to the lowest paid, or the ratio of the lowest paid executives to the highest paid executives, then so be it. However, since establishing CEO compensation is an art and not a science, internal pay equity should at least be considered by the compensation committee.

LAKE WOBEGON EFFECT

> **BEST PRACTICE**
>
> Avoid the Lake Wobegon Effect: Not all executives are better than average.

Compensation committees should avoid what has been characterized as the Lake Wobegon Effect (after the mythical Minnesota village dreamed up by radio personality Garrison Keillor, where "all the children are above average.") Not all executives are above average and not all executives deserve to be at or above the 50th percentile in compensation.

Establishing an appropriate peer group and benchmarks is only the beginning of the methodology to establish competitive compensation for executives. The next chapter discusses the new wild card in executive compensation: the influence of private equity.

---

[7]Compensation Standards (Spring 2007); E. I. du Pont de Nemours and Company Schedule 14A, filed on March 19, 2007, p. 19.

Benchmarking with Medians

BEST PRACTICE

Consider the use of median compensation of peer group executives, rather than mathematical averages.

The use of a mathematical average of the compensation of peer group executives can distort the so-called "average" for peer group executive compensation if there are members of the peer group who have either exceedingly high or exceedingly low compensation levels. A median (the middle number in a series) avoids the distortion caused by executives whose compensation is outside the normal range.

After assembling an appropriate peer group and benchmarking, compensation committees should consider potential competition for executive talent from private equity funds, as discussed in the next chapter.

CHAPTER 4

Competing With Private Equity Funds

Assuming the compensation committee wishes to retain the services of the CEO and the rest of the management team, a competitive compensation policy must be adopted. This requires not only compensation surveys of other direct competitors, but also a consideration of other opportunities in different industries or with private equity groups that might be available to the executive.

BEST PRACTICE

Executive compensation packages must take into consideration, among other items, the potential competition from private equity funds for talented management groups.

There is at least anecdotal evidence that the increasing number of private equity takeovers of public companies is partly due to the greater rewards available to management in a private equity setting. In a private equity merger, management is typically permitted to rollover its existing public company stock into the private company and, in addition, enjoys equity incentive rewards which constitute a significant percentage of the total equity of the private company. Although the higher amount of equity incentives typically available to management from private equity mergers is subject to greater potential risk because of the high debt leverage employed by private equity funds, this higher risk has not deterred management groups from seeking such mergers.

In many cases, the total equity incentives available to senior management as part of a private company significantly exceed the equity incentives granted to management in the public company. For example, Richard D. Kinder, Kinder Morgan's Chairman and Chief Executive Officer, increased his beneficial ownership in Kinder Morgan, Inc. from 17.9% to 30.73%[1] of the private company by virtue of an equity rollover of his public company stock as a result of the private equity transaction organized by Mr. Kinder and affiliates of GS Capital Partners V Fund, L.P., American International Group, Inc., The Carlyle Group, and Riverstone Holdings LLC. At Dunkin' Brands (home of Dunkin' Donuts), which is co-owned by Bain Capital, Carlyle, and Thomas H. Lee Partners, the 40 officers of the company have a substantial amount of their personal money invested in the company, which creates more of an ownership mentality rather than a corporate mentality.[2]

Indeed, in many situations, it is the management of the public company who introduces the private fund buyers to the board of directors of the public company. Although the primary motivation of management is to increase their equity stake by taking the public company private, there are many nonequity rewards for management in going private.

The following is a short list of the nonequity rewards to management in causing the public company to go private:

- No need to show quarterly growth in revenue and earnings; management is not crucified for earnings blips[3]
- No need to meet with securities analysts
- No need to hold shareholders meetings or deal with activist shareholders[4]
- No need to deal with the media

---

[1]Kinder Morgan, Inc. Schedule 14A filed on November 15, 2006.

[2]"Private Equity, Private Lives," CNNMoney.com, November 27, 2006.

[3]"Firms Go Private In Search of Deeper Pockets," D. Cho, washingtonpost.com, January 1, 2007.

[4]"Investors Who Are Too Bolshy for Their Own Good," L. Stout, FT.com, April 23, 2007.

- Reporting solely to a small group of sophisticated directors (typically the board is far more involved in assisting the company)
- Eliminating all the substantial costs of being public, which can be in the millions
- No need to report financial information to the Securities Exchange Commission (SEC) (unless there is publicly-traded debt)
- No longer subject to most of the provisions of the Sarbanes-Oxley Act of 2002, including the necessity of personal certifications of financial information required under Sections 302 and 906 of that statute (unless there is publicly-traded debt after the private equity transaction).

The benefits of not being subject to SEC reporting requirements and the Sarbanes-Oxley Act of 2002 can be short-lived if the exit planned by the private equity fund is an initial public offering (IPO). However, the other benefits of being part of a private organization are very real and can be very significant to management.

An article in the Harvard Law School Corporate Governance Blog suggests that too much "shareholder democracy" and shareholder activism has been driving public companies into the arms of private equity firms.[5] It was suggested that this increased shareholder power is actually beginning to harm the very shareholders it was designed to protect by inducing management groups to seek refuge with private equity.

The competition for management talent from private equity funds should cause public companies to review their entire compensation program. In many cases there is not sufficient equity incentives given to management compared to what would be available in a private company setting. Therefore, it is not sufficient solely to benchmark compensation with peer groups. Rather, compensation packages, particularly equity incentives, should be reviewed in light of the increasing competition from private equity funds.

It is arguable that a public company could never provide the same percentage of equity to a management team as can a private company controlled by a private equity fund. This is because the private equity fund typically cashes out the public shareholders, primarily using debt to finance the going

---

[5]"Is Shareholder Democracy Encouraging Private Buyouts of Public Firms?" by L. Stout, The Harvard Law School Corporate Governance Blog.

private transaction, thereby reducing the total number of equity holders of the private company. Because of the smaller number of shares outstanding in a private company after the completion of the going private transaction, the number of public company shares "rolled over" by management constitutes a larger percentage of the total equity of the private company than was previously owned in the public company by management. Most of the going private transactions do not reflect the percentage of the private company owned by management after the closing, with the possible exception of the Kinder Morgan transaction referred to earlier in this chapter.

In order to compete with the equity incentives provided to management by private equity funds, the public company would generally have to leverage itself with debt and use the proceeds of such debt to repurchase sufficient shares to provide equal management equity incentives. Many public companies are not willing to incur such debt and, as a result, it may be difficult for a public company to match the equity offers to management by a private equity fund. Public companies can point to the higher debt leverage ratios of private equity fund mergers to argue that management should accept lower equity percentages in the public company since the lower leverage ratio provides management with a much safer investment. Unfortunately, some management groups are not always impressed with this argument and are willing to "roll the dice" in order to obtain higher equity rewards.

The potential competition from private equity funds for management talent will have its ebbs and flows. During periods in which there is generous debt leverage available to private equity funds, private equity funds will be active in seeking mergers with public companies having talented management groups. However, when significant debt leverage becomes difficult to obtain for private equity funds, the potential returns of these funds from public company mergers deteriorate and fewer mergers occur. Therefore, in judging the potential competition from private equity funds for management groups, the compensation committee should consider the likelihood of a private equity merger in light of the then current availability of debt leverage.

The result of failing to match the equity incentives provided to management by private equity funds may well be that the public company shareholders will be unable to obtain the same long-term rewards as are available to the private equity fund and its equity holders. The following article from *The New York Times* of January 8, 2007 illustrates clearly some of the challenges now facing compensation committees in establishing a competitive compensation framework for executives.

Private Firms Lure C.E.O.'s With Top Pay

—By Andrew Ross Sorkin and Eric Dash

Robert L. Nardelli's unceremonious departure from Home Depot may spell the end of the era of super-size pay packages for chief executives of public companies, but a new refuge for lavish compensation and private jets is emerging elsewhere.

Flush with hundreds of billions of dollars, private equity firms are beginning to offer compensation on a previously unimaginable scale to the chief executives who run the once-public companies that the firms have bought out. At the privately held firms, the executives still get salaries and bonuses, but a crucial difference lies in the ownership positions they can secure, which can turn into particularly bountiful riches when these businesses are sold or go public again.

While executives like Mr. Nardelli are being deposed, other public company chieftains are deciding that they no longer want to be judged by their shareholders and regulators, and are going to work for businesses owned by private equity. The imperial chief executive is still very much alive and well in the private realm.

"Five or 10 years ago, it used to be that private company C.E.O.'s wanted to return to the public markets because they wanted to run their own ship, not have private equity managers second-guessing their decisions," said Jeffrey A. Sonnenfeld, associate dean of the Yale University School of Management.

Now, that pattern has reversed. "You regularly hear public company C.E.O.'s talk about how they can make two or three times the money in what they feel is half the effort because they don't have the same degree of scrutiny," Mr. Sonnenfeld said.

David Calhoun, a 50-year-old vice chairman at General Electric who ran the company's $47 billion aircraft unit, left G.E. last year to become chairman and chief executive of privately held VNU, a $4.3 billion media company whose holdings include Nielsen Media Research and The Hollywood Reporter.

Mr. Calhoun, who was a contemporary of Mr. Nardelli's at General Electric, was offered a compensation package worth more than $100 million, according to executives involved in negotiating the agreement. VNU, which up until last year was a public company, is controlled by a consortium of private equity firms led by Kohlberg Kravis Roberts & Company.

Private equity investors "think about compensation differently. They will spend the money to get the right person," said George B. Paulin, an executive pay consultant at Frederic W. Cook & Company. They are "not under pressure to reform the same way big public companies are," he said.

This willingness to pay big money may bolster the argument of defenders of corporate pay practices who have contended that companies have simply been paying the going rate in the market to attract top talent. At the same time, however, private equity may be quicker than a public company to fire an executive if he is not getting results.

"There's also huge risk," said Mr. Paulin, whose firm advised on some of the richest pay packages for executives at a number of big public companies. "It's the classic pay-for-performance model."

Of course, the great irony is that private equity executives usually get their biggest paydays when a private company is either sold or taken public again. Then they again find themselves in the public view.

Mark P. Frissora is an example of the risk being worth it. Up until last year, Mr. Frissora was the chairman and chief executive of Tenneco, the auto parts manufacturer. He was making only a few million dollars a year at Tenneco when executive recruiters approached him last year with several job offers. Among them was one to lead a big public company.

But then he was offered the chief executive's job at Hertz, the rental car chain owned by a group of big private equity firms, including Carlyle Group, Clayton, Dubilier & Rice, and an investment arm of Merrill Lynch. The public company offers could not compete.

Mr. Frissora left Tenneco for Hertz in July and was granted a $4 million "make-whole" cash award and a guaranteed bonus of almost $1 million for 2006. He also was given millions in stock options and the chance to buy company stock—both at very steeply discounted prices—and a special dividend that would put another $1.2 million in his pocket.

Less than six months and an initial public offering later, Mr. Frissora is more than $33 million richer on paper, according to an analysis by Brian Foley, an independent compensation consultant in White Plains. He stands to make even more money if Hertz's share price goes up.

"It's nice work if you can get it," Mr. Foley said. And Mr. Frissora is not the only one to reap such riches.

Millard S. Drexler made hundreds of millions of dollars and his reputation as the merchant prince in his 16 years running the Gap retail chain. Now, four years after the Texas Pacific Group, a private equity firm, recruited him in to turn around J. Crew, he has made a princely sum of money: at least $300 million, and growing.

Mr. Drexler took $200,000 in annual salary and received no bonus, but he was granted millions of stock options and shares of restricted stock. Those awards are now worth $190 million after J. Crew's initial public offering last June. Over the last three years, the company also reimbursed Mr. Drexler hundreds of thousands of dollars for moving expenses, a personal chauffeur and business use of a personal jet, according to public filings.

Even more lucrative was the chance to invest $10 million of his own money. That investment is now worth at least $120 million today, and has helped him solidify a 12 percent ownership stake—a size virtually unheard of for a public company chieftain who is not the company's founder.

That kind of money is exacerbating the tension at public companies, where directors weigh the demands of top officers, who are aware of the riches elsewhere, against the demands of shareholders, who expect to see some gains in return.

"You have conflicting pressures where people in the private markets are driving up the numbers of compensation at public companies," said William W. George, the former Medtronic chairman who serves on the boards of Exxon Mobil and Goldman Sachs.

It is probably not surprising that some of the best examples of imperial chief executives of the recent past—John F. Welch Jr. of General Electric, Louis V. Gerstner of I.B.M. and Lawrence A. Bossidy of Honeywell International—have all since ventured into private equity after their retirement as advisors. Even Mr. Nardelli, who departed abruptly on Wednesday and will exit with a $210 million pay package, has already received phone calls, e-mail messages and letters from the nation's largest private equity firms, all seeking his services and dangling the possibility of even more money, according to people in private equity who approached him.

"He will wind up making a lot more money with a lot less grief in the private equity world," Leon Cooperman, one of Home Depot's largest shareholders, said on CNBC about an hour after news of Mr. Nardelli's departure. "I think it will be a long time before Bob Nardelli gets involved in a public company again."

Some worry that with executives all rushing to take their companies private, the United States is going to become less competitive. Last month, the Committee on Capital Markets Regulation published a report, which was endorsed by Henry M. Paulson Jr., the Treasury secretary, calling for a lightening of the regulatory burden on public companies.

Henry Silverman, who spent the last decade building Cendant into an $18 billion conglomerate—it owned dozens of the nation's most prominent businesses like Century 21, Avis, Days Inn and Orbitz—through a number of stock deals, says being public is no longer attractive. He broke up Cendant into four pieces and last month sold Realogy, its former real estate unit, to Apollo Management, a private equity firm.

"There is no reason to be a public company anymore," he said.

"You don't need access to the public market," because, he said, of the enormous amount of money sloshing around private equity and hedge funds.

Like Mr. Nardelli, Mr. Silverman of Cendant had been accused of being an imperial chief executive with an outsized pay package. He is estimated to have made $36.6 million in salary and bonus and reaped $223 million from exercising options between 1998 and 2002. And he will make $135 million more as a result of selling Realogy.

"Wherever I show up next, it will not be at a public company," Mr. Silverman said.

A key function of the compensation committee is to create a transparent executive compensation package which is easily explained to shareholders, as discussed in the next chapter.

CHAPTER 5

Explaining Executive Compensation to Shareholders

BEST PRACTICE

Executive compensation processes must be clearly explained to share-holders as well as to the executive. Charts and graphics are helpful aids to disclose.

INTRODUCTION

The executive compensation program of the company must be clearly explained to shareholders in the "Compensation Discussion and Analysis" (CD&A) section of the proxy statement of Form 10-K. The purpose of the CD&A is to provide transparency to the executive compensation process. A salutary effect of the CD&A is likely to be the use of better corporate governance practices by the compensation committee.

One of the best explanations the authors of this book have uncovered is in the Schedule 14A (proxy statement) filed by Bank of America Corporation with the Securities and Exchange Commission (SEC) on March 19, 2007. The following are excerpts from the CD&A:

"Overview

"We operate a large, global business in a very competitive environment. To best meet the challenges of running a business of our size and scope, we have designed our executive compensation program, under the direction of the Compensation Committee of the Board, to attract and retain the highest quality executive officers and directly link pay to our performance. This pay-for-performance mandate results in a compensation program that:

- provides pay that varies depending on performance;
- aligns our executive officers' interests with those of our stockholders; and
- can be easily understood by our stockholders

The key elements of compensation for our executive officers are annual cash incentive awards, restricted stock awards (which can be granted as shares or units) and stock option awards. These awards make up most of the total annual compensation opportunity and are based on an annual performance review. Base salary, retirement benefit accruals and perquisites or other fringe benefits make up only a minor portion of the total annual compensation opportunity. Our executive officers are not covered by employment, severance or change in control agreements.

The annual performance review for determining cash incentive, restricted stock and stock option awards follows a principled, structured framework for analysis. This analysis focuses on financial performance measures that the Committee believes collectively best indicate successful management of our business. The analysis takes into account both performance against internal business goals and relative performance against our competitors over one-year and multi-year periods.

We provide most of the total annual compensation opportunity in stock, because stock ownership is the simplest, most direct way to align our executive officers' interests with those of our stockholders. The vesting and other design features of these awards, together with our stock ownership guidelines, encourage long-term stock ownership by our executive officers to further motivate them to create long-term stockholder value. . .

"Examples of Commitment to Pay-for-Performance

"We believe that our actions in recent years demonstrate our commitment to our pay-for-performance mandate:

- We do not have any employment, severance, or change in control agreements with any of our executive officers. In recent years, both Mr. Lewis and Mr. Moynihan have voluntarily cancelled employment agreements that would have provided potential severance benefits.

- We encourage long-term stock ownership by our executive officers, with award features such as no vesting on restricted stock and stock option awards until the third anniversary of the grant and an additional three-year hold requirement on net proceeds from stock option exercises.
- Our executive officers are subject to formal stock ownership guidelines. They all currently comply with these requirements.
- We began expensing stock options in 2003, before we were required to do so by generally accepted accounting principles. We were also a leader in the shift from stock options to restricted stock as part of a balanced approach to stock compensation.
- Our Key Associate Stock Plan prohibits discounted stock options, reload stock options or stock option re-pricing.
- We have an annual stock option award process that provides for a pre-established, regular grant date in accordance with written policies and procedures. If stock options are awarded other than as part of the annual award process, those awards also have a pre-established regular grant date in accordance with written policies and procedures.
- During 2002, we adopted a policy regarding executive severance agreements which states that we will not enter into employment or severance agreements with our named executive officers that provide severance benefits exceeding two times base salary and bonus, unless the agreement has been approved by our stockholders.
- Executive officers do not accrue any additional benefits under any supplemental executive retirement plans. In addition, employer contributions under all qualified and nonqualified retirement plans are limited to the first $250,000 in annual compensation. Accordingly, the Committee's decisions to award annual performance-based cash incentive compensation, restricted stock awards and stock option awards do not create any additional retirement benefit accruals.
- Beginning in 2006, we made it more expensive for executive officers who use corporate aircraft for personal travel by requiring income to be imputed to them for such travel using a third-party "charter value," rather than the more common Internal Revenue Service "Standard Industry Fare Level" (or SIFL). This practice also benefits our stockholders by helping us avoid lost tax deductions for the related aircraft operating expenses."

The proxy statement of Bank of America Corporation then proceeds to discuss methods of measuring performance and uses a chart to explain its measurement metrics:

"Measuring Performance

"We rigorously evaluate our performance each year against a set of financial metrics that provide a complete picture of the results we achieved. We evaluate our results relative to the expectations we set in our annual business plans and compared to the performance of our key competitors over one-year and multi-year periods. The central element of this analysis is a review of the following five measures of stockholder satisfaction, which the Committee believes collectively best indicate successful management of our business:

Performance Measures	Reason For The Measure
Revenue	Our financial success begins with our ability to grow revenue.
Net Income	Revenue growth is not sufficient, however, unless it leads to growth in our net income.
Operating Earnings Per Share	We look to this measure to make sure that our net income growth is being achieved over time in a manner that is accretive for our stockholders
Shareholder Value Added	This performance measures specific focus on whether the investments we make in our businesses generate returns in excess of the cost of capital associated with those investments.
Total Stockholder Return	We use this measure, which takes into account both stock price performance and dividends, as the ultimate means to compare our performance for our stockholders relative to our competitors.

"The Committee applies the following core principles in its annual performance analysis:

• The Committee reviews the extent to which our internal business goals for revenue, net income, operating earnings per share and shareholder value added have been achieved, taking into account the quality of our earnings. We establish these goals at a level which we believe, if achieved, will result in our delivering value to our stockholders and out-performing our competitors.

- The Committee reviews our performance relative to that of our primary competitor group in the areas of revenue growth, net income growth, operating earnings per share growth and shareholder value added growth, as well as total stockholder return.
- The Committee also reviews performance over a one-year, three-year and five-year period, and for our Chief Executive Officer, over his full tenure. We intend this multi-year approach to focus our executive officers on consistent performance over time, and not just short-term returns.

"In order to achieve target or above target compensation awards, the Committee must determine that:

- internal business goals for the performance measures were attained; and
- we outperformed our primary competitor group over time.

"We believe this structured, principled framework for analysis requires strong performance to achieve target or above target compensation awards.

"As part of its analysis, the Committee looks to how the financial goals were achieved, taking into account the quality of our earnings. The Committee also considers objective data on the successful implementation of strategic initiatives that position us for future growth while also delivering positive total stockholder returns.

"For those executive officers who lead a line of business, the Committee considers how that line of business has performed against its internal business goals. In addition, as part of the annual performance review for our executive officers other than the Chief Executive Officer, the Committee considers the Chief Executive Officer's perspective on each executive officer's individual performance as well as on the performance of our various lines of business."

The proxy statement of Eli Lilly and Company contains a number of charts that are helpful in explaining the executive compensation process.[1]

---

[1] Eli Lilly and Company Schedule 14A, filed March 5, 2007.

The Coca-Cola Company used the following graphic in its 2007 proxy statement to help shareholders better understand its compensation program:

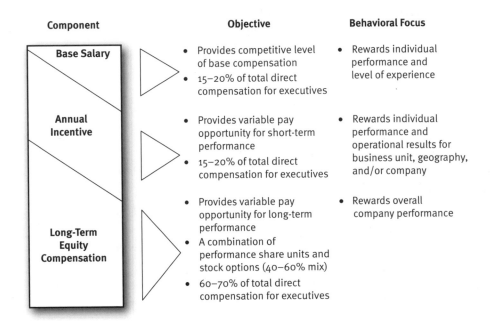

Component	Objective	Behavioral Focus
Base Salary	• Provides competitive level of base compensation • 15–20% of total direct compensation for executives	• Rewards individual performance and level of experience
Annual Incentive	• Provides variable pay opportunity for short-term performance • 15–20% of total direct compensation for executives	• Rewards individual performance and operational results for business unit, geography, and/or company
Long-Term Equity Compensation	• Provides variable pay opportunity for long-term performance • A combination of performance share units and stock options (40–60% mix) • 60–70% of total direct compensation for executives	• Rewards overall company performance

---

BEST PRACTICE

If the disclosure of performance targets would not cause competitive harm, a comparison of actual achievement of the executive to each performance target should be contained in the proxy statement, together with a disclosure of how each performance target affected compensation.

SEC rules permit the omission of performance targets if their disclosure would result in competitive harm. The SEC standard for determining competitive harm is very rigorous. Despite this, a number of companies have chosen to omit performance targets based upon competitive harm. For example, IBM refused to disclose the performance targets for its executives because such disclosure would "give competitors insight to areas where IBM is changing investments or divestments and impair IBM's ability to leverage these actions for competitive advantage. . ."[2]

The SEC staff is currently questioning whether companies who omitted performance targets because of competitive harm can actually justify their position on competitive harm.[3] Even if the performance targets are in fact protected by this exclusion and thus do not need to be disclosed, then the company "still must provide investors with a sense of how hard the targets are to achieve or how likely it is they will be met."[4]

However, a number of other companies have chosen to disclose performance targets in charts and compared the actual achievement of the executive to the performance target, and the consequent performance payout to the executive. This is very helpful disclosure in explaining to shareholders exactly how performance-based compensation was determined. A good example may be found in the ACCO Brands Corporation 2007 proxy statement, which calculates exactly how much payout was received for each individual performance measurement.[5] The General Electric Corporation 2007 proxy statement contains a comparison of the financial, strategic, and operational objectives and goals for Jeffrey R. Immelt (CEO) against his actual performance but does not specifically detail how each of these goals and objectives affected his compensation, except to disclose that he was awarded a bonus payment of $5 million for his performance.[6]

If the company elects not to disclose performance targets because of competitive harm, the company is required by the SEC rules to disclose "how difficult it will be for the executive or how likely it would be for the registrant to achieve the undisclosed target levels or other factors." The Google, Inc. 2007 proxy statement[7], in response to this SEC instruction, stated as follows: "While performance targets are established at levels that

---

[2]IBM Schedule 14A filed on March 12, 2007, p. 31.

[3]K. Scannell and J. Lublin, "SEC Asks Firms to Detail Top Executives' Pay", *The Wall Street Journal* (August 31, 2007).

[4]Speech by John W. White, Director of Division of Corporation Finance, U.S. Securities and Exchange Commission, May 3, 2007. http://sec.gov/news/speech/2007/spch050397jww.htm

[5]ACCO Brands Corporation Schedule 14A filed on April 5, 2007, p. 15.

[6]General Electric Corporation Schedule 14A filed on February 27, 2007, p. 19.

[7]Google, Inc. Proxy Statement Schedule 14A filed on April 4, 2007.

are intended to be achievable for both the Company Multiplier and the Individual Multiplier, a maximum bonus payout would require very high levels of both individual and company performance which we believe are possible but highly unlikely to be achieved. In the three years of operating the executive bonus plan, we have not paid the maximum amount to an executive."

RECONSTRUCTING EXECUTIVE COMPENSATION DISCLOSURE FOR SHAREHOLDERS

BEST PRACTICE

If the SEC mandated Summary Compensation Table distorts the compensation of an executive, consider adding an alternative Summary Compensation Table or using footnotes to clarify the distortion.

On July 26, 2006, the SEC adopted revisions to its rules governing disclosure of executive compensation in order to provide a clear and more complete picture of compensation to principal executive officers, principal financial officers, other highest paid executive officers, and directors. These rules, which are designed to create greater transparency in the executive compensation process, are summarized in Appendix B.[8]

One significant feature of the amended disclosure rules was the adoption of a "Summary Compensation Table" which would include a "Total" column that aggregated the total dollar value of each form of compensation quantified in the other columns. A Director Compensation Table, modeled on the Summary Compensation Table, was also adopted. The "Total" column is given prominence by the financial press and shareholders.

The Summary Compensation Table initially required that the table include the full dollar value from all equity awards based on the grant date

---

[8]Executive Compensation and Related Persons Disclosure, Release No. 33-87323A (Aug. 29, 2006) [71 FR 53158]. These revisions originally became effective on November 7, 2006, but were amended by Release No. 33-8765 (Dec. 22, 2006).

fair value of the equity award determined pursuant to FAS 123R, even though FAS 123R required that value to be spread over the years of service. On December 22, 2006, the SEC changed its mind and required that the Summary Compensation Table only include the accounting amount recognized in that year under FAS 123R. Thus, if stock options that were awarded in 2005 had a four year vesting period, the amount shown in 2007, and subsequent proxy statements through 2009, would be allocable FAS 123R charges to income resulting from the original grant in 2005.

Thus, when shareholders look at the "Total" column for a 2007 or a subsequent year proxy statement, the executive's compensation would include the allocable share of the 2005 option grant under FAS 123R. This figure could substantially inflate the "Total" column for 2007 or subsequent years, leading unsophisticated shareholders or financial writers to the conclusion that this amount was received in 2007, when in fact the option grants were received in 2005. If 2007 were a particularly bad year financially for the company or for shareholders' stock values, there could be a hue and cry that this was another example of excessive CEO compensation.

To avoid this erroneous inference, some companies have included an alternative Summary Compensation Table in their proxy statement that attempts to show what was actually received by the CEO during a specific year as well as the SEC's official Summary Compensation Table. An example of this can be found on page 38 of the proxy statement filed by EMC Corporation with the SEC on April 20, 2007.[9] Although the official Summary Compensation Table showed a "Total" column of $20,213,028 for the Chairman, President, and CEO, the alternative "received" Summary Compensation Table showed $5,586,177.

NYSE Euronext proxy statement presented a supplemental compensation table that they entitled "Compensation Earned in 2006," which reflected $4 million of *additional* compensation for the CEO than the Summary Compensation Table. The difference was due to the presentation of time-vested equity awards based on fair value rather than FAS 123R.[10]

Another example of where the official Summary Compensation Table can distort equity compensation is in connection with potential forfeitures

---

[9]EMC Corporation Schedule 14A filed April 20, 2007, p. 38.
[10]NYSE Euronext Schedule 14A filed on May 7, 2007.

of service-based equity awards. In its December 22, 2006 release, the SEC stated as follows:

> "In determining the amount recognized, FAS 123R requires a company to estimate at the grant date the number of awards that ultimately will be earned. Those estimates are revised each period as awards vest or are forfeited. The interim final rules that we adopt today are not intended to change the method a company uses to estimate forfeitures under FAS 123R. However, under the amendments, the compensation cost disclosed for Item 402 purposes will not include an estimate of forfeitures related to service-based vesting conditions. Compensation costs for awards containing service-based vesting conditions will be disclosed assuming that a named executive officer will perform the requisite service to vest in the award. If the named executive officer fails to perform the requisite service and forfeits the award, the amount of compensation cost previously disclosed in the Summary Compensation Table will be deducted in the period during which the award is forfeited."

At a minimum, footnote disclosures should be added to the official Summary Compensation Table that reflects the fact that forfeitures are disregarded in valuing service-based vesting of equity awards. Such a footnote appeared on page 52 of the proxy statement of EMC Corporation filed April 20, 2007.[11]

Another example of an alternative or supplementary Summary Compensation Table can be found in the proxy statement of ConocoPhillips for 2007. That proxy statement included a "Supplement to Summary Compensation Table" which reconciled the targeted and actual amounts considered by the compensation committee under each of the company's compensation programs with the amount that was required to be reported in the official Summary Compensation Table.[12]

BEST PRACTICE

Consider disclosing in the company's proxy statement the Associated Press' methodology of computing executive compensation.

---

[11]EMC Corporation Schedule 14A filed April 20, 2007, p. 52.
[12]ConocoPhillips Schedule 14A filed on April 2, 2007.

The SEC permits the Summary Compensation Table to include items that the public and the media may not perceive as fairly valuing the total compensation. This can result in media reports of CEO compensation that are much higher or much lower than the SEC total.

For example, the Associated Press reported the total compensation of John Hammergren, the Chairman and CEO of McKesson Corp., as $22.6 million for its fiscal year ended March 31, 2007.[13] This was substantially below the approximately $31 million total figure in the SEC Summary Compensation Table.[14] The Associated Press's calculations of total pay "include executives' salary, bonus, incentives, perks, above-market returns on deferred compensation and the estimated value of stock options, and awards granted during the year. This approach often results in figures that differ from the totals that companies report to the Securities and Exchange Commission."[15] The approximately $8.4 million difference apparently resulted from the Associated Press not including the column entitled "Change in Pension Value and Nonqualified Deferred Compensation Earnings" in the McKesson proxy statement and using the Grant of Planned Based Awards Table total instead of the total of the Stock Awards and Option Awards columns of McKesson's SEC's Summary Compensation Table.

The SEC's Summary Compensation Table can be misleading. Many shareholders would not count changes in pension value and nonqualified deferred compensation earnings as part of the current annual compensation of the CEO. These amounts typically represent the increase in annual actuarial present value of pension benefits and above-market interest earned from amounts deferred in the company's nonqualified deferred compensation plans. Moreover, the stock awards and option awards columns of the SEC's Summary Compensation Table tend to overstate the value of these awards because of the use of the FAS 123R figure without regard to potential forfeitures or the inclusion of an accounting allocation from prior years' option grants.

---

[13]Liedtke, "McKesson CEO Gets $22.6M Pay Package," Houston Chronicle, June 13, 2007.

[14]McKesson Corp. Schedule 14A filed on June 13, 2007.

[15]Liedtke, "McKesson CEO Gets $22.6M Pay Package," Houston Chronicle, June 13, 2007.

Moody's Investment Service has published a "User Guide to the SEC's new Rules for Reporting Executive Pay" which also reconstructs executive compensation disclosures for credit rating purposes. Interestingly, Moody's analysis agrees with the Associated Press' analysis that includes the full FAS 123R grant date fair values in executive compensation (not just the FAS 123R cost allocated to that year as contained in the Summary Compensation Chart) and also removes the annual change in defined benefit plan values and above market or preferential earnings on deferred compensation from their computation of executive compensation.

BEST PRACTICE

The company and the compensation committee should be sensitive to "headline risk" resulting from any distortion by the media or activist shareholders of the CEO's compensation and be prepared to promptly respond to any such distortion.

Obviously, McKesson did not respond to the Associated Press' compensation number because it was significantly lower than the figure in the SEC Summary Compensation Table. However, recalculations of executive compensations by the media or activist shareholders could result in a significantly higher figure than the SEC's Summary Compensation Table and even the Associated Press' methodology could, on rare occasions, lead to a higher figure.

For example, the Stock Awards and Option Awards columns of the Summary Compensation Table could result in a negative number, thereby causing the Total column to be lower than the Associated Press' computation. A negative number would result if the value of awards forfeited in a fiscal year by a named executive officer exceeds the value of other awards recognized in the Summary Compensation Table for that same named executive officer.

Companies should therefore be prepared to respond to unfair or distorted criticism by the media or activist shareholders of CEO compensation.

BEST PRACTICE

Members of the compensation committee should be present at all meetings of shareholders at which questions on executive compensation may arise.

It is typical for activist shareholders to criticize CEO compensation at meetings of shareholders. Any response to shareholder questions by the CEO is not as effective as a response by members of the independent compensation committee. Therefore, at least the chairman of the compensation committee, and preferably the entire committee, should be present at annual meetings of shareholders and at any other shareholders meetings at which such questions may arise.

Compensation committees must use best practices in their operations and in negotiating executive employment and severance agreements, as discussed in the next two chapters.

Compensation Committee Ordinary Operations

This chapter should be read in conjunction with other chapters of this book, particularly Chapter 7 entitled "Negotiating Executive Employment and Severance Agreements," Chapter 8 entitled "Compensation Committee Structure and Process," Chapters 9 entitled "Equity Incentive Choices," and Chapter 10 entitled "Option Granting Practices."

> **BEST PRACTICE**
>
> The compensation committee should have a tally sheet of all executive compensation components, which should be created by the HR Department and verified by the internal auditor. The tally sheet should include the cash, accounting, and tax effect of each of the executive compensation decisions, and should include all the information that is required in the Securities and Exchange Commission (SEC) mandated Summary Compensation Table.

Executive compensation packages are complex. The compensation committee must understand all aspects of an executive's compensation package. Likewise, the compensation committee should understand the maximum payment due to the executive under different scenarios, such as change in control, retirement, termination with or without cause, and so on. Each executive compensation decision involves a cash, accounting, and tax effect and each of these effects must be understood by the compensation committee.

An analysis of the cash, accounting, and tax effect should be obtained by the compensation committee, including the maximum payout due under each of the different scenarios. This analysis should be presented in tally sheets prepared for the compensation committee. The analysis is typically performed by the HR Department, often with the assistance of counsel and either the internal or external auditor.

The tally sheets should include all elements of compensation, including the annual increase in the value of pension plans as well as annual gains from deferred benefit plans.[1] The tally sheet should also include, at a minimum, all of the information that is required to be inserted in the Summary Compensation Table to be used in the proxy statement.

Any analysis should be verified by the internal auditor and presented to the compensation committee annually. The analysis should include not only the cash payments to the executive under various potential scenarios, but also the accounting effect so that shareholders are not shocked by a very material charge to income.

The Exxon Mobil Corporation 2007 proxy statement not only describes the use by the compensation committee of tally sheets but also provides greater detail on the preparation of the tally sheet in the following passage:

> "The Committee uses tally sheets to assess total compensation for the Corporation's senior executives. The tally sheets value all elements of cash compensation; incentive awards, including restricted stock grants; the annual change in pension value; and other benefits and perquisites.

---

[1]Lucian A. Bebchuk, "How Much Does the Boss Make,"*The Wall Street Journal* (January 18, 2006) and the study by Bebchuk and Robert J. Jackson entitled "Executive Pensions," http://papers.ssrn.com/sol3/papers.cfm?abstract_id=694766. The SEC has proposed disclosure of the increase in pension value but excluded defined contribution plans for reasons which are not clear. Securities Exchange Act Release No. 34-53185 (January 27, 2006) and the study by Lucian A. Bebchuk and Robert J. Jackson entitled "Executive Pensions," http://papers.ssrn.com/sol3/papers.cfm?abstract_id=694766. The SEC has proposed disclosure of the increase in pension value but excluded defined contribution plans for reasons that are not clear. Securities Exchange Act Release No. 34-53185, January 27, 2006.

The tally sheets also display the value of outstanding awards and lump sum pension estimates. For tally sheet purposes, the Committee considers restricted stock awards on the basis of grant date fair value as shown in the 'Grants of Plan-Based Awards' table, not on the financial accounting method used for the 'Summary Compensation Table.' "[2]

The reference in the last sentence to using the "Grants of Plan-Based Awards" valuation, rather than the FAS 123R allocation to a particular year contained in the Summary Compensation Table, was intended to reflect the fact that equity awards are valued on the grant date for tally sheet purposes and their value is not spread over the life of the equity instruments.

The Wal-Mart Stores, Inc. proxy statement for 2007 indicates that they review what is called "realized compensation" when establishing compensation levels for their 2008 fiscal year. "Realized compensation" includes cash incentive payments received, the value of restricted stock that vested in that fiscal year, the value of stock option vested during that fiscal year, the value of any performance-based shares that were paid out during that fiscal year, and other realized compensation components.[3]

BEST PRACTICE

The compensation committee should annually review each executive officer's total compensation package.

Every year the compensation committee should review each executive officer's total compensation package including base salary; cash and stock incentive awards; accumulated realized and unrealized stock option and restricted stock (or phantom unit) gains; qualified and nonqualified retirement and deferred compensation benefit accruals; and the incremental cost to the company of all perquisites. This analysis, including the tally sheet for each executive, should be provided to the full board of directors.

---

[2] Exxon Mobil Corporation Schedule 14A filed on April 11, 2007 at p 7.
[3] Wal-Mart Stores, Inc. Schedule 14A filed on April 19, 2007 at p 25.

According to the 2007 proxy statement of Bank of America Corporation,[4] this is the exact process followed by that company.

BEST PRACTICE

Compensation committees should consider the "headline" risk involved in the CEO compensation package, particularly unusually high guaranteed payments and perquisites for the CEO and the CEO's family.

Public interest in CEO compensation is so great today that the compensation committee must consider the "headline" risk involved in the CEO's compensation package (i.e., the risk that some newspaper or other media reporter will publicly critique the package). One area of media interest is the amount of any guaranteed payments, particularly any signing bonus and severance payments which are unusually high.

A "hot button" for the media is perquisites.[5] The most popular perquisite for top executives of 250 large companies included in the S&P 500 is personal use of corporate aircraft, which is offered by 76.4% of these companies.[6] This expense is typically justified by saying that the perquisite provides flexibility for executives and increased travel efficiencies, allowing more productive use of executive time and providing greater security and safety for executives. Other popular perquisites include supplemental executive retirement plans, tax and financial planning, and automobile allowances. Somewhat less popular perquisites include club memberships, home security monitoring systems, and medical examinations.

Perquisites for CEO's spouses and other family members are raw meat for newspaper reporters.[7] Nothing is more irritating to shareholders than media disclosure that a CEO, who is making over $10 million a year, did not have to pay for a spouse's or other family members corporate airplane

---

[4]Bank of America Corporation Schedule 14A filed on March 19, 2007.
[5]White and Lublin "Companies Trim Perks for Senior Executives," *The Wall Street Journal* (January 17, 2007).
[6]Compliance Week, July 3, 2007.
[7]Lublin, "Company Jets, Lifetime Discounts Are among the Perks for CEO's Kin," *The Wall Street Journal* (July 3, 2007).

trips that cost the company $75,000. It is much simpler to raise the CEO's base salary to avoid these media disclosures. However, raising the base salary by $75,000 may cost three or four times this amount because of the impact this has on bonuses and pensions among other things. Therefore, any increase in the base salary to compensate for the loss of perquisites must adjust for these other items.

The SEC's executive compensation rules provide that perquisites and personal benefits may be excluded from disclosure as long as the total value of all perquisites and personal benefits for a named executive officer is less than $10,000. If the total value of all perquisites and personal benefits is $10,000 or more for any named executive officer in the proxy statement, then each perquisite or personal benefit, regardless of its amount, must be identified by type. If perquisites and personal benefits are required to be reported for a named executive officer pursuant to this rule, then each perquisite or personal benefit that exceeds the greater of $25,000 or 10% of the total amount of perquisites and personal benefits for that officer must be quantified and disclosed in the footnote to the Summary Compensation Table included in the company's proxy statement.

An item is not a perquisite or personal benefit if it is integrally and directly related to the performance of the executive's duties. Otherwise, an item is a perquisite or personal benefit if it confers a direct or indirect benefit that has a personal aspect, without regard to whether it may be provided for some business reason or for the convenience of the company, unless it is generally available on a nondiscriminatory basis to all employees.

Examples of disclosable perquisites include the following:

- Club memberships not used exclusively for business entertainment purposes
- Personal financial planning or tax advice
- Personal travel using vehicles owned or leased by the company
- Personal travel otherwise financed by the company
- Personal use of property owned or leased by the company
- Housing and other living expenses (including, but not limited to, relocation assistance and payments for the executive to stay at his or her personal residence)
- Security provided at a personal residence or during personal travel and commuting expenses (whether or not for the company's convenience or benefits)

- Discounts on the company's products or services not generally available to employees on a nondiscriminatory basis

Examples of nondisclosable perquisites include a Blackberry or laptop computer provided by the company if it is an integral part of the executive's duties to be accessible by e-mail. There is some dispute whether partial personal use of a single secretary's time is disclosable, with most law firms taking the position that it is not disclosable if the single secretary is essential to the performance of the executive's duties.

To minimize "headline" risk for perquisites, the proposed perquisites should either be limited or structured as additional base salary (taking into account the effect of an increase in base salary on bonuses, pensions, etc.) For example, it was reported that Exxon Mobil Corp. and Lockheed Martin Corp. had stopped paying country club dues for executives, effective January 1, 2007.[8] Adding the value of the perquisite to base pay avoids having to discuss in the proxy statement details such as the number and model of automobiles received by the CEO, the free use of an apartment by the CEO, the country and dining clubs whose dues are paid by the company for the CEO, the sports boxes and other facilities made available to the CEO, the free corporate aircraft perquisites for the CEO's spouse and other family members, and so on.

The Council of Institutional Investors believes that executives should be responsible for paying personal expenses and that compensation committees should consider capping all perquisites at a de minimis level.

UnitedHealth Group, Incorporated, a company that suffered from an option backdating scandal, advertised in its 2007 proxy statement that the company had eliminated all perquisites for its new CEO other than those generally made available to all employees and executive officers.[9]

SEC Action against Tyson Foods

The SEC is particularly concerned about the failure to properly disclose and value all compensation elements in the proxy statement sent to the company shareholders. For example, the SEC has taken the position in

---

[8]White and Lubin, "Companies Trim Perks For Senior Executives," *The Wall Street Journal* (January 17, 2007).

[9]UnitedHealth Group, Incorporated Schedule 14A filed on April 30, 2007, p 31.

litigation against Tyson Foods, Inc. and Don Tyson (who is a director and a member of the executive committee of the board) that there was a failure of internal controls because of inadequate disclosure of Don Tyson's perquisites in the company's proxy statement.

According to the SEC complaint, Tyson Foods' internal accounting controls were deficient because they failed to cause the disclosure of approximately $424,000 in perquisites and because $1,500,000 in personal benefits and perquisites had not been raised with or authorized by the compensation committee of the board of directors. The SEC alleged that the company's proxy statement mischaracterized certain perquisites as "performance-based" bonuses whereas in fact, they were not performance-based. According to the SEC, some of Tyson's personal expenses and his use of homes owned by Tyson Foods should have been specifically reported in the footnotes to the compensation disclosures in the proxy statement, but were not. The SEC also alleged that Tyson's use of a company airplane was improperly valued because it did not take into consideration the incremental cost of his private use of the airplane and instead used the Standard Industry Fare Level (SIFL) method of calculated value. When the sole purpose of the flight is for the individual's personal use, the incremental cost will significantly exceed the SIFL valuation.[10]

BEST PRACTICE

The total compensation package of the CEO should not be established without considering the total compensation packages of the members of the CEO's team, particularly including the next most important senior executives.

The compensation committee must, prior to finalizing the CEO's compensation package, consider the compensation packages of other members of the CEO's team. No CEO can operate alone and be effective. Other senior executives who are key members of the CEO's team

---

[10]U.S. Securities and Exchange Commission, Litigation Release No. 19208 (April 28, 2005) http://www.sec.gov/litigation/litreleases/lr19208.htm.

must have competitive compensation packages which bear some relationship to the CEO's compensation.[11]

BEST PRACTICE

The board of directors or a board committee should be familiar with the compensation of middle-level employees in order to determine if the compensation structure is consistent with an ethical, law-abiding culture as well as the goals and strategic plan of the company.

It is typical for the compensation committee to only deal with the compensation of top executives. If that is the case, then another board committee, such as the corporate governance committee, should make itself familiar with the compensation of middle-level employees. The purpose of such review is to determine if the compensation structure is consistent with establishing an ethical, law-abiding culture as well as the goals and strategic plan of the company. To establish such a culture, rewards should be given not only for "hitting the numbers" but also for ethical behavior such as jeopardizing one's career to report legal risks and evidence of wrongdoing.

EARNINGS ON DEFERRED COMPENSATION

BEST PRACTICE

Interest on deferred compensation by executives should not exceed 120% of the applicable federal long-term interest rate and dividends on phantom equity or similar equity plans should not exceed the dividend rate on the company's common stock.

Under SEC rules, no disclosure is required for nonqualified deferred compensation earnings except to the extent that they are "above market

---

[11]See Berger and Berger, "The Compensation Handbook," McGraw-Hill, 4th Ed. (1999) p 261 et sec for "Team-Based Pay" and pp 287–288 for "Key Issues and Best Practices When Designing Team-Based Incentives."

or preferential." Under SEC rules, interest on deferred compensation is considered above market or preferential to the extent that such interest exceeds 120% of the applicable federal long-term rate, with compounding interest (as described under section 1274[d] of the Code) at the rate that corresponds most closely to the rate under the company's plan at the time the interest rate or formula was set. Dividends (and dividend equivalents) on deferred compensation denominated in the company's stock, such as phantom stock plans, are preferential only if earned at a rate higher than dividends on the company's common stock.

Practical Steps for Compensation Committees

Good corporate governance requires that the board of directors establish an independent compensation committee that in turn creates a substantial record of good faith and due diligence in making its decisions. Consideration should be given by the compensation committee to obtain separate independent counsel to help create such a record.

Decisions of the compensation committee will only be fully respected by the courts if the members are truly independent. This may suggest that the compensation committee members should have no interrelationships with management, even relationships that are permitted by the rules of the New York Stock Exchange or The NASDAQ Stock Market.

It is important that the compensation committee think and act independently with regard to compensation issues. Compensation committees should adhere to the words of Chief Justice Veasey of the Delaware Supreme Court, who stated that "directors who are supposed to be independent should have the guts to be a pain in the neck and act independently."[12]

To create a record of good faith and due diligence, the compensation committee should do the following:

> **BEST PRACTICE**
>
> Choose an independent compensation consultant.

---

[12]Veasey, "What's Wrong with Executive Compensation," Harvard Business Review, pp. 68, 76 (January 2003).

This subject is discussed further in Chapter 8.

BEST PRACTICE

Obtain independent verification that the compensation actually paid to the top executives is not greater than what was approved by the compensation committee (i.e., avoid a Tyco situation) by using an independent auditor or an independent internal auditor for such verification. Public companies should verify that any proxy statement filed with the SEC fully reflects all of the compensation elements and that they are properly valued.

In Tyco, massive compensation that was paid to both the CEO and other executive officers was allegedly never authorized by the compensation committee. An independent auditor, or an independent internal auditor, hired by the audit committee, should verify that the actual compensation paid was authorized.

Dr. LeMaistre, Chairman of Enron's Compensation Committee, testified before a Congressional committee that he had tremendous difficulty in obtaining information on Mr. Fastow, Enron's CFO. An independent auditor or an independent internal auditor, hired and compensated by the audit committee, and reporting directly to the audit committee, should be the eyes and ears of the compensation committee as well as the audit committee.

The compensation committee should also use an independent internal auditor to verify that all compensation information contained in the proxy statement is correct, complete, and properly valued.

BEST PRACTICE

Obtain information on the compensation of lower level employees to determine if the compensation arrangements reward not only financial performance but also being good corporate citizens.

The compensation incentives granted to lower level employees affect the corporate culture. Enron, WorldCom, and many other companies that suffered from corporate corruption had a "number only" culture. To instill an ethical, law-abiding culture, lower level employees must receive rewards and punishment not merely for financial performance but also for being good corporate citizens. The compensation committee (or corporate governance committee) is best suited to making inquiry of management as to whether the compensation incentives to lower level employees are consistent with an ethical, law-abiding culture.

BEST PRACTICE

Carefully oversee the operation of ERISA Plans.

Compensation committee members may be considered ERISA fiduciaries and therefore be subject to personal liability for ERISA plan operations. In Enron, the court held that since the compensation committee appointed members of the ERISA plan committee, the members of the compensation committee were themselves fiduciaries. The Enron directors paid $1.5 million from their own pockets to settle the case against them, in addition to the almost $100 million paid by the fiduciary insurer. The moral of the story: pay attention to the operation of ERISA plans.

COMPENSATION COMMITTEES OF NON-PROFIT ORGANIZATIONS

Compensation of executives of tax-exempt organizations has become a major issue in the media, Congress and state attorney generals. For example, the *New York Times* of February 11, 2006 disclosed a state investigation into the finances of the J. Paul Getty Trust in Los Angeles, the nation's third largest private foundation, resulting from a $3 million severance payment to the director of the Getty Museum and a $250,000 severance payment to another trust executive. Information about the severance payments came to light after the trust's President and CEO resigned amid questions about his leadership and possible abuse of expenses and perquisites.

In 2004, the IRS described its Tax Exempt Compensation Enforcement Project, an aggressive audit and compliance check program in which 2,000 charities and foundations will be asked about their compensation practices. In 2005, the IRS' Exempt Organizations Division's new compliance unit sent an estimated 1,250 letters to a wide range of charities and private foundations inquiring about executive compensation, insider transactions (e.g., loans or sales of property to officers or directors), 990 reporting and other issues that impact compensation.

To maintain tax-exempt status under Section 501(c)(3), an organization must be both organized *and* operated so that no part of its net earnings inures to the benefit of any private shareholder or individual.[13] In addition, a charity must not be organized and operated for the benefit of private interests such as designated individuals, founders of the organization or their family members, shareholders, or persons controlled (directly or indirectly) by such interests.[14]

Excessive compensation is one form of private inurement or impermissible private benefit. Whether a particular compensation arrangement is excessive or reasonable is a question of fact, to be determined based on the facts and circumstances of each case. For tax purposes, "reasonableness" is determined according to the standard applicable to business deductions under Section 162 of the Internal Revenue Code ("Code"), taking into account the aggregate benefits provided to a person and the rate at which deferred compensation accrues.[15] In this context "reasonable" compensation for services is the amount that would ordinarily be paid for like services by like enterprises (whether taxable or tax-exempt) under like circumstances (i.e. reasonable compensation).

The principal enforcement tools available to the IRS are known as "Intermediate Sanctions" (Section 4958 of the Code) for public charities (organizations described in Section 501(c)(3) or 501(c)(4) of the Code) and the "Self-Dealing Excise Tax" (Section 4941 of the Code), which applies to private foundations. In addition, the IRS can revoke the tax-exempt status of the organization.[16]

---

[13]Treas. Reg. Section 1.501(c)(3)-1(c)(2).

[14]Treas. Reg. Section 1.501(c)(3)-1(d)(1)(ii).

[15]Treas. Reg. Section 53.4958-4(b)(1)(ii)(A).

[16]See Miller, "Rebuttable Presumption is Key to Easy Intermediate Sanctions Compliance" Tax Notes, Vol. 91, Issue 11 (June 4, 2001).

Section 4958 imposes taxes on so-called "excess benefit transactions" with "disqualified persons". Excess benefit transactions refer generally to transactions in which the economic benefit, directly or indirectly, to the disqualified person exceeds the value of the services or other consideration received by the tax-exempt organization. The additional tax, which is imposed on the disqualified person, can be as much as 25% of the excess benefit and can rise to 225% of the excess benefit if the transaction is not corrected within the taxable period. Disqualified persons include (among others) persons who are in a position to exercise substantial influence over the affairs of the organization (e.g. CEOs, CFOs, etc.) and members of their families (as defined in the Code and the regulations).

In cases where an initial 25% tax has been imposed on disqualified persons, a 10% tax is imposed by Section 4958 on the organization managers (e.g. directors and officers) who participate in the transaction knowing that it was an excess benefit transaction, unless the participation is not willful and is due to reasonable cause.

> **BEST PRACTICE**
>
> If there is the slightest doubt as to the reasonableness of executive compensation, compensation committees of non-profit organizations should receive a reasoned written opinion as to the reasonableness of executive compensation from an independent compensation professional.

There is a safe harbor under which participation by an organization manager in a transaction will ordinarily not be subject to the 10% tax, even though the transaction is later held to be an excess benefit transaction. Specifically, an organization manager is ordinarily not considered to have knowingly participated in a transaction, to the extent that, after full disclosure of the factual situation to an appropriate professional, the organization manager relies on a reasoned written opinion of that professional regarding the elements of the transaction within the professional's expertise.

We next turn to one of the most important functions of the compensation committee, namely negotiating employment and severance agreements with new and existing executive officers.

CHAPTER 7

Negotiating Executive Employment and Severance Agreements

This chapter deals with best practices in negotiating employment and severance agreements with both new CEO candidates and existing CEOs, including, but not limited to, the subject of termination clauses, clawback provisions, golden parachutes, gross–up clauses, and retirement arrangements.

NEGOTIATING WITH NEW CEO CANDIDATES

BEST PRACTICE

Compensation committees should establish a range of compensation at the outset of a search for a new CEO, with the help of an independent compensation consultant.

By setting a compensation range before commencing the CEO search, the compensation committee provides a guidepost for itself of what it considers to be reasonable compensation. Failing to set such a compensation range at the beginning of the search leaves the compensation committee vulnerable to unreasonable demands from a CEO candidate.

The Wall Street Journal of May 21, 2007 reported that the directors of Sharper Image Corp., after ousting its founder and CEO, sought to replace him without paying "big bucks — even if that meant foregoing potential stars." Ultimately, they landed an experienced outsider "without giving away the store," according to the article, since his contract lacked typical CEO perks such as a supplemental pension plan. By establishing a range of compensation at the onset of the CEO search process, the board of directors of Sharper Image Corp. was able to hire a competent CEO without paying excessive compensation.

For purposes of the CEO search process, an independent compensation consultant should be hired by the compensation committee who does not have any relationship with management. The use of a compensation consultant that has a prior relationship with management should be avoided.

BEST PRACTICE

The CEO search should include back-up candidates so that the compensation committee has alternatives if the compensation demanded by the first choice is unreasonable.

One method to avoid having to cave-in to unreasonable compensation demands from a proposed CEO is to have back-up candidates who may be less desirable from the first choice but are nevertheless reasonable choices. A compensation committee that fixes solely on a single candidate makes itself vulnerable to oversized compensation demands and limits the bargaining power of the compensation committee.

It is recognized that there may be situations in which quick action is required to hire a new CEO and to pay whatever the candidate requires. This should be a very rare situation and many times results from inadequate CEO succession plans.

On April 27, 2007, it was reported that the Dean of Admissions at MIT had quit because she misrepresented her academic credentials when she applied for her job at MIT 28 years earlier. She claimed on her resume

BEST PRACTICE

Carefully check and recheck the resume of any prospective CEO candidate in whom you are interested. Have the CEO represent the accuracy of the resume in any employment agreement.

to have degrees from Union College, Rensselaer Polytechnic Institute, and the Albany Medial College, but in fact had no degrees from any of those institutions, or anywhere else. *The Wall Street Journal* stated that the Dean had "embellished her own credentials."[1] Remarkably, the Dean was a prominent crusader at MIT against pressure on students to build their resumes for elite colleges.[2]

In February 2006, the CEO of RadioShack Corp., David J. Edmondson, resigned following the revelation that he had lied on his resume. The CEO claimed that he had received degrees in theology and psychology from Pacific Coast Baptist College in California (subsequently renamed "Heartland Baptist Bible College"). Unfortunately, the school had no record of the degrees and the registrar of the school stated that the CEO had completed only two semesters and the school never offered degrees in psychology. The CEO had served in various positions with RadioShack starting in 1994 and became CEO in May 2005.[3]

In October 2002, Kenneth Lonchar, the CFO of Veritas Software, was forced to resign after making false claims that he was a Stanford MBA graduate. On the day of his resignation, Veritas Software stock price fell approximately 16%. In November 2002, Bausch & Lomb, the eye care company, announced that Chairman and Chief Executive Ronald Zarrella would forfeit $1.1 million because his resume falsely noted an MBA from New York University. In November 2002, MSG Capital Chairman and

---

[1] The Wall Street Journal (April 27, 2007).

[2] "A Noted MIT Dean Quits for Falsifying Her Credentials," The Philadelphia Inquirer, April 27, 2007, p. A5.

[3] "Departing RadioShack CEO to get $1 million," The Associated Press (February 21, 2006).

CEO, Brian Mitchell, admitted falsifying a degree from Syracuse University and, although he was continued as CEO, the stock price fell 37% after the announcement, hitting a 52-week low.[4] On February 1, 2000, Jeffrey P. Papows quit as president of IBM's Lotus unit because of discrepancies in his education and military records.[5]

People lie on their resumes. Approximately 30% of all job applicants make material representations on resumes. ADP Screening and Selection Services says that in performing 2.6 million background checks in 2001, it found that 44% of applicants lied about their work histories, 41% lied about their education, and 23% falsified credentials or licenses.[6] The lying extends not merely to their prior positions but also to their educational background. Nothing is more embarrassing than hiring a CEO only to find that they have misrepresented their background.

The cost to check a resume is relatively small compared to the potential damage that can occur if the resume is false in any material respect.

Requiring the prospective CEO to make a legal representation as to the accuracy of his or her resume will force the prospective CEO to think hard about any inaccuracy or exaggeration in the resume as well as providing legal protection to the company.

BEST PRACTICE

If a CEO is recruited from another company and the CEO demands a signing bonus to compensate for the loss of benefits, the executive should be required to represent in the employment agreement the exact amount of the CEO's current compensation package from the existing employer of the CEO as well as the CEO's compensation package during the past three to five years.

---

[4]"Resume Fraud in The Corner Office" (Penn State College of Business (November 2002); see also "School Lies: Why Do So Many Executives Lie About Their Education." (Slate Magazine, October 22, 2002).

[5]"Lotus CEO Resigns." (Computerworld, January 10, 2000).

[6]"Spotting Lies." (HR Magazine, October 2003, Vol. 48, No. 10).

The written representation by a CEO candidate of his or her compensation package currently and for the past three to five years permits the company to perform an investigation of the truthfulness of the CEO candidate. Many CEO candidates will not want their current employer to know that they are looking for new employment. The written representation of the proposed CEO in the employment or severance agreement will permit the CEO to be hired without first checking with the current employer of the CEO, while preserving the legal rights of the company if the representation is false. Once the employment agreement is signed, the company should check with the proposed CEO's current employer quickly and preferably before any public announcement that the new CEO has been hired.

The reason for asking for the compensation package for the last three to five years is to determine if the prospective CEO's current employer was loading the candidate up with options and other compensation in anticipation of providing the candidate with more bargaining power with a new employer. For example, it was reported in *The Wall Street Journal* of January 4, 2007 that much of the rich compensation package given to Robert Nardelli was due to his prior employer, Jack Welch of General Electric Company, loading him up with stock options in anticipation of his leaving General Electric. Allegedly, Mr. Welch convinced his board of directors to give Mr. Nardelli, one of three finalists to succeed Jack Welch, large batches of stock options to permit Mr. Nardelli, as well as the other runner-up, to negotiate pay at their next jobs. According to *The Wall Street Journal*: "'Mr. Welch convinced his board to give all three finalists large batches of stock options, telling board members they would have to make good on only one man's options,' one director says."

BEST PRACTICE

Any employment agreement with a new CEO should contain warranties and representations about their resume, and any agreements with prior employers that might affect their ability to perform services for the company.

If the compensation committee is basing its hiring decision on the resume of the CEO, the employment agreement should so state as such and should contain a warranty and representation by the new CEO as to the contents of his or her resume. Likewise, the new CEO should warrant and represent in the employment agreement that there are no agreements with prior employers that would interfere with the performance of his or her duties for the company. If there are such agreements with prior employers, they must be carefully examined to determine if they will restrict the executive in any material manner in his or her new position.

Negotiating With Existing CEOs

The negotiation of an existing CEO differs markedly from negotiation with a CEO candidate. The compensation committee is familiar with the strengths and weaknesses of the existing CEO and can tailor any agreement accordingly. However, the compensation committee should consider competitive factors in negotiating with an existing CEO who has other opportunities and may be willing to take advantage of these opportunities.

Although some activist shareholders have been stressing internal pay equity, any such metrics must consider the other opportunities available to the CEO that are not necessarily available to either other executives or to the workforce in general. Although internal pay equity can be considered, such consideration cannot be used to make the CEO's compensation less than competitive.

More important than internal paid equity is the relationship of the CEO's compensation to other members of the CEO's team who are important to the company's operations. Team compensation structure must be considered in establishing CEO compensation and the terms of any employment agreement. In addition, compensation committees should avoid the Lake Wobegon effect discussed in Chapter 3, since not all executives deserve to be at or above the 50th percentile in compensation.

Some prominent CEOs have voluntarily canceled their existing employment agreements. Included among those CEOs who have voluntarily given up their existing employment agreements are the CEOs of Bank of America, Wachovia Corp., and ConocoPhillips.[7]

---

[7]"Exit Pay Best Practices in Practice," Institutional Shareholder Services (March 2007).

Best Practices Applicable to New and Existing CEOs

The following best practices apply to employment and severance agreements for both new and existing CEOs.

BEST PRACTICE

The compensation committee should attempt, where feasible, to avoid any employment agreement with a new or existing CEO and if an employment or severance agreement is required, its term should be limited. Severance agreements should be preferred over employment agreements.

Although a majority of Fortune 100 companies have an employment agreement with at least one named executive officer, there are prominent examples of companies who have no employment agreement with their CEO. Jeffrey R. Immelt, Chairman and CEO of General Electric Company, is an example of the CEO without an employment contract. Other prominent companies without an employment agreement for their CEO include: Exxon Mobil Corp., PepsiCo, Inc., Pfizer, Inc., Wm. Wrigley, Jr. Co., CitiGroup, Inc., Procter & Gamble Co., Intel Corp., Cisco Systems, Health Management Associates, and Masco Corp.[8]

However, in most situations, it is likely that an employment or severance agreement will be required with a new CEO. A severance agreement should be preferred over an employment agreement since it does not bind the company to any period of employment, but does protect the new CEO from the effect of a severance of the relationship. if an employment agreement is required because the new CEO would like to clarify in writing the exact compensation and benefits to which he or she is entitled as well as other applicable employment provisions,. the term of the employment agreement should be typically limited to not more than three years.

---

[8]"Exit Pay Best Practices in Practices," Institutional Shareholder Services (March 2007).

Multiyear employment agreements should be avoided. Jeffery R. Immelt, General Electric's CEO, has spoken out against CEOs with multi-year employment agreements that could lead to large payoffs if they are terminated.[9]

COUNCIL OF INSTITUTIONAL INVESTORS

The Council of Institutional Investors represents 130 institutional investors with $3 trillion under management. According to the Council of Institutional Investors, the following are the best practices:

BEST PRACTICE

Employment contracts: Companies should only provide employment contracts to executives in limited circumstances, such as to provide modest, short-term employment securities to a newly hired or recently promoted executive. Such contracts should have a specified termination date (not to exceed three years); contracts should not be "rolling" on an open-end basis.

Severance payments: Executives should be entitled to severance payments in non-control change situations only in the event of wrongful termination, death, or disability. Termination for poor performance, resignation under pressure, or failure to renew the contract should not qualify as wrongful termination.

Employment agreements and severance agreements can be very similar. Notwithstanding the fact that the executive has an employment agreement, the law permits the company to terminate employment of the executive even though this may violate the employment agreement. Effectively, all that an employment agreement typically affords an executive are certain rights during the period of his or her employment and certain protections after their employment terminates. The court will almost never specifically enforce an employment agreement (i.e., they

---

[9]Chrystia Feeland and Francesco Guerrera, "GE Head Wades into Pay Debate," *Financial Times*, November 3, 2006, Front Page – Companies and Markets, p. 17.

will almost never force the company to rehire the executive, but will only merely limit the executive to money damages).

Severance agreements provide what happens in the event the executive's employment is terminated. Unlike an employment agreement, there is no guarantee of the duration of employment. However, in view of the company's ability to terminate employment any time it wishes, the benefits provided by an employment agreement are somewhat illusory.

From a public relations' prospective, a severance agreement is easier to explain to shareholders than a long-term employment agreement. if the executive is given a list of his salary and benefits by a letter from the company describing them, the severance agreement will, in all practical respects, provide the executive with the protections he would have received under an employment agreement, without the public relations issues resulting from long-term employment agreements.

BEST PRACTICE

The compensation committee should select an experienced negotiator to finalize the terms of any proposed CEO employment or severance agreement.

Many compensation committee members do not have the expertise to negotiate employment or severance agreements and, even if a compensation member has such expertise, he or she may not have the time. Therefore, it is important to hire an experienced negotiator, typically an attorney, to assist the compensation committee in this process. Many CEOs hire very experienced attorneys to represent their interests and it is important that the compensation committee have attorneys who are counterparts of the CEO's attorney.

BEST PRACTICE

Expand the termination for "cause" rights of the company in the employment or severance agreement.

It has been traditional to limit terminations for "cause" rights of the company very narrowly to include only conviction for certain felonies and willful misconduct. However, there may be other situations that would justify a termination for "cause." For example, Robert Iger, the CEO of Walt Disney Co., can be terminated for "cause" if he refuses to give testimony or cooperate with an investigation into his or the company's business practices. Obviously, this is a sensitive area of negotiation since the company can refuse to pay severance benefits in the event of termination for "cause."

BEST PRACTICE

The compensation committee should consider a proactive approach to disclosing CEO compensation by crafting their own press release that contains the justifications for the compensation package.

The Securities and Exchange Commission (SEC) requires full disclosure of CEO compensation in its regulatory filings. If the company is followed by securities analysts, unions, or other corporate governance activists, they should anticipate that the information contained in the SEC regulatory filings will be headline worthy. It is therefore appropriate for companies to take a proactive approach to media interests in CEO compensation. A proactive approach would require the company to use its own press releases to report new hires and to craft a justification for the CEO compensation, making it less newsworthy.

Public outrage over executive compensation has extended to new CEO hires as well as ongoing compensation packages. For example, the following appeared in a newspaper in April 2007:

> "Ford Motor Co. paid Alan Mulally $28.2 million in his first four months as chief executive officer after recruiting him from the Boeing Co.
>
> "Mulally's compensation included $666,667 in salary, a $7.5 million hiring bonus, $11 million for payments he would have gotten from running Boeing's commercial-Aircraft business, $8.68 million in stock

options and awards, and $334,433 in other compensation, the company said in a U.S. regulatory filing yesterday."[10]

According to the April 6, 2007 issue of *The Wall Street Journal*, a spokesperson for Ford Motor Co. stated that part of Mr. Mulally's compensation related to him forfeiting performance stock option awards at Boeing.

The bad publicity received by Mulally's compensation package could have been partially blunted by a fuller disclosure by Ford Motor Co. of the benefits that Mulally gave up at Boeing to join Ford. In order to make such a public disclosure, Ford would have had to obtain a representation from Mulally as to his existing compensation package in his employment agreement. This representation from Mulally could then be used to justify the signing bonus that Ford was required to pay Mulally.

BEST PRACTICE

The executive employment agreement must contain provisions relating to confidentiality, nonsolicitation of customers and employees, and noncompetition. If there is no executive employment agreement, there should be separate agreements with key executives covering confidentiality, nonsolicitation of customers and employees, and noncompetition.

Although provisions relating to confidentiality, nonsolicitation of customers and employees and noncompetition are contained in almost all executive employment agreements, these provisions are not standard among law firms. Slight differences in the wording of these provisions can make a major difference in the ability to effectively enforce these clauses. Therefore, these provisions should be carefully reviewed by the compensation committee and should not be considered "boilerplate" legal clauses.

For example, the authors of this book have been involved in situations in which the executive leaves the company and joins a competitor.

---

[10]"New Ford CEO Received $28 Million in 4 Months," *The Philadelphia Inquirer* (April 6, 2007).

The executive's employment agreement contains a one-year noncompete provision. Legal action is then taken to enjoin the executive from violating the noncompetition provision. However, by the time the court acts, a number of customers have left to join the competitor and it is difficult to prove damages caused by the executive with the mathematical precision required by the courts. Therefore, the company may not be able to secure a money damage remedy and is limited to an injunction. The injunction, however, will not last longer than the balance of the one-year noncompete period, which may only have months until it expires. If the noncompetition provision stated that the executive who violates it would be required to not compete not only for the one-year period but for one year *plus the amount of time the executive violated the noncompete provision*, the company would have been protected from competition far longer.

BEST PRACTICE

Insert so-called "clawback" provisions in employment or severance agreements.

Many employment agreements contain salary or bonus provisions that are based upon financial results. Suppose that a bonus is paid based upon the net income for a particular fiscal year, and subsequently those results are changed or otherwise restated to show a lower net income as a result of an auditor review, government action or otherwise. A clawback clause would require the executive to refund all or a portion of the bonus in the event of a subsequent change or other restatement of the financial statement on which the bonus was based.

Section 304(a) of the Sarbanes-Oxley Act of 2002 provides as follows:

"(a) ADDITIONAL COMPENSATION PRIOR TO NONCOMPLIANCE WITH COMMISSION FINANCIAL REPORTING REQUIREMENTS. – If any issuer is required to prepare an accounting restatement due to the material noncompliance of the issuer, **as a result of misconduct**, with any financial reporting requirement under the securities laws, the chief executive officer and chief financial officer of the issuer shall reimburse the issuer for –

"(1) any bonus or other incentive-based or equity-based compensation received by that person from the issuer during the 12-month period following the first public issuance or filing with the Commission (whichever first occurs) of the financial document embodying such financial reporting requirements, and

"(2) any profits realized from the sale of securities of the issuer during that 12-month period."

[Emphasis supplied]

The law requires that the clawback only applies if there is "misconduct" by the executive. However, there is nothing to prevent a company from drafting the clawback clause so that it applied whether or not the change or other restatement of the financial statement occurred as a result of misconduct.

UnitedHealth Group Incorporated has adopted the following clawback policy in 2007:[11]

"Material Restatements

- "The clawback policy applies to a defined list of approximately 30 members of senior management, including all executive officers, and applies to both incentive cash and equity compensation.

- "Annual or long-term cash incentives: Any designated executive must repay the Company the entire amount of his or her annual or long-term cash incentive payment if the Board determines that he or she has engaged in fraud or misconduct that caused, in whole or in part, a material restatement of the Company's financial statements and the executive would have received a lower annual or long-term cash incentive payment if it had been based on the restated financial results.

- "Equity compensation: If it is determined that a designated executive has engaged in fraud that causes, in whole or in part, a material restatement of the Company's financial statements, the Company will cancel his or her then-outstanding vesting and unvested options/SARs or other unvested equity awards subject to the

---

[11]UnitedHealth Group Incorporated Schedule 14A, filed on April 30, 2007, pp. 38–39.

clawback policy, and the executive must return to the Company all gains from equity awards realized during the twelve-month period following the filing of the incorrect financial statements.

"Violation of Noncompetition Covenants

- "The clawback policy with respect to violations of noncompetition covenants, applies to a broader group of executives, and applies only to equity compensation.
- "The policy requires cancellation of unvested options/SARs or other unvested equity awards and forfeiture of all equity awards which vested within one year prior to termination of employment or anytime thereafter if the employee violates a restrictive covenant."

All employment and severance agreements should contain reasonable clawback clauses.

BEST PRACTICE

If the compensation committee determines to provide a golden para-chute to an executive, a double trigger should be required.

A golden parachute is typically a clause in the executive's employment or severance contract specifying what they will receive if their employment is terminated under certain conditions, usually (but not always) following a change in control.

According to a Towers Perrin Report for 2005 of 973 companies, 79% had golden parachute protection provisions in 2005, compared to 70% in 1999 and only 35% in 1997.[12] Thus, it is unlikely that most companies can avoid golden parachute provisions.

The golden parachute payments are subject to different types of triggers, including the following:

- Single trigger: Benefit becomes payable automatically upon a change in control or upon a voluntary termination by the executive for any reason within a specified time period following the change in control.

---

[12]Towers Perrin, Executive Compensation Resources, July 6, 2006.

- Double trigger: Benefits become payable after both a change in control and the subsequent termination of the executive's employment, either by the company without "cause" or by the executive for "good reason" (i.e., a "constructive termination").
- Modified single trigger: Benefits become payable subject to a double trigger. In addition, the executive may voluntarily terminate employment for any reason during a specified "window period" (typically the 30-day period following the one-year anniversary of the change in control).

The argument for requiring a double trigger is that the change in control should not in itself accelerate benefits or entitle the employee to compensation unless the employee is harmed by the change in control. The employee can be harmed because he is terminated without cause or he is "constructively" terminated (e.g., reduced compensation, reduced authority and responsibility, change in title, etc.).

Moody's Investors Service, Inc. has focused on "single-trigger" change in control payout provisions stating that "such mechanisms have the potential to encourage acquisitive behaviors that are not in the overall interests of the company."[13]

> **BEST PRACTICE**
>
> Change in control provisions should be carefully tailored to situations in which there is an actual change in control.

Some change in control provisions permit a change of 20% of the stock ownership by a single person or group to constitute a change in control, even if there is no change of the board of directors. The change in control clause should be tailored to situations in which there is an actual change in control and, typically, no change in control occurs at the 20% level.

---

[13]"A User's Guide to the SEC's New Rules for Reporting Executive Pay," April 2007, Note 1.

The following is a typical change in control clause at the 50% level which, while not perfect, is at least reasonable:

Change in Control. For the purpose of this Agreement, a "Change in Control" shall mean:

(a) The acquisition by any individual, entity or group (within the meaning of Section 13(d)(3) or 14(d)(2) of the Securities Exchange Act of 1934, as amended (the "Exchange Act")) (a "Person") of beneficial ownership (within the meaning of Rule 13d-3 promulgated under the Exchange Act) of more than 50% of either (i) the then-outstanding shares of common stock of the Company (the "Outstanding Company Common Stock") or (ii) the combined voting power of the then-outstanding voting securities of the Company entitled to vote generally in the election of directors (the "Outstanding Company Voting Securities"); provided, however, that for purposes of this subsection (a), the following acquisitions shall not constitute a Change in Control: (i) any acquisition directly from the Company, (ii) any acquisition by the Company, (iii) any acquisition by any employee benefit plan (or related trust) sponsored or maintained by the Company or any corporation controlled by the Company, or (iv) any acquisition by any corporation pursuant to a transaction which complies with clauses (i), (ii) and (iii) of subsection (c); or

(b) Individuals who, as of the date hereof, constitute the Board (the "Incumbent Board") cease for any reason to constitute at least a majority of the Board; provided, however, that any individual becoming a director subsequent to the date hereof whose election, or nomination for election by the Company's shareholders, was approved by a vote of at least a majority of the directors then comprising the Incumbent Board shall be considered as though such individual were a member of the Incumbent Board, but excluding, for this purpose, any such individual whose initial assumption of office occurs as a result of an actual or threatened election contest with respect to the election or removal of directors or other actual or threatened solicitation of proxies or consents by or on behalf of a Person other than the Board; or

(c) Consummation of a reorganization, merger or consolidation or sale or other disposition of all or substantially all of the assets of the Company (a "Business Combination"), in each case, unless, following such Business Combination, (i) all or substantially all of the individuals and entities who were the beneficial owners, respectively, of the Outstanding Company Common Stock and Outstanding Company Voting

Securities immediately prior to such Business Combination beneficially own, directly or indirectly, more than 50% of, respectively, the then-outstanding shares of common stock and the combined voting power of the then outstanding voting securities entitled to vote generally in the election of directors, as the case may be, of the corporation resulting from such Business Combination (including, without limitation, a corporation which as a result of such transaction owns the Company or all or substantially all of the Company's assets either directly or through one or more subsidiaries) in substantially the same proportions as their ownership, immediately prior to such Business Combination of the Outstanding Company Common Stock and Outstanding Company Voting Securities, as the case may be, (ii) no Person (excluding any corporation resulting from such Business Combination or any employee benefit plan (or related trust) of the Company or such corporation resulting from such Business Combination) beneficially owns, directly or indirectly, more than 50% of, respectively, the then-outstanding shares of common stock of the corporation resulting from such Business Combination, or the combined voting power of the then-outstanding voting securities of such corporation except to the extent that such ownership existed prior to the Business Combination and (iii) at least a majority of the members of the Board of Directors of the corporation resulting from such Business Combination were members of the Incumbent Board at the time of the execution of the initial agreement, or of the action of the Board, providing for such Business Combination; or

(d) Approval by the shareholders of the Company of a complete liquidation or dissolution of the Company.

Section 409A of the Internal Revenue Code has its own change in control definitions which, in the absence of an exemption from that section, must be complied with at a minimum in order to avoid any violation of Section 409A. These are discussed more fully in Chapter 13. However, to avoid inadvertent violations of Section 409A, it is recommended that the change in control clauses be drafted so that, in the absence of an exemption from Section 409A, a change in control would have to also meet the definitions in Section 409A in addition to the definitions in the employment or severance agreement. Failure to do so may subject the executive to a total federal income tax rate of 55% (plus interest retroactive to the vesting date), consisting of a maximum federal income rate of 35% for 2007 plus 20% additional tax on the deferred compensation which violates Section 409A. The tax rate could be as high as 85% for California residents, since California has adopted its own version of Section 409A. For an example, see Appendix D.

BEST PRACTICE

Require shareholder approval of executive severance agreements that would constitute an excess golden parachute payment under Section 280G of the Internal Revenue Code.

Companies that have adopted this policy or a variant include the Coca-Cola Company, Bank of America Corp., Raytheon Co., Hewlett-Packard, Electronic Data Systems, American Electric Power, Union Pacific, and AutoNation.[14] No deduction is allowed under the Internal Revenue Code to a public company with respect to an "excess parachute payment," which is typically a payment to a disqualified individual (generally officers or other highly compensated individuals) contingent on a change in the ownership or effective control of the corporation, or in the ownership of a substantial portion of the assets of the corporation, which equals or exceeds three times the "base amount" of such individual.

This policy has the incidental benefit of deterring requests for "excess parachute payments" from executives or so-called "gross up" clauses to cover the golden parachute taxes. The disadvantage of this policy is that the cost of the shareholders meeting can sometimes exceed the golden parachute payment and can interfere with the hiring of key executives. However, on the whole, seeking shareholder approval is generally going to be the best policy in today's atmosphere.

---

[14]Morgenson, "Severance Pay Doesn't Go Better With Coke," *The New York Times* (December 25, 2005).

GROSS-UP CLAUSES

BEST PRACTICE

So-called "gross-up" clauses (covering any excise or additional taxes payable upon the receipt of severance, change-in-control or similar payments) should be carefully considered. Companies should only agree to "gross-up" clauses if there is a maximum placed on the amount of the gross-up.

Section 4999 of the Internal Revenue Code of 1986 ("Code") imposes a 20% excise tax on so-called "excess parachute payments," which in general refers to payments contingent upon a change in the ownership or effective control of the corporation or in the ownership of a substantial portion of the assets of the corporation. A gross-up clause reimburses the executive for these additional excise taxes payable or other taxes payable upon receipt of severance, change-in-control or similar payments.

Some companies have eliminated tax gross-up clauses entirely, such as Sara Lee, E-Trade, Prudential, and Wyeth.[15] The Council of Institutional Investors opposes any compensation to executives for excise or additional taxes payable upon receipt of severance, change in control, or similar payments. An argument may be made that this is the best practice; however, it is not always feasible to avoid gross-up clauses.

Some compensation consultants argue that gross-up clauses are needed to fix a flawed tax law. If an executive exercises stock options for significant profit gains during the base period (used for purposes of computing the maximum golden parachute payment under Section 280G of the Internal Revenue Code), thereby increasing the base period compensation, the executive is more likely to escape or minimize the excise tax under Section 280G for "a parachute payment" (generally not more than 2.99 times the base amount). However, if the same executive continues to hold the stock options instead of exercising them during the base period, the excise taxes will likely apply or be larger.

---

[15]Compensation Standards (Spring 2007).

Institutional Shareholders Services (ISS) has taken the position that gross-ups are quite costly to companies because the gross-ups hit them with "a one-two punch."[16] The first punch is the payment itself, which can amount to a large number of dollars. The second punch is the fact that the company can lose eligibility for the corporate tax deduction on the excess parachute payments caused by the gross-up under Section 280G of the Internal Revenue Code. The effect of the one-two punch is that the cost to the company may exceed the benefit to the executive. ISS has also noted that companies with gross-up clauses will not necessarily escape the application of this clause by limiting severance payments to 2.99 times salary and bonus, since a typical provision for accelerated vesting of stock options may cause the total parachute payment to exceed the 2.99 limitation.

Despite the ISS position, a Towers Perrin study has indicated that 77% of companies with golden parachute agreements provide for excess tax gross-ups.[17]

The amount which has to be paid under the gross-up clause is extremely difficult to determine. For example, a golden parachute payment which exceeds the limits of Section 280G of the Code may be based upon the total compensation (including bonus during the year) prior to the change of control. Since the change of control has not occurred and may not occur for many years, there is no way that the compensation committee can calculate the amount of the change of control payment and, accordingly, they are unable to determine the total gross-up payment. Moreover, federal income or excise tax rates can change in the interim.

Accordingly, if a gross-up clause is required in an employment or severance contract, it should be subject to an overall dollar limitation or possibly a limitation which prevents the payments from exceeding the limits of Section 280G of the Code. Some would argue that there should be no such limitations where the transaction that triggers the gross-up payment is beyond the control of the executive and over the executive's objections. The counter-argument is that such an exception would permit the executive to easily avoid the limitation on the gross-up by merely objecting to the transaction that triggered the gross-up clause.

---

[16] "Exit Pay Best Practices in Practice," Institutional Shareholders, Inc. (March 2007).

[17] Towers Perrin, Executive Compensation Resources, July 6, 2006.

The following is an example of a gross-up clause with an overall dollar limitation:

"7. Certain Additional Payments by the Company.

(a) Anything in this Agreement to the contrary notwithstanding and except as set forth below, after a Change in Control and as a result of a termination of employment, in the event it shall be determined that any payment or distribution by the Company to or for the benefit of the Executive (whether paid or payable or distributed or distributable pursuant to the terms of this Agreement or otherwise, but determined without regard to any additional payments required under this Section 7) (a 'Payment') would be subject to the excise tax imposed by Section 4999 of the Code or any interest or penalties are incurred by the Executive with respect to such excise tax (such excise tax, together with any such interest and penalties, are hereinafter collectively referred to as the 'Excise Tax'), then the Executive shall be entitled to receive an additional payment (a 'Gross-Up Payment') in an amount such that after payment by the Executive of all taxes (including any interest or penalties imposed with respect to such taxes), including, without limitation, any income taxes (and any interest and penalties imposed with respect thereto) and Excise Tax imposed upon the Gross-Up Payment, the Executive retains an amount of the Gross-Up Payment equal to the Excise Tax imposed upon the Payments.

(b) Subject to the provisions of Section 7(c), all determinations required to be made under this Section 7, including whether and when a Gross-Up Payment is required and the amount of such Gross-Up Payment and the assumptions to be utilized in arriving at such determination, shall be made by PricewaterhouseCoopers LLC or such other certified public accounting firm as may be designated by the Executive (the 'Accounting Firm') which shall provide detailed supporting calculations both to the Company and the Executive within 15 business days of the receipt of notice from the Executive that there has been a Payment, or such earlier time as is requested by the Company. In the event that the Accounting Firm is serving as accountant or auditor for the individual, entity or group effecting the Change in Control, the Executive shall appoint another nationally recognized accounting firm to make the determinations required hereunder (which accounting firm shall then be referred to as the Accounting Firm hereunder). All fees and expenses of the Accounting Firm shall be borne solely by the Company. Any Gross-Up Payment, as determined pursuant to this

Section 7, shall be paid by the Company to the Executive within five days of the receipt of the Accounting Firm's determination. Any determination by the Accounting Firm shall be binding upon the Company and the Executive. As a result of the uncertainty in the application of Section 4999 of the Code at the time of the initial determination by the Accounting Firm hereunder, it is possible that Gross-Up Payments which will not have been made by the Company should have been made ('Underpayment'), consistent with the calculations required to be made hereunder. In the event that the Company exhausts its remedies pursuant to Section 7(c) and the Executive thereafter is required to make a payment of any Excise Tax, the Accounting Firm shall determine the amount of the Underpayment that has occurred and any such Underpayment shall be promptly paid by the Company to or for the benefit of the Executive.

(c) The Executive shall notify the Company in writing of any claim by the Internal Revenue Service that, if successful, would require the payment by the Company of the Gross-Up Payment. Such notification shall be given as soon as practicable but no later than ten business days after the Executive is informed in writing of such claim and shall apprise the Company of the nature of such claim and the date on which such claim is requested to be paid. The Executive shall not pay such claim prior to the expiration of the 30-day period following the date on which it gives such notice to the Company (or such shorter period ending on the date that any payment of taxes with respect to such claim is due). If the Company notifies the Executive in writing prior to the expiration of such period that it desires to contest such claim, the Executive shall:

(i) give the Company any information reasonably requested by the Company relating to such claim,

(ii) take such action in connection with contesting such claim as the Company shall reasonably request in writing from time to time, including, without limitation, accepting legal representation with respect to such claim by an attorney reasonably selected by the Company,

(iii) cooperate with the Company in good faith in order to effectively contest such claim, and

(iv) permit the Company to participate in any proceedings relating to such claim;

provided, however, that the Company shall bear and pay directly all costs and expenses (including additional interest and penalties) incurred in connection with such contest and shall indemnify and hold the Executive harmless, on an after-tax basis, for any Excise Tax or income tax (including interest and penalties with respect thereto) imposed as a result of such representation and payment of costs and expenses. Without limitation on the foregoing provisions of this Section 7(c), the Company shall control all proceedings taken in connection with such contest and, at its sole option, may pursue or forgo any and all administrative appeals, proceedings, hearings, and conferences with the taxing authority in respect of such claim and may, at its sole option, either direct the Executive to pay the tax claimed and sue for a refund or to contest the claim in any permissible manner, and the Executive agrees to prosecute such contest to a determination before any administrative tribunal, in a court of initial jurisdiction and in one or more appellate courts, as the Company shall determine; provided, however, that if the Company directs the Executive to pay such claim and sue for a refund, the Company shall advance the amount of such payment to the Executive, on an interest-free basis and shall indemnify and hold the Executive harmless, on an after-tax basis, from any Excise Tax or income tax (including interest or penalties with respect thereto) imposed with respect to such advance or with respect to any imputed income with respect to such advance; and further provided that any extension of the statute of limitations relating to payment of taxes for the taxable year of the Executive with respect to which such contested amount is claimed to be due is limited solely to such contested amount. Furthermore, the Company's control of the contest shall be limited to issues with respect to which a Gross-Up Payment would be payable hereunder and the Executive shall be entitled to settle or contest, as the case may be, any other issue raised by the Internal Revenue Service or any other taxing authority.

(d) If, after the receipt by the Executive of an amount advanced by the Company pursuant to Section 7(c), the Executive becomes entitled to receive any refund with respect to such claim, the Executive shall (subject to the Company's complying with the requirements of Section 7(c)) promptly pay to the Company the amount of such refund (together with any interest paid or credited thereon after taxes applicable thereto). If, after the receipt by the Executive of an amount advanced by the Company pursuant to Section 7(c), a determination is made that the Executive shall not be entitled to any refund with respect to such claim and the Company does not notify the Executive in writing of its intent to contest such denial of refund prior to the expiration of 30 days after such determination, then such advance shall be forgiven and shall not be required to be repaid and the amount of such advance shall offset, to the extent thereof, the amount of Gross-Up Payment required to be paid.

(e) Notwithstanding the foregoing, in no event shall the total payments made by the Company pursuant to this Section 7 exceed $500,000."

RETIREMENT ARRANGEMENTS

BEST PRACTICE

Executive retirement arrangements should be consistent with programs offered to the general work force but should permit executives whose compensation exceeds limits under the Internal Revenue Code to receive reasonable supplemental retirement benefits.

The Internal Revenue Code places limits on the amount of compensation that can count for tax qualified retirement plans. It is appropriate to provide a supplemental executive retirement plan (SERP) for executives whose compensation exceeds the IRS limits. However, SERPs should not contain special provisions, such as above-market interest rates and excess service credits, and should not count incentive compensation in computing SERPs unless that benefit is also provided in the tax-qualified retirement plan for other employees.

The Council of Institutional Investors believes that, with respect to deferred compensation plans for executives, the investment alternatives "should mirror those offered to employees in broad-based deferral plans." The Council also believes that retired executives should not be entitled to special perquisites, such as apartments, automobiles, use of corporate aircraft, security, financial planning, etc.

Section 409A impacts supplemental retirement plans of public companies and is more fully discussed in Chapter 13. Section 409A may prevent payments to certain "specified employees" of public companies for a period of six months after their retirement, except for payments that are exempted from Section 409A.

THE GRASSO CASE

Dick Grasso, Chairman and Chief Executive Officer of the New York Stock Exchange (NYSE), was ousted from his position in September 2003 as a result of a public outcry over his compensation package. The NYSE is a not-for-profit organization, formed under New York law. Prior to his ouster, it was determined that Mr. Grasso's $187.5 million pay package was excessive. A suit was subsequently filed by New York state's Attorney General, Eliot Spitzer, to recover some of the money.

According to *The Wall Street Journal* of July 20, 2005, 9 of the 12 directors who served on the compensation committee of the NYSE during a crucial period in 2001 and 2002 did not realize that the big pay raises awarded to Grasso would cause his retirement benefits to soar when his total compensation rose to $26.8 million in 2000 and $30.6 million in 2001. Many of the members of the compensation committee were reportedly surprised by how large the pension package had become. The growth in Grasso's pension plan was not envisioned when the SERP was established because the plan was modeled after one for U.S. government employees earning far less money.

The moral of this story is that the compensation committee of the board of the NYSE apparently failed to fully understand Grasso's entire pay package when they gave him large increases in his compensation and should have placed a cap on his SERP.[18] Had the compensation committee used tally sheets that reflected the maximum payment due to Grasso under different scenarios, a best practice discussed in Chapter 6, they would have discovered the potential for enormous compensation to be paid pursuant to Grasso's SERP.

---

[18]Langdon and Anderson "Report Details Huge Pay Deal Grasso Set Up," *New York Times*, 3 February 005, A1 and Crawford, "Spitzer seeks $100 million from Grasso,"*CNNMoney*, 24 May 2004. http://money.cnn.com/2004/05/24/markets/spitzer_grasso (6 April 2005). See also Donaldson, William, "Statement by the Chairperson: Letter to NYSE Regarding NYSE Executive Compensation," U.S. Securities and Exchange Commission, Washington, D.C. (2 September, 2003).

SECTION 409A OF THE INTERNAL REVENUE CODE

BEST PRACTICE

All employee agreements, severance agreements, and retirement arrangements should be reviewed by a tax attorney for compliance with Section 409A of the Internal Revenue Code.

Section 409A of the Internal Revenue Code and the final regulations issued by the IRS under that section substantially impact the design of all employee agreements, severance agreements and retirement arrangements. See Chapter 13. The provisions of Section 409A and the final regulations are extremely complex and are easily violated. If the employee agreement, severance agreement or retirement arrangement violates Section 409A, the executive may have to pay a 20% additional tax plus interest on any "deferred compensation," thereby raising the total potential federal tax to the executive to 55% (35% maximum federal income tax based on current rates plus 20% additional tax) plus interest retroactive to the vesting date. This figure can rise potentially to 85% for California residents. Moreover, it is expected that, in the future, the company will have an obligation to identify on Form W-2, issued to an executive, any compensation that violates Section 409A. Chapter 13 of this book contains a fuller discussion of Section 409A but such chapter is only a summary of certain highlights of Section 409A and is not a substitute for seeking advice from a tax attorney.

OTHER BEST PRACTICES IN NEGOTIATING EMPLOYMENT OR SEVERANCE AGREEMENTS

If the determination of the compensation committee on an executive employment or severance agreement are legally challenged, the court will look closely at the process and procedures followed by the committee. Such a challenge occurred in the Disney case discussed in Chapter 11. The following specific best practices should be followed by the compensation committee in negotiating employment and severance agreements along with the more general best practices discussed in Chapter 11.

BEST PRACTICE

Members of the compensation committee must receive materials well in advance of any meeting at which compensation is to be discussed and the package should include a full draft of the proposed agreement, a summary of the key provisions, an analysis of the aggregate cost of the agreement to the company and any other documents that shed light on the reasonableness of **its** terms.

BEST PRACTICE

The minutes should reflect a record of arms-length negotiations with the executive and his or her attorney, with each proposal and counteroffer fully documented.

BEST PRACTICE

If the final form of the agreement differs materially from the version submitted to the compensation committee, a separate meeting should be held to consider the material changes.

BEST PRACTICE

The report of the compensation consultant must compare the compensation package with industry standards.

The structure and process of the compensation committee is a key ingredient of the corporate governance process. This is our next topic.

CHAPTER 8

Compensation Committee Structure and Process

> **BEST PRACTICE**
>
> The compensation committee should consist solely of independent directors.

Stock market rules generally require an independent compensation committee. As a matter of good practice, and in keeping with a favorable public perception, all members of the compensation committee should be independent directors, whether or not required by stock market rules. Unlike the public company audit committee that cannot include controlling shareholders, the compensation committee can include them if they are otherwise independent.

> **BEST PRACTICE**
>
> The compensation committee should have a charter that reflects its authority and responsibilities. The charter should be reviewed annually.

A compensation committee charter helps to focus the efforts of the committee and articulates the authority and responsibilities of the committee.

Annual review of the charter is essential. A sample compensation committee charter for a public company is contained in Appendix A.

The Securities and Exchange Commission (SEC) rules now require a statement in the proxy statement or Form 10-K as to whether the compensation committee of public companies has a charter.

BEST PRACTICE

The compensation committee's responsibilities should include overseeing the organization's overall compensation structure, policies, and programs (including board compensation); establishing or recommending to the board performance goals and objectives for the chief executive officer (CEO) and other members of senior management; and establishing or recommending to the independent directors compensation for the CEO and senior management.

The compensation committee is as equally important as the audit committee in the corporate governance structure. Since the culture of an organization is reflective of its compensation policies, the policies adopted by the compensation committee can be instrumental in establishing an ethical, law-abiding culture.

The compensation committee (or possibly the corporate governance committee) must study the entire compensation system within the organization to determine whether the incentives and disincentives are consistent with an ethical, law-abiding culture. Unfortunately, many compensation committees limit their activities to just the compensation of the top executives. This is a mistake unless some other committee (e.g., corporate governance committee) has been assigned the duty of monitoring the entire compensation structure of the organization.

The compensation committee should, at a minimum, establish the compensation for all executive officers whether they are named executive officers for purposes of the Summary Compensation Table or not. SEC rules under Item 404 of Regulation S-K require approval of executive officer compensation by the compensation committee (or a recommendation for approval to the full board by the compensation committee) as a condition to avoid disclosure of such compensation under Item 404. In the absence of such approval, annual compensation of such executive officers which exceeds $120,000 would have to be disclosed as a transaction with a related person under Item 404, even though such executive officer does not have to be named in the Summary Compensation Table because they are neither the principal executive or financial officer nor one of the next three most highly compensated executive officers.

BEST PRACTICE

The compensation committee should have the authority to retain independent compensation consultants, counsel, and other advisors to provide the committee with independent advice.

The compensation committee cannot rely on experts provided by management and should have its own independent access to outside experts, including compensation consultants, counsel, and other advisors. To avoid conflicts of interest, it is particularly important for the compensation committee to use independent experts to assist the committee in establishing reasonable compensation for the members of the board of directors.

Some corporate governance experts believe that all companies should embrace the two compensation consultant models, that is, executive compensation should be set by the board with the help of a consultant hired by the board and all other compensation should be set by management using a separate consultant and not duplicating the same work. The authors of this book do not subscribe to the position that this is universally necessary. Aside from the potential duplication of services and additional costs, the use of two separate compensation consultants may have the effect of having no single compensation consultant knowledgeable concerning the entire operations of the company. Judgment should be exercised by the compensation committee on this issue.

Likewise, some corporate governance experts believe that compensation consultants should be rotated every five years. We believe that this is an arbitrary rule and is not universally necessary. Hiring a new compensation consultant every five years has a disadvantage of losing the accumulated knowledge of the prior compensation consultant and requiring the new compensation consultant to go through a learning period, at the company's expense. Again, judgment should be exercised by the compensation committee on this issue.

The Toronto-Dominion Bank proxy statement dated March 30, 2006 contains the following statements concerning its compensation consultant, which can serve as a model for disclosure:

> "The Committee utilizes an independent advisor to assist in making the best possible decisions on executive compensation for the Bank as well as to help keep the Committee current with best possible decisions on executive compensation. For the past several years, the Committee has engaged Frederic W. Cook & Co., Inc. as the Committee's independent consultant. Frederic W. Cook & Co., Inc. is a compensation consulting firm based in New York City, New York, which consults to a large number of Fortune 500 firms throughout the United States and Canada, including in the financial services industry. To ensure independence of the Committee's consultant, the firm does not accept other retainers from the Bank. For the period of October 2004 – November 2005, Frederic W. Cook & Co., Inc. was paid U.S. $46,488 for the services provided."

BEST PRACTICE

If the compensation committee determines to hire a compensation consultant that also provides services to management, all services provided by the compensation consultant to management should be voluntarily disclosed to shareholders and the compensation consultant should keep the compensation committee informed of all new assignments.

There is language in the SEC release adopting the Compensation Discussion and Analysis (CD&A) requirements that suggest that the involvement with management of compensation consultants employed by the compensation committee is material information to shareholders.[1]

---

[1]SEC Release No. 33-8732, p. 178.

Whatever ambiguity may exist in the SEC release, it is clearly a best practice to make disclosure to shareholders of other relationships that the compensation committee consultant has with management that may undermine his or her independence. Such disclosures have been voluntarily made by such companies as CVS, Caremark, DTE Energy, General Electric, and Pfizer.[2]

DTE Energy has adopted a policy requiring the compensation committee to preapprove all engagement with management by the compensation consultant employed by the compensation committee.[3] Preapproval should not be necessary so long as the compensation consultant is required to keep the compensation committee advised of all new management engagements.

BEST PRACTICE

The procedures followed by the compensation committee should be clearly explained to shareholders.

To maintain creditability for the compensation committee procedures, they should be clearly explained to shareholders in the proxy statement or Form 10-K Report of the company, typically under the section entitled "Compensation Committee Discussion and Analysis." The following is an excerpt from the proxy statement of Bank of America Corporation filed with the SEC for its 2007 stockholders meeting[4]:

> "*Compensation Committee.* The Compensation Committee currently consists of four directors, all of whom are independent under the NYSE listing standards and our Director Independence Categorical Standards. During 2006 the Compensation Committee held six meetings. Duties of the Committee include:
>
> • Overseeing the establishment, maintenance and administration of our compensation programs and employee benefit plans;

---

[2]*Compensation Standards,* Summer 2007, p. 3
[3]Id.
[4]Bank of America Corporation Schedule 14A filed on March 19, 2007.

- Reviewing our Chief Executive Officer's performance, approving and recommending to the Board our Chief Executive Officer's compensation and approving compensation for our other executive officers; and
- Making recommendations to the Board on director compensation.

"The Committee may create subcommittees with authority to act on the Committee's behalf. The Committee has delegated to the Stock Plan Award Subcommittee (which consists of the Chairman of the Committee) the Committee's authority to make awards and determine the terms and conditions of stock options, stock appreciation rights and restricted stock awards (both shares and units) under the Bank of America Corporation 2003 Key Associate Stock Plan (the "Key Associate Stock Plan") that was most recently approved by stockholders in April 2006. However, this delegation of authority does not extend to awards to our executive officers.

"The Committee may delegate to management certain of its duties and responsibilities, including with respect to the adoption, amendment, modification or termination of benefit plans and with respect to the awards of stock options under certain stock plans. Significant delegations made by the Committee include the following:

- The Management Compensation Committee has the authority to direct the compensation for all our associates and officers except for those persons serving as our executive officers.
- The Corporate Benefits Committee has overall responsibility for substantially all of our employee benefit plans.
- The Chief Administrative Officer has the authority to make awards of stock options and stock appreciation rights under the Key Associate Stock Plan to other associates who are not "insiders" or "named executive officers" as defined in the Key Associate Stock Plan, provided the awards are on terms and conditions that have been pre-approved by the Committee or the Stock Plan Award Subcommittee.

"The Committee actively engages in its duties and follows procedures intended to ensure excellence in the governance of our pay-for-performance mandate:

- The Committee regularly meets throughout the year. Generally at each meeting it reviews: (i) year-to-date personnel expense versus plan; (ii) year-to-date financial performance versus plan; (iii) year-to-date and multi-year performance versus competitor group performance;

(iv) stock plan usage and effect on dilution relative to our competitor group; (v) executive officer and director stock ownership levels; (vi) each executive officer's target total compensation for the year; and (vii) other topics as appropriate.

- At least once a year, the Committee reviews each executive officer's total compensation package, including base salary, cash and stock incentive awards, accumulated realized and unrealized stock option and restricted stock gains, qualified and nonqualified retirement and deferred compensation benefit accruals and the incremental cost to us of all perquisites. The Committee utilizes, and makes available to the full Board, an executive compensation statement, or "tally sheet," for each executive officer for this purpose.

- The Committee members receive materials for meetings in advance and participate in individual pre-meetings with management to review the materials. If resolutions to consider new or amended plans or agreements are included, the Committee members receive when possible advance copies of the actual plan documents or agreements under consideration with appropriate summaries.

- The Committee retains a compensation consultant, which it meets with regularly without the presence of management.

- The Committee regularly meets in executive session without the presence of management or the compensation consultant.

- The Committee reports on its meetings to the full Board. After a performance review, the Board approves the total annual compensation awards for our executive officers.

"The form and amount of compensation paid to our non-employee directors is reviewed from time to time by the Committee. Competitive data is provided to the Committee by its compensation consultant using the same competitor groups that are used in making compensation decisions for our executive officers. Any changes to non-employee director compensation are recommended by the Committee to the Board for approval.

"Our executive officers are not engaged directly with the Committee in setting the amount or form of executive officer or director compensation. However, as part of the annual performance review for our executive officers other than the Chief Executive Officer, the Committee considers the Chief Executive Officer's perspective on each executive officer's individual performance as well as the performance of our various lines of business.

"We operate a large company in a dynamic, competitive global environment, and the Committee has responsibility for our global compensation and benefit programs that support this business. To perform its duties, the Committee requires assistance from a compensation consultant who has broad skills and experience, including experience with global compensation and benefits programs, and who has sufficient resources to meet our needs. The Committee has the sole authority and responsibility under its charter to approve the engagement of any such compensation consultant.

"In addition to possessing the necessary skill, experience and resources to meet our needs, the consultant must have no relationship with us that would interfere with its ability to provide independent advice. The Committee reviews any relationships between management and the consultant, as well as the amount of work performed for us by the consultant in areas other than executive officer and director compensation. Given that there are a limited number of compensation consultants with the broad skills, experience and resources necessary to support a company of our size and global scope, the Committee believes that its compensation consultant may have other relationships with us, so long as those relationships do not interfere with its ability to provide independent advice. If the compensation consultant provides services to us other than in connection with the evaluation of director, chief executive officer or senior executive compensation and benefits, the Committee will approve the annual amount of aggregate fees permitted for such other services.

"Mercer Human Resource Consulting served as the compensation consultant for the Committee for the last several years. In October 2006, the Committee hired Towers Perrin. While the Committee highly valued Mercer's services, the change in consultants was a result of the Committee's continuing review of its needs and the exercise of its discretion.

"Towers Perrin provides other services to us in the areas of global retirement and healthcare benefits, for which the Committee has oversight responsibility. Towers Perrin also provides a small amount of services to us in other areas. The Committee took these services into account when it retained Towers Perrin to serve as its compensation consultant and concluded that these other relationships with us would not interfere with Towers Perrin's ability to provide independent advice. The Committee has approved an annual amount of aggregate fees for Towers Perrin for all services, and at least annually the Committee will review the services performed by, and the actual fees paid to, the firm."

> ### BEST PRACTICE
>
> Compensation committees must be familiar with the SEC's disclosure rule that requires a "Compensation Discussion and Analysis" (CD&A) section to be included in the company's proxy statement or Form 10-K and be prepared to discuss the rationale for each element of the compensation package, any changes that are made during the year, and any differences in the compensation packages of named executive officers.

The compensation committee should fully understand the disclosure requirements of the CD&A (see Appendix B) and be sensitive to the fact that their actions will be required to be described to shareholders in the CD&A prepared in the following years' proxy statement or Form 10-K. They must be able to articulate how each compensation element and the amount paid for that element fits into the company's overall compensation objectives. If they make any changes in any such element during the year, they should have a clear rationale for such changes that can be explained to shareholders.

The compensation committee should also be prepared to clearly explain the rationale for differences between the various components of the compensation packages for each of the executive officers required to be named in the proxy statement or Form 10-K.

> ### BEST PRACTICE
>
> On any major executive compensation issue, the compensation committee should have more than one meeting so that they have time to reflect on the issues.

It is important that the compensation committee have time to reflect on any major executive compensation issue. Therefore, at least two or more compensation committee meetings should be held to discuss any major issue with a sufficient separation in time between meetings to permit new insights and thoughtful discussion.

> **BEST PRACTICE**
>
> Given the pressures on compensation committees, it is helpful to have a securities lawyer available for compensation committee meetings.

The SEC executive compensation rules require a full description of the procedures followed by the compensation committee in determining executive compensation. A securities lawyer who is familiar with these rules can be helpful in assisting the committee to consider all of the issues for which SEC disclosure will be required.

Moreover, legal actions against compensation committees can be expected in the future, particularly where major executive compensation issues are resolved or executive employment or severance agreements are negotiated and finalized. The presence of a securities lawyer who is familiar with executive compensation issues, and can advise the committee as to its fiduciary duties, can be helpful in mitigating the risks of such litigation.

CREATING INCENTIVES FOR GOOD CORPORATE GOVERNANCE

If the only incentives given to top management by the compensation committee are numbers driven, the board of directors should not be surprised if the corporate culture of the organization is also numbers driven. An excessively numbers-driven culture will produce an Enron or a WorldCom.

The board must recognize that top management of public companies is under greater pressure than ever before from securities analysts to hit the numbers in order to keep the share price up. The board must balance this pressure by creating incentives for ethical behavior and good corporate governance as well as incentives that are driven by financial results.

Most boards of directors would be loath to reward top management whose economic performance is poor just because they have also accomplished corporate governance goals. Therefore, there has to be a balance in the compensation system between rewards created for financial performance and rewards for satisfying corporate governance objectives. At a minimum, even if the compensation committee does not reward reaching

BEST PRACTICE

Incentives must be provided by the compensation committee for top management of all organizations (whether public, private, or not-for-profit) to create good corporate governance. These incentives should include significant economic rewards for achieving these goals:

- Creating an ethical, law-abiding corporate culture
- Assisting the board in establishing an effective internal control function that monitors management on financial statement issues

corporate governance goals, top management should be penalized for the failure to achieve such objectives.

How does the compensation committee measure the achievement of corporate governance goals for the purpose of determining management rewards or penalties? Such measurements may require the use of outside consultants on corporate culture, input from the internal auditor, and direct conversations between board or compensation committee members and lower-level employees. The attitude of the sales and marketing group within the organization is of particular importance, since such employees may have some of the greatest incentives for unethical behavior.

It is crucial to good corporate governance that the board balance management incentives to satisfy financial goals with the incentives to accomplish corporate governance objectives. However, the financial incentive to management for good governance will never equal the financial incentives to management for creating shareholder value—nor should they. Therefore, other mechanisms for overseeing management must be utilized (e.g., internal audit).

BEST PRACTICE

The compensation committee should hold executive sessions, without management present, at meetings.

Executive sessions permit the members of the compensation committee to speak more freely about members of management and facilitate the exchange of views among committee members.

BEST PRACTICE

Make certain that the minutes of the compensation committee meeting reflect a full consideration of each of the elements of the current compensation structure (not just base salary and bonus but all of the pension benefits (including SERPs), fringe benefits, and other perquisites) of the executive and the total value of the existing compensation package, and allow adequate time at different compensation committee meetings to discuss each of these elements.

DISNEY LITIGATION

The importance of the compensation committee using proper process and procedure is illustrated by the Disney case.

The Disney case involved allegations that the Disney compensation committee and the full board approved a compensation agreement with Disney's former president, Michael Ovitz, *without having ever seen a draft of the agreement,* only an incomplete summary, following a compensation committee meeting that lasted over an hour. The complaint also alleged that: there were no analyses to show the potential compensation over the term of the agreement; there were no analyses of the potential cost of the severance package under various termination scenarios, including no-fault termination; no outside consultant advised the board; comparable peer compensation was not considered; and there was no review of the final employment or stock option agreements, which differed from the summaries previously provided.

The Delaware Chancery Court in 2003 initially denied Disney's motion to dismiss the complaint against the directors, holding that "[w]here a director consciously ignores his or her duties to the corporation, thereby causing economic injury to its shareholders, the director's actions are either 'not in good faith' or 'involve international misconduct.'"

In August 2005, after a full trial, (including 37 days of testimony) the Delaware Chancery Court dismissed the complaint against the directors and others because the plaintiffs failed to prove the factual allegations in the complaint, holding that ordinary negligence by the directors is not sufficient to prove lack of good faith. The Court found that, although the Board's conduct fell significantly short of the "aspirational ideal of best practices," the directors did not breach their fiduciary duties.

Although the Disney directors were successful after a full trial, the Disney case would probably have been dismissed at an earlier stage (or perhaps not brought to trial at all) had the Disney compensation committee used best practices in approving Michael Ovitz's compensation agreement. Use of best corporate practices would have avoided the distraction and disruption of Disney's operations and of the lives of its director defendants resulting from lengthy depositions and the full trial.

Some commentators have noted that the actions of the Disney board took place in the twentieth century, and that the application of twenty-first century notions of best practices for compensation committees might have changed the result. Therefore, compensation committees should update and improve their practices to current standards to safeguard themselves from personal liability.[5]

Equity should play a significant role in any competitive executive compensation package and this is discussed in our next chapter.

---

[5]In re Walt Disney Company Derivative Litigation, No. 15452 (Del. Ch. Aug. 9, 2005).

CHAPTER 9

Equity Incentive Choices

OVERVIEW OF EQUITY INCENTIVES FOR KEY EMPLOYEES

If you want to grant equity incentives only to key employees, you have five major choices:

1. Stock Options—Either Incentive Stock Options or Nonqualified Stock Options (with or without Stock Appreciation Rights)
2. Stock Appreciation Rights Payable in Stock or Cash (or alternatively for limited liability companies, a "profits interest")
3. Performance Share Plans Payable in Stock or Cash
4. Restricted Stock Bonus and Award Plans
5. Phantom Stock Plans Payable in Stock or Cash

The term "phantom stock plans" is used in this book to refer to a wide variety of bonus plans including so-called performance share/unit plans that are keyed to the increases in the value of the stock or other performance goals.

Some large companies permit their key employees to make their own selection among the various equity choices, so long as such choices have the same accounting charge attached to them. This is not necessarily the best practice since executives will tend to select time-restricted stock awards which provide them with free stock if they are employed by the company through the vesting date even if the stock price during that period has not risen.

There is no universal single best choice for an equity incentive for executives of all companies. The exact equity incentive chosen depends upon the culture and compensation philosophy of the company and its

> ### BEST PRACTICE
>
> The equity incentives provided to executives should be tied to the strategic plan of the company and should be consistent with the culture and compensation philosophy of the company.

strategic plan. The terms of whatever equity incentive is chosen should be tied to the strategic plan. For example, if a company expects an exit within five years, the vesting of the equity incentive should coincide with the expected exit date or at least be accelerated by the exit event.

The following table (see page 115) provides a comparison of equity incentive plans which can be limited to key employees of the company.

DILUTION

> ### BEST PRACTICE
>
> Compensation committees should develop and disclose to shareholders their philosophy concerning dilution resulting from equity incentives to employees.

Equity incentives to employees potentially dilute the interest of shareholders in the company. Compensation committees should determine the total potential dilution they will permit from equity incentives and be prepared to explain their philosophy to shareholders. For purposes of determining total potential dilution, peer group comparisons should be considered. Many companies buy back their own stock in order to minimize dilution from equity incentives. If that is part of the company's philosophy, this also should be explained to shareholders.

STOCK OPTION VERSUS STOCK APPRECIATION RIGHTS

A stock option permits an executive to acquire equity at the market value on the date of grant. As a result of Section 409A of the Internal Revenue Code, options issued at exercise prices below the fair market

Incentive Stock Options	Nonqualified Stock Option Plans	Stock Appreciation Rights	Performance Share/Unit Plans	Restricted Stock Plans	Phantom Stock Plans
Description					
A right granted by employer to an employee to purchase stock at a stipulated price during a specified period of time in accord with Section 422 of Internal Revenue Code.	A right granted by employer to purchase stock at stipulated price over a specific period of time.	A right granted to employee to realize appreciation in value of specified number of shares of stock. No employee investment required. Time of exercise of rights is at employee's discretion.	Awards of contingent shares or units are granted at beginning of specified period. Awards are earned out during the period that certain specified company performance goals are attained. Price of company stock at end of performance period (or other valuation criteria) determines value of payout.	Shares of stock are subject to restrictions on transferability with a substantial risk of forfeiture, and shares are granted to employee without cost (or at a bargain price).	Employee is awarded units (not any ownership interest) corresponding in number and value to a specified number of shares of stock.
Characteristics					
• Option price is not less than fair market value on date of grant.	• May be granted at price below fair market value.*	• May be granted alone or in conjunction with stock options.	• Awards earned are directly related to achievement during performance period.	• Shares become available to employee as restrictions lapse-generally upon completion of a period of continuous employment.	• Award may be equal to value of shares of phantom stock or just the appreciation portion.

*Options granted at price below fair market value create Section 409A issues. See Chapter 13.

(Continued)

Incentive Stock Options	Nonqualified Stock Option Plans	Stock Appreciation Rights	Performance Share/ Unit Plans	Restricted Stock Plans	Phantom Stock Plans
• Option must be granted within ten years of adoption or shareholder approval, whichever is earlier, and granted options must be exercised within ten years of grant. • $100,000 limitation on total amount that first becomes exercisable in a given year (measured on date of grant). • Previously acquired stock may be used as payment medium for the exercise of incentive stock options.	• Option period is typically ten years. • Vesting restrictions are typical. • Previously acquired company stock may be used as full or partial payment for the exercise of nonqualified stock options. • May be granted to non-employees.	• A specified maximum value may be placed on amount of appreciation that may be received. • Distribution may be made in cash or stock or both in amount equal to the growth in value of the underlying stock. • May be granted to non-employees.	• Performance periods are typically from three to five years. • Grants usually are made every one to two years as continuing incentive device. • Payments are made in cash or stock or combination. • May be granted to non-employees.	• Individual has contingent ownership until restrictions lapse. • Dividends can be paid or credited to the employee's account. • May be granted to non-employees.	• Dividend equivalents may be credited to account or paid currently. • Benefit can be paid in cash or stock or both. • May be granted to non-employees.

• Written approval of shareholders (within 12 months before or after adoption).			
Employer			
• No tax deduction allowed to employer on exercise.	• Tax deduction in the amount, and at the time, the employee realizes ordinary income.	• Tax deduction in the amount, and at the time, the employee realizes ordinary income.	• Tax deduction in the amount, and at the time, the employee realizes ordinary income.
			• Tax deduction in the amount, and at the time, the employee realizes ordinary income.
Accounting Considerations			
• Fair value accounting under FAS 123R	• Fair value accounting under FAS 123R	• Fair value accounting under FAS 123R	• Fair value accounting under FAS 123R

value on the date of grant will be subject to a potential additional tax of 20%, bringing the maximum total federal income tax rate up to 55% (plus interest retroactive to the vesting date) from 35%. Therefore, it is no longer practical to issue stock options which have exercise prices that are lower than the fair market value on the date of grant.

A stock appreciation right (SAR) typically permits the executive to receive the appreciation in equity over the grant date fair market value. For example, assume that the fair market value on the date of grant of the SAR is $10.00, the number of shares subject to the SAR is 100,000 shares, and upon exercise of the SAR three years later, the fair market value of the stock is $20.00 per share. The SAR therefore has a value of $1 million (100,000 shares multiplied by $10.00 appreciation per share) upon its exercise and the executive would receive 50,000 shares upon exercise of the SAR. In contrast to a stock option, the 50,000 shares are received pursuant to the exercise of the SAR by the executive without having to pay an option exercise price of $10.00 per share.

If under these same facts a stock option had been granted with an exercise price of $10.00 per share on the date of grant, the executive would have to come out of pocket for $1 million in order to exercise the option and would have received 100,000 shares pursuant to the option exercise. One may argue that it is better to have the executive pay the $1 million option exercise price, thereby forcing him or her to use some personal funds to invest in the company. However, that is not the way stock options work. What typically happens is that the option exercise is "cashless," with the broker selling enough shares to fund the option exercise price (i.e., selling 50,000 shares at $20.00 per share), leaving the executive with a balance of 50,000 shares. This is exactly the same number of shares that the executive would have received under the SAR.

The effect of using the stock option is that the company has more shares outstanding in the marketplace, namely 100,000 shares (50,000 shares sold by the broker and 50,000 shares held by the executive), whereas only 50,000 additional shares are outstanding under a SAR. (This example ignores any tax issues resulting from the exercise of the SAR or the stock option.) In view of the smaller dilution to existing shareholders arising from a SAR, using SARs instead of stock options may be viewed as a best practice.

Why then, you may ask, were so many stock options issued in the past rather than SARs? The answer is that the accounting rules have changed.

Prior to FAS 123R, which is the current accounting rule, there was no charge to income from the grant of an option which satisfied the requirements of APB25 (namely an exercise price equal to at least fair market value on the date of grant and time vested), whereas there was a charge to income for a SAR and so-called "variable accounting" could produce a large charge against income depending upon the stock price. All of that has changed with the adoption of FAS 123R which produces the same accounting result for a stock option or a SAR.

The disadvantage of a SAR to the executive is the absence of any potential federal long-term capital gains treatment for the appreciation in the stock, as more fully discussed later with respect to incentive stock options. Many executives who are granted incentive stock options never achieve long-term capital gains treatment for one of three reasons:

1. To avoid alternative minimum tax, the executive sells or otherwise makes a disqualifying disposition of the stock received under an incentive stock option in the year of exercise.
2. The executive sells or otherwise makes a disqualifying disposition of the stock before the end of the required holding periods for an incentive stock option because of the need for cash.
3. The size of the option grant exceeds the $100,000 per year limitation contained in Section 422(d) of the Code for incentive stock options.

Although SARs may also be settled in cash as well as equity, for purposes of this book, the preference for SARs is for those SARs that are settled solely in stock. A phantom stock plan that rewards the executive solely for appreciation in stock value above the grant date stock value, and which is settled solely in stock, is the equivalent of a SAR. For purposes of this book, we call this a "Phantom Appreciation Plan."

BEST PRACTICE

If the choice is between stock options and SARs that are settled solely in stock, SARs are preferable because they involve less dilution to shareholders.

RESTRICTED STOCK VERSUS SARS OR PHANTOM APPRECIATION PLANS

Restricted stock plans provide for the actual grant of shares of stock to executives and other employees, without cost to the grantee, subject to restrictions on transferability and to a substantial risk of forfeiture. The substantial risk of forfeiture can consist of the continuation of employment for specified time periods, the satisfaction of certain performance goals, or both. Executives who make an election on Section 83(b) of the Internal Revenue Code and pay the appropriate amount of federal income tax can achieve long-term capital gains on the appreciation at the time the forfeiture provisions lapse.

One advantage of restricted stock is that, if the company stock loses value, the executives really share the loss. This is in contrast to a SAR or stock option. If the SAR goes underwater (i.e. the SAR base price is above the current trading price) or if the exercise price of the stock option exceeds the current trading price, the executives do not suffer the same loss as they would if they held restricted stock.

The disadvantages of a restricted stock plan compared to a SAR or Phantom Appreciation Plan are as follows:

- The executive becomes a shareholder immediately and is entitled to the rights and privileges of a shareholder, which includes the rights to dividends, as opposed to a SAR which is merely an option and does not entitle the executive to any rights as a shareholder.
- The restricted stock rewards executives who have not contributed to the past growth of the company; in contrast, a SAR only rewards employees for appreciation in the value of the company after the SAR grant date.
- The grant of restricted stock increases the issued and outstanding stock and reduces basic earnings per share, whereas the SAR is only reflected in fully diluted earnings per share.
- Restricted stock which is vested solely by time (i.e., the executive must work for a certain number of years for the forfeiture provisions to lapse) rewards executives even if the value of the company does not increase or in fact goes down; in contrast, a SAR or stock option only rewards the executive for increases in value.

To avoid some of the disadvantages of restricted stock, some companies have inserted performance goals that must be satisfied in order for the restrictions to lapse. The Exxon Mobil Corporation, while not requiring performance goals, has a very long vesting period. For most of their senior executives, 50% of each grant of restricted stock is subject to a five year restricted period and the balance is restricted for ten years or retirement, *whichever is later*. In addition, the company provides a ceiling on annual restricted stock awards so that the overall number of shares granted represents a dilution of only 0.2%.

Some companies use restricted stock as a substitute for cash compensation, particularly start-up companies that have cash flow problems. Restricted stock may also be used by more developed companies that may not be paying a competitive salary as a cash substitute. Private equity firms typically use restricted stock as a management retention incentive.

PHANTOM PLANS

A phantom plan is a notional plan which typically consists of a document that creates an equity equivalent award to the executive. A bookkeeping account is typically maintained for each award. The equity equivalent award is usually subject to vesting conditions and, when vested, may be settled in stock, cash, or some combination. The vesting conditions may just involve the continuation of the employment of the executive for a specific time period. An example would be a phantom award of 1,000 units which vest at the rate of 20% per annum and are convertible into an equal number of shares of common stock upon vesting. This phantom plan would be similar to a grant of restricted stock that is time-vested, but would not have the disadvantage of a restricted stock award which typically provides the executive with all the rights of a shareholder.

The greatest advantage of a phantom plan is the ability to defer federal income taxation until cash or shares are actually delivered or are constructively received by the holder of the phantom units (except that payroll taxes may be due upon vesting). The award of phantom units which are settled in shares uses fewer shares than a SAR or stock option to deliver equivalent value. The principal disadvantage to the executive of phantom units is that the executive does not have voting or dividend rights; however, the award may include a dividend equivalent feature.

Time-vested phantom plans reward the executive merely for continuing employment with the company, without regard to the accomplishments of either the executive or the company. The typical time-vested phantom plan does not require the payment of any exercise price. This contrasts with stock options that require the executive to pay an amount equal to the fair market value at the date of grant.

A time-vested phantom plan (similar to a time-vested restricted stock award) rewards the executive even if there has been no appreciation in the equity since the grant of the phantom award. The reward is solely given for continuing employment with the company.

Phantom plans can also contain performance conditions, as can stock options and SARs. For example, the phantom plan may require as a condition to vesting not only that the executive remain with the company, but that the company or the executive achieves certain financial goals. Phantom plans can also be made similar to a SAR or stock option by rewarding the executive only for appreciation in the stock value after the grant date.

Many phantom plans also contain so-called "dividend equivalent rights." This is also a bookkeeping entry that credits the executive with additional phantom units based upon cash dividends that are paid by the company prior to vesting. This is a desirable clause for companies with a high dividend payout which reduces the potential appreciation of the equity.

> ### BEST PRACTICE
>
> Dividend equivalent rights for the holder of phantom stock should be considered when the company maintains a high dividend payout that impairs the appreciation of the equity.

ISOs versus Non-ISOs

The advantage of an incentive stock option (ISO) is that it permits the key employee to achieve long-term capital gain treatment on the appreciation of the stock after the grant date, provided two requirements are satisfied:

1. The stock is not sold or otherwise disposed of in a "disqualifying disposition" for two years after the option grant and for one year after the exercise date.

2. The option holder is an employee of the company at all times from the grant date until three months prior to the exercise of the stock option (one year in the case of death or "disability" as defined in the Internal Revenue Code")

SCENARIO 9.1

Executive Joe received an ISO grant on January 1, 2008 for 5,000 shares of common stock, at an exercise price of $5 per share (its fair market value at the grant date). The option becomes fully vested in five years and expires in ten years. Joe continues to be employed by the company until January 2, 2013, when he exercises his fully vested option on February 1, 2013 at the price of $5 per share. Joe sells the stock on February 2, 2014 at the price of $25 per share. Joe would treat the $20 per share gain as long-term capital gain for federal income tax purposes and be taxed 15% (assuming long-term capital gains rate remains the same as year 2007). If Joe had sold the stock on February 2, 2013 at $25 per share, the $20 per share gain would be treated as ordinary income, because Joe sold the stock within one year after exercise.

If Joe qualifies for long-term capital gains by selling on February 2, 2014, the company does not obtain a federal income tax deduction for this $20 gain per share. If Joe receives ordinary income treatment because he sold on February 2, 2014, the company would obtain a federal income tax deduction for the $20 per share due to the ordinary income recognized by Joe.

If the company is a "C" corporation in the 35% federal income tax bracket, the company loses a deduction which would lower its federal income taxes by $7.00 per share. If the company is a Subchapter S corporation (an "S corporation") and the shareholders are in the 35% federal income tax bracket, the shareholders lose a tax deduction worth $7.00 per share to you (35% × $20). Limited liability companies produce similar tax results.

The cost of giving Joe long-term capital gains in this example is the *loss* by the company (or shareholders of an S corporation) of federal income tax savings of $7.00 per share. The answer remains substantially the same if we factor in state income taxes.

How much does Joe benefit by having long-term capital gains on the appreciation? Answer: A lot less than the company (or shareholders of an

(Continued)

S corporation) loses. If Joe would have paid federal income tax of 35% had the gain been ordinary income, and instead pays a 15% long-term capital gain on the $20 appreciation, Joe saves only 20% of $20, or $4.00 per share.

Is it worthwhile for the company (or shareholders of an S corporation) to give up a federal income tax deduction of $7.00 per share so that Joe can save $4.00 per share? The answer is probably no. For this reason, many public companies grant non-ISOs instead of ISOs

Still, that is not the end of the story.

THE ADVANTAGE OF ISOs

Most employees will not satisfy the one year holding period on ISOs—they cannot afford to hold the stock for one year after paying the exercise price. Many highly paid executives can afford to hold the stock for the one year holding period. Nonetheless, doing so may subject these executives to paying alternative minimum taxes which apply to ISOs. As a result, many executives make disqualifying dispositions of stock acquired under ISOs in the year of exercise in order to avoid alternative minimum tax.

Consequently, by granting an ISO, the company can give an employee the *potential* of long-term capital gains treatment, but in most cases that is not the reality. When an employee makes a sale or other disqualifying disposition of the stock within one year after option exercise, the company (and/or the shareholders of an S corporation) will generally obtain the same income tax deduction as if the employee originally received a non-ISO.

Moreover, if an employee receives a non-ISO and exercises it, the company will have to withhold on the exercise date an amount sufficient to pay the employee's federal income tax withholding and the employee's share of other payroll taxes on the share appreciation (unless the shares are subject to vesting conditions, in which case the tax is postponed until the vesting conditions are satisfied or a Section 83(b) election is made). Using an ISO avoids the result, since there is no withholding tax upon an employee's exercise of the ISO.

The lead author of this book generally recommends that ISOs be issued to employees, rather than non-ISOs, because they give the employee at least the potential of long-term capital gains treatment. Even though the employee will in most cases not achieve that potential because of personal sale decisions, the ISO is generally viewed as a more valuable option by knowledgeable employees who will avoid all federal withholding on option exercise.

Section 422(d) of the Code limits the amount of long-term capital gains that an employee can receive on an incentive stock option. The limitation is measured each calendar year by multiplying the option price of the incentive stock options received by the optionee by the number of option shares that first become exercisable during that calendar year. To the extent that this multiplication exceeds $100,000 in any calendar year, the excess numbers of shares are not entitled to long-term capital gains investments.

Appendix E, entitled "What an Employee Should Know about His or Her Stock Options," contains a guide for executives and other employees.

Non-ISOs with Tax Reimbursement

A few companies have opted to grant non-ISOs with tax reimbursement to executives and other employees. The tax reimbursement assists the employee in paying the federal income tax withholding upon exercise of the non-ISO. Nevertheless, there is withholding due on the tax reimbursement itself, so that the tax reimbursement must be sufficient to permit the employee to pay withholding on both the exercise of the non-ISO and the tax reimbursement.

SCENARIO 9.2

In the previous example, suppose executive Joe received a non-ISO which he exercised on January 2, 2013, and there was appreciation of $20 per share. Assume further that the required federal income tax withholding is 28% or $5.60. Under these circumstances, Joe should receive tax reimbursement of approximately $7.78 per share, which after tax withholding of 28% of that amount, would result in Joe receiving $5.60 per share. The $7.78 tax reimbursement to Joe should ordinarily be deductible by the company. The net after federal income tax benefits to the company (or shareholders of an S Corporation, assuming they are in the 35% federal income tax bracket) on the non-ISO

(Continued)

exercise, after subtracting tax reimbursement, would be $1.94 per share, computed as follows:

$7.00	Federal Income Tax benefit of non-ISO tax deduction (35% × $20 per share)
+2.72	Federal Income Tax benefit of tax reimbursement (35% × $7.78 per share)
$9.72	
−7.78	Less cash cost of tax reimbursement
$1.94	Net Cash Federal Income Tax Benefit.

Thus, the company (or the shareholders of an S corporation) save $1.94 per share using a non-ISO in this example, *even after reimbursing Joe's federal income tax withholding*. If we factor in state income taxes, the answer remains substantially the same.

There is a slight difference in the tax result between ISO stock prematurely sold and a non-ISO. If on the exercise date of an ISO the appreciation is $20 per share and Joe sells the stock the next day at a price that produced a gain of $19 per share (the market value dropped $1), the company's federal income tax deduction (or the shareholders' deduction in an S corporation) and Joe's ordinary income tax is limited to the $19 gain per share. However, if Joe receives a non-ISO, Joe is taxed on the $20 per share gain on the date of exercise and the sale at $1 less produces a short term capital loss for Joe for federal income tax purposes. In this case, the company's federal income tax deduction (or the shareholders' deduction in an S corporation) equals the $20 recognized by Joe on the date of exercise of the non-ISO.

A federal income tax reimbursement provision only works if the company pays federal income taxes. If the company has losses or loss carryovers, there are no current federal income tax savings from the exercise of a non-ISO. The tax deduction from the exercise of the non-ISO would only increase the company's loss carryovers.

If Joe executive is given an ISO and violates the one-year holding period, the company's federal income tax savings (or the savings of the shareholders of an S corporation) is even greater than $1.94 per share and equals $7.00 per share (35% × $20). This is the same tax benefit as if Joe executive received a non-ISO without any tax reimbursement whatsoever.

The use of tax reimbursement provisions with non-ISOs will require the company to accrue the liability under the tax reimbursement provision on the company's statement of income for accounting purposes.

THE TAX BENEFIT TO THE COMPANY

The company receives a federal income tax deduction equal to the amount of income realized by its employee when they exercise a non-ISO or when they sell or make another disqualifying disposition of stock previously acquired within one year after exercising an ISO. These savings can be quite substantial. If the company is a Subchapter S corporation, these tax deductions accrue to the personal benefit of the shareholders.

Section 162(m) of the Internal Revenue Code limits, in the case of a publicly held corporation, the tax deductions available to the company with respect to certain employee remuneration to the extent that the remuneration for a taxable year exceeds $1 million. This provision is applicable to the chief executive officer (or an individual acting in such a capacity) and the four highest compensated officers (other than the chief executive officer).

These federal income tax deductions have in the past eliminated all of the federal income tax of both Microsoft and Cisco Systems.[1]

BEST PRACTICE

All forms of equity incentives, and any amendments to such forms, should be checked for compliance with Section 409A of the Internal Revenue Code.

The complex provisions of Section 409A of the Internal Revenue Code and the final regulations under that section require companies to structure their equity incentives (and any amendments) so that they can rely on one of several exemptions from Section 409A.[2] See Chapter 13 for additional information. In general, incentive stock options and employee stock purchase plans under Section 423 of the Code are exempted from Section 409A.

The scandals over option backdating practice have tainted many public companies. Our next chapter discusses best option backdating practices.

---

[1]G. Morgenson, "The Consequences of Corporate America's Growing Addition to Stock Options," *The New York Times* (June 13, 2000).

[2]See Jones and Tyson, "Effect of Final Code Section 409A Regulations on Equity Plans," June 14, 2007, Womble Carlyle Sandridge & Rice, www.wcsr.com/

CHAPTER 10

Option Granting Practices

In 1997, Professor David Yermack of New York University (NYU) published an article in the *Journal of Finance* that documented peculiar price patterns around executive stock option grants. He and other researchers speculated that the stock price rise after the grant date might be due to corporate executives who knew that good news was on the horizon and made sure options were granted before the release of that information.

In May 2005, Professor Eric Lie of the University of Iowa published in *Management Science,* a paper that collected a much larger sample of data than Professor Yermack. Professor Lie noted that stock prices perform worse than what was normal immediately *before* option grants and performed better than what was normal immediately *after* option grants. He concluded that "unless corporate insiders can predict short-term movements in the stock market, my results provided further evidence in support of the backdating explanation." Professor Yermack wrote that he did not believe it at first as "the whole idea was so sinister."

Professor Lie started his research for the May 2005 paper in 2003 and sent an early version of his backdating hypothesis to the Securities and Exchange Commission (SEC) in 2004, which found the hypothesis "very interesting." The analysis by Professor Lie, and his coauthor, Professor Herron, indicated that 13.6% of options grants to top executives between January 1, 1996 and December 1, 2005 were backdated or manipulated, out of a total of approximately 40,000 option grants studied. The professors concluded that 23% of unscheduled option grants were backdated before the new 2-day filing requirements for Form 4 took effect in August 2002, while 10% of unscheduled option grants were backdated after the rules changed. A higher frequency of backdating was found among technology firms, small firms, and firms with high stock price volatility.

The Wall Street Journal Scorecard through September 11, 2006 reflects more than 105 companies that have publicly disclosed option backdating issues. The backdating controversy led to a record number of late filings. The early findings of Professor Yermack are now called "spring-loading" or "front-running," and the subsequent findings by Professor Lie are now called "bullet-dodging" (i.e., intentionally delaying option grants until negative news has been released, as well as pure backdating).

Three researchers at the University of Michigan estimated that back-dating stock options between 2000 and 2004 helped sweeten the average executive's pay by more than 1.25%, or about $600,000. But the fallout from the recent options investigations has caused those executives' companies to fall in market value by an average of 8%, or $500 million each. "For about $600,000 a year to the executives, shareholders are being put at risk to the tune of $500 million," the study concludes.

Option backdating has far-reaching legal, accounting, and tax implications. The most recent implication appeared in The Wall Street Journal of August 29, 2006 that revealed that UnitedHealth Group had been warned by a group of hedge funds who held their bonds that those bonds would become immediately due and payable if UnitedHealth Group did not file its 10-Q within 60 days. The quarterly reports of UnitedHealth Group as well as many other companies had been delayed because of this option backdating scandal and the subsequent investigation by the audit committee and by the SEC.

The U.S. Department of Justice has formed an Options Backdating Task Force. The Chairman of the SEC has testified before Congress that there are over 100 companies that are currently being investigated by the SEC for option backdating practices. This does not include the many other public companies who are not being investigated by the SEC but who have engaged in internal investigations.

A study of option grants during the period 1996-2005 released November 16, 2006 by the Harvard Law School Program on Corporate Governance entitled "Lucky CEOs" states as follows:

- 1,150 "lucky grants" (defined as option grants given at the lowest price of the month) were manipulated.

- 720 public companies (12% of all public companies studied) provided one or more "lucky grants."
- 850 CEOs (about 10% of all public CEOs) received "lucky grants" produced by opportunistic timing.

The internal audit committee investigations and the SEC investigations have lead to the resignations of senior executives at a number of public companies, including the following: the Chairman, CEO and General Counsel of UnitedHealth Group, Inc.; a director and former CFO of Apple Computer; the CEO of McAfee, Inc.; the CEO of CNet Networks, Inc.; the Chairman and CEO of Sapient Corp; the Chairman and CEO of KP Home; the CEO of Monster Worldwide, Inc.; the CEO of HCC Insurance Holdings, Inc; the CEO of Cyberonics, Inc.; the CEO of Affiliated Computer Services, Inc.; the CEO of Brocade Communications Systems; and the Chairman and CEO of Selectica, Inc.

Appendix E to this book includes a document entitled "Search Terms Typically Required to be Researched By Public Company in Option Backdating Investigations by the Securities and Exchange Commission." This is a typical discovery request by the SEC for electronic searching by companies which the SEC is investigating for backdating. The reader will be blown away by the extensive list of electronic search terms that are being required by the SEC as part of its option backdating investigations.

BEST PRACTICE

Compensation committees should meet in person or by teleconference to grant options and other equity instruments, either before the stock market opens or after it closes, and should avoid the use of unanimous written consents (including e-mail consents).

The grant of a stock option by a compensation committee should be a formal process and is typically time-sensitive, that is, the option exercise price should be equal to the market price at the time of the grant. A unanimous written consent (including e-mail consents) is typically not legally effective until the last signature is received (either by fax, mail, or e–mail) by the company from the last member of the compensation committee to sign the consent. The exact time that the written consent was received may not be easily determined, especially if the company does not open its mail immediately upon receipt.

Therefore, to avoid any question as to the exact time of the option grant, it is better practice to have an in–person meeting or a teleconference meeting at which a quorum is present, with prior written notice of the meeting or teleconference time to all members. The exact time at which the approval has been given by the compensation committee can then be determined by the secretary of the compensation committee by virtue of the time of the vote of the members in person or by teleconference.

It is preferable to have the meeting before the market opens in the morning or after it closes at night. A meeting of the compensation committee in the early morning before the market opens could utilize the closing price of the day before. A meeting of the compensation committee after the market closes, either in the late afternoon or at night, could use the closing price of that day.

If the meeting is held during the time that the market is open, a question could arise as to what the actual market price was at the exact moment of the compensation committee approval. For example, if the approval occurred at 11:30 A.M. (Eastern Time), was the market price the sale at 11:28 A.M. (Eastern Time) or the sale at 11:31 A.M. (Eastern Time)?

Of course, the compensation committee could avoid this problem by setting the market price as the closing price on the day of their approval of the stock option. However, this procedure has the disadvantage that the compensation committee does not know the actual exercise price of the option at the time they approve its grant. For example, if the compensation committee approved the stock option grant at 11:30 A.M. (Eastern Time) based upon the closing price at 4:00 P.M. (Eastern Time) that day, there could be significant fluctuation in the market price between 11:30 A.M. (Eastern Time) and 4:00 P.M. (Eastern Time) that might have changed the decision of the compensation committee.

There is an advantage of establishing the option exercise price at the exact time of the compensation committee decision and this can be done with certainty if the compensation committee meets before the market opens or after it closes. At either time, the compensation committee will know the exact market price and therefore the exact option exercise price which it is approving.

Item 402(d) (Instruction 3) of SEC Regulation S-K requires that the public company describe the methodology for determining the exercise or base price of options (or presumably SARs) if the closing market price on the grant date is not used in determining such exercise or base price.

BEST PRACTICE

Generally grant stock options or other equity instruments at the same time or times each year, with the possible exception of new hires, promoted executives or other extraordinary circumstances, such as mergers and acquisitions.

By establishing a fixed date or dates to grant stock options or other equity instruments each year, the compensation committee will help avoid a charge that they utilized inside information in establishing the grant date. This helps avoid charges of "spring-loading" or "bullet-dodging." Even though neither of these practices is arguably illegal, using a fixed granting date helps to avoid criticism by shareholders and corporate governance rating agencies. It should be noted that in *Ryan v Gifford*[1] the Delaware Chancery Court stated in a footnote that spring-loading "encompasses an element of intentional dissembling."[2]

The problem with using fixed granting dates to avoid criticism is that it may be necessary to create an exception for new hires, promoted executives, and other extraordinary circumstances, such as a merger or acquisition. Typically, a new hire will want to have their option grant price based upon the date of the commitment to hire them. If there is a rise in the price of the stock between the commitment date and the fixed grant date, the new hire may be very unhappy. Some companies are now picking a fixed date for grants to new hires or for promoted executives; still, this does not solve the problem of the new hire or promoted executive who sees the stock price rise before the fixed grant date.

---

[1] *Ryan v. Gifford*, 2007 WL 1018208 (Del. Ch. 2007).
[2] Id note 59.

It may, therefore, be best to permit new hires to receive their stock option based upon the commitment date market price or possibly the first day of employment market price. In order to permit a potential hire who has received a commitment for stock option to receive the market price on the commitment date, the plan must so provide. The option given to the new hire would, by its terms, automatically terminate if he or she does not join the company on the proposed date of first employment and the option could not be exercised prior to the new hire joining the company.

Promoted executives may also be excluded from the fixed grant date requirement by selecting as the grant date the effective date of the promotion.

In the case of a major merger or extraordinary transaction, it may be necessary to grant stock options to employees joining the company as a result of the merger. It would be bad for the acquired company's employee morale and could actually make the merger negotiations more difficult if these new employees had to wait until the fixed grant date to receive a stock option. This would be particularly true if these new employees were required to surrender a stock option granted by the acquired company as a result of the merger.

In describing the company's granting practices in documents filed with the SEC, it would be important to stress that there are exceptions from the general rule that stock options and other equity instruments are granted on a fixed date or dates each year.

BEST PRACTICE

The compensation committee or audit committee should require a preliminary review of all past stock option granting practices to determine if there has been an option backdating problem.

The paper by Professor Bebchuk entitled "Lucky CEOs" suggests that there can be as many as 720 companies that may have option backdating problems. These companies include both "old economy" as well as technology and other "new economy" companies. There is no identification in the paper as to who these companies are. However, it does not take much imagination to realize that sooner or later they will be identified.

Some boards of directors take the position "don't ask, don't tell." They would prefer not to uncover issues that will cause problems for the company. This attitude ignores the probability that this problem is unlikely to go away and could result in the loss of a key executive. If the board were to at least preliminarily investigate whether the company has had an option backdating issue in the past, the board could exercise better control over the results of the investigation than if the investigation were performed by the SEC or another government agency. Moreover, accounting firms are asking companies about the backdating issue in connection with their annual audits and are required to do so by the Public Company Accounting Oversight Board (PCAOB).

A preliminary view of option granting practices should extend for a ten-year period and attempt to trace the extent to which stock options were granted at the low market prices during a given month, quarter, or year. The procedures followed should be similar to the procedures performed by Professor Lie in his original paper.

OPTION GRANTING PRACTICES

BEST PRACTICE

Stock option plans and other equity plans must clearly address the following topics and should grant broad authority to the board of directors:

- Who is authorized to administer the plan (the board of directors or the compensation committee)?
- Who is eligible to receive option grants under the plan?
- Does the plan provide for the delegation of authority to an officer of the company with respect to certain grants (i.e., which officers and what authority do they have)?
- Can options be granted at an exercise price that is different from the market price on the date of the grant, and how is market price defined in the plan?
- Are there special provisions governing the grant of options to directors?

Option and other equity plans must specify the exact authority of the administrator of the plan, including the eligibility requirements. For example, are part time employees and consultants eligible for an equity grant? Are prospective employees eligible for an equity grant conditioned on the start of their employment, as discussed below?

Any equity incentive plan should provide broad authority to the board of directors and to any administrator of the plan. An example of such a broad authority plan is contained in Appendix D.

The purpose of granting broad authority in an equity incentive plan is to provide maximum flexibility to the board and to any plan administrator to deal with unusual situations and to avoid amendments to the plan which require shareholder approval. No one can foresee all of the future circumstances that may arise. Any material amendment to the plan will typically require shareholder approval by reason of stock market listing rules, the Internal Revenue Code, or the terms of the plan itself. Such shareholder approval involves significant time and expense and can cause push-back from shareholders. By initially establishing a broad authority plan, these disadvantages can be avoided.

Appendix D contains a Public Company Equity Incentive Plan that includes both part-time and prospective employees as well as full-time current employees, directors, and consultants. Part-time executives (such as women executives in job sharing arrangements or an executive on partial family leave) can be extremely valuable to the company and the company should retain flexibility to provide them with equity incentives.

Obviously, any equity grant to a prospective employee should provide for its automatic termination in the event the prospective employee never commences employment and should not be vested prior to such date.

It is preferable to grant the plan administrator the authority to make option grants below fair market value on the grant date. Circumstances may arise where it is desirable to do so, even if such an option grant creates issues under Section 409A of the Internal Revenue Code. For example, if a key prospective employee receives an offer of stock options and the market price is $20.00 per share and on the grant date (which is the same as the employment start date), the market price is $30.00 per share, the compensation committee should have the flexibility of granting the stock with a $20.00 per share exercise price. Obviously, this should be a very limited and rare situation, but there is no reason to deny the compensation committee this flexibility for addressing the problems of a key employee.

Another reason to give the administrator the authority to make option grants below fair market value is illustrated in the Delaware Chancery Court decision in *Ryan v. Gifford*.[3] *Ryan* concerned allegations of backdating involving the stock of Maximum Integrated Products, Inc. In a shareholder derivative action, the complaint alleged that members of the company's board of directors and compensation committee breached their duties of due care and loyalty by approving or accepting backdated options that violated a provision of a shareholder-approved stock option plan requiring that the exercise price of all stock options granted would be no less than the fair market value of the company's stock on the grant date. The Court refused to dismiss the plaintiff's backdating claims, citing the provision of the shareholder-approved plan that required option exercise prices be no less than fair market value on the grant date. A plan provision that authorizes option grants below fair market value provides a legal defense against inadvertent option granting practices that do not satisfy the fair market value test.

Similarly, it may not be the best practice to delegate authority to the CEO to grant stock options, nevertheless it may be important for the compensation committee to have this authority in limited circumstances. Should the compensation committee delegate such authority, the boundaries of the delegation should be carefully spelled out. For example, the compensation committee might delegate to the CEO authority for approving new hire grants subject to certain limitations established by the committee. In addition, the compensation committee should carefully monitor the grants made by the CEO to ascertain whether the CEO has adhered to the boundaries of the delegation.

For instance, the proxy statement filed by Bank of America Corporation for its 2007 stockholders' meeting contained the following sentence relating to delegation of authority to grant stock option and stock appreciation rights: "The Chief Administrative Officer has the authority to make awards of stock options and stock appreciation rights under the Key Associate Stock Plan to other associates who are not 'insiders' or 'named executive officers' as defined in the Key Associate Stock Plan, provided the awards are on terms and conditions that have been pre-approved by the Committee on the Stock Plan Award Subcommittee."

---

[3] *Ryan v. Gifford*, 2007 WL 1018208 (Del. Ch. 2007).

The "Compensation Discussion and Analysis" required under SEC compensation rules, effective December 15, 2006, requires the disclosure of:

- Whether the company has any program to time option grants to its executives in coordination with the release of material nonpublic information
- How such a program to time option grants to executives fits in the context of the company's program with regard to option grants to other employees
- The role of the compensation committee in approving and administering such a program
- Whether the company has timed, or plans to time, its release of material nonpublic information for the purpose of affecting the value of executive compensation.

BEST PRACTICE

The corporate secretary or other designated member of the compensation committee should be in charge of properly documenting all actions taken at meetings in the minutes, which then should be filed in the company's record book. Minutes should be reviewed by corporate counsel familiar with the option granting rules and other requirements to ensure all appropriate steps are taken and correctly documented.

The board of directors of United Healthcare Group recently hired a secretary to the board after they had serious option backdating practices problems that led to the resignation of their CEO. Although it is not necessary for every company to do so, it is important to have very precise documentation of all actions taken in connection with the granting of stock options and other equity incentives. The purpose of the documentation is to provide the basis for the accounting for the equity grants and to avoid backdating issues.

BEST PRACTICE

The amount and size of equity awards to various classes of executives and other employees should be subject to written compensation guidelines.

The compensation committee of every company, in consultation with management, should develop written guidelines for the amount and size of equity awards for different classes of executives and other employees. Such written guidelines will help avoid having disparate treatment of executives and other employees at the same level, which tends to cause resentment among executives and employees.

BEST PRACTICE

Once equity awards are approved, they should be entered into an award tracking database that will also track any exercises of equity awards.

If there are a significant number of equity awards, software should be purchased to assist the administrator in tracking both the granting of and the exercising of awards. Manual tracking of information is inefficient unless there are extremely few awards. Some companies have outsourced the administration of equity awards to third party vendors which may make sense if there are a significant number of such awards. Executives subject to Section 16 of the Securities Exchange Act of 1934 should not be permitted to exercise their awards electronically.

BEST PRACTICE

Persons receiving equity awards should be required to accept their awards with a manual signature.

Requiring acceptance of equity awards is important to avoid disputes with executives and other employees. Some equity awards contain supplemental requirements imposing confidentiality duties on employees, preventing them from soliciting customers or other employees shortly after termination of employment, and other provisions that are important to the company. Obtaining a manual signature indicating acceptance is vital to the legal enforceability of these provisions. Using electronic means to accept such awards may create uncertainty as to the legal enforceability of such acceptance and should be avoided.

BEST PRACTICE

Promptly send a summary of the key terms and conditions of the equity grant to the recipients. Set a reasonable time frame in which the paperwork reflecting the grant of an equity award is distributed and establish deadlines which comply with FAS 123R.

Under the FASB Staff Position[4] on the grant date under FAS 123R, a mutual understanding of the key terms and conditions of an award is presumed to exist on the date the award is approved in accordance with the relevant corporate governance requirements *if* both of the following conditions are met:

- The award is a unilateral grant and, therefore, the recipient does not have the ability to negotiate the key terms and conditions of the award with the employer.
- The key terms and conditions of the award are expected to be communicated to an individual within a relatively short time period from the date of approval.

A "relatively short time period" is the period that the organization "could reasonably complete all actions necessary to communicate the awards to the recipients in accordance with the entity's customary human resource practices."

---

[4]FAS 123(R)-2, October 18, 2005.

Technically, the FASB Staff Position does not require the distribution of the grant paperwork, only the "key terms and conditions" of the equity grant. Accordingly, it is a best practice to promptly send a summary of the key terms and conditions to the recipients of the equity grant. However, unless there is a summary provided to the employee of the key terms and conditions, it is the grant paperwork that will reflect all of the key terms and conditions. In addition, sending the complete grant paperwork avoids any question by the auditor as to whether the summary of key terms and conditions was adequate.

The date of distribution of the grant paperwork to employees receiving equity grants therefore can impact the grant date and the fair market value calculation under FAS 123R. Accordingly, the company and its auditors should collectively establish a time frame that they believe will satisfy the grant date requirements under the FASB Staff Position.

If a manual signature is required from the person receiving the equity grant, a similar deadline must be established by the company and its auditor. The paperwork should indicate that the equity grant is automatically cancelled if the paperwork with the manual signature of the equity grant recipient is not received by the deadline.

BEST PRACTICE

Companies that have suffered from stock option backdating problems should take special care to list the remedial steps they have taken to prevent this problem in the future.

For example, UnitedHealth Group, which suffered a major stock option scandal in 2006, took great care in its 2007 proxy statement to explain to shareholders the changes it had made in its equity reward program. These included engaging an outside professional services firm to conduct regular testing of the company's equity award controls.

Private companies should obtain an independent appraisal of their stock prior to granting stock options to their employees. Section 409A of the Internal Revenue Code (discussed in Chapter 13) exempts from its provisions options granted with exercise prices at or above fair market value.

BEST PRACTICE FOR PRIVATE COMPANIES

In the case of private companies granting stock options to employees, the compensation committee should obtain an independent appraisal to determine the fair market value of the option stock in order to establish the option exercise price.

An independent appraisal provides evidence of what is fair market value in case of the IRS audit. In the case of incentive stock options, which must be granted with exercise prices at or above fair market value, the independent appraisal is also helpful in case of an IRS audit. Finally, an independent appraisal is helpful in supporting the accounting charge for stock option under FAS 123R.

THE COUNCIL OF INSTITUTIONAL INVESTORS

The Council of Institutional Investors has developed its own best practices for granting stock options. These practices are divided between those that are preferred practices and those that are inappropriate practices.

The preferred practices include the following:

- *Performance options:* Stock option prices should be indexed to peer groups, performance-vesting and/or premium-priced to reward superior performance based on the attainment of challenging quantitative goals.
- *Dividend equivalents:* To ensure that executives are neutral between dividends and stock price appreciation, dividend equivalents should be granted with stock options, but distributed only upon exercise of the option.

The inappropriate practices include the following:

- *Discount options:* No discount options should be awarded.
- *Reload options:* Reload options should be prohibited.
- *Option repricing:* "Underwater" options should not be repriced or replaced (either with new options or other equity awards), unless

approved by shareowners. Repricing programs, for shareowner approval, should exclude directors and executives, restart vesting periods, and mandate value-for-value exchanges in which options are exchanged for a number of equivalently valued options/shares.

EQUITY RETENTION PRACTICES

> **BEST PRACTICE**
>
> Require executives who receive stock options or stock grants to hold the profit (net of taxes and transaction costs) in the form of stock for a period of time and cease granting stock options or other equity rewards once the executive receives a competitive level of equity.

The proxy statement filed by Bank of America Corporation in 2007 states the following as its policy: "Any gains realized by an executive officer upon exercise of the stock option (net of taxes and transaction costs) must be held in the form of shares of our Common Stock for an additional three-year period following exercise or until termination of employment, if earlier."

Some companies are implementing hold-until-retirement provisions in their stock options and stock grants and placing an overall limit on the equity rewards to executives. The advantage of the hold-until-retirement provisions is that they align the interest of the executive with the interests of the long-term shareholders. Any such provisions should contain an exception for personal emergencies of the executive, as determined by the board of directors.

Some argue that a cap should be placed on the total amount of equity rewards in order to limit the total amount of equity received by the executive to an amount sufficient to motivate him or her properly, but not in excess of that amount. Unfortunately, it is almost impossible to determine in advance the exact amount of the cap that still provides competitive compensation to the executive. The level of equity compensation that is competitive tends to change over time and circumstances and, therefore, placing a cap may not be realistic.

We next turn to the issue of director compensation.

CHAPTER 11

Director Compensation

There is a saying that you will "get the board that you pay for." In general, to attract motivated, experienced, and well connected (and thus busy) persons to a board of directors, the company must provide an attractive compensation package to its directors.

According to a 2006 Report of the NACD Blue Ribbon Commission on Director Compensation[1] (NACD Report), there have been recent years of dramatic growth in the pay levels of directors of public companies because of major changes in shareholder expectations and heightened regulatory requirements.

BEST PRACTICE

Nonemployee director compensation policies should accomplish the following goals:

- Attract highly qualified candidates
- Retain highly qualified directors
- Align directors' interests with those of the long-term owners of the corporation
- Provide complete disclosure to shareowners regarding all components of director compensation including the philosophy behind the program and all forms of compensation.

---

[1]"Report of the NACD Blue Ribbon Commission, Director Compensation," (2006 Edition).

The Council of Institutional Investors believes that nonemployee director compensation should exist of a combination of cash retainer and equity-based compensation and opposes the use of meeting attendance fees, whether for board meetings or committee meetings. Their theory is that the cash retainer should cover all meetings. The Council also believes that directors should have their own individual capital at stake in the company, but supports equity-based compensation plans that provide a supplemental means of obtaining long-term equity holdings.

The NACD Report recommends, as a best practice, that equity should represent 50% to 100% of total director compensation.

The Coca-Cola Company has taken the position of the Council of Institutional Investors and the NACD Report one step further and has eliminated, starting the year 2006, any cash retainer for nonemployee directors. No employee who serves as a director is paid for their services as a director. The 2006 Directors' Plan provided that "each director was credited with the number of share units equal to the number of shares of Common Stock that could be purchased on February 16, 2006 with $175,000. On each dividend date the number of units was adjusted as though the dividends had been reinvested. In February 2009, performance for the three-year period 2006–08 will be certified. If the performance target is met, the units will be paid in cash equal to the number of units multiplied by the fair market value of the shares of Common Stock. If the performance target is not met, the Directors will receive nothing."[2]

There is no universal agreement as to the desirability of performance compensation for directors. The Council of Institutional Investors and many corporate governance advocates do not support performance measures in director compensation on the grounds that performance-based compensation for directors has a significant potential to conflict with the director's primary role as an independent representative of shareholders. Accordingly, the Council would not favor the 2006 Directors' Plan of The Coca-Cola Company.

Although The Coca-Cola Company may be able to attract and retain highly qualified directors with a pure equity plan, it is unlikely that smaller and less prestigious companies can do so. Some compensation consultants

---

[2]The Coca-Cola Company Schedule 14A filed on March 9, 2007, p. 26.

have privately criticized the plan as most companies will have to use a cash component to permit them to attract and retain directors. Director compensation plans must be tailored to the unique circumstances of each company. Nevertheless, at least one component of director compensation should include equity in order to better align the interests of directors with the interests of shareholders.

BEST PRACTICE

Director compensation plans should include an equity component in addition to a cash component in order to better align the interests of directors with the interests of shareholders. Generally, directors who are employees should not receive additional compensation for serving on the board of directors.

RETAINER AND DIFFERENTIAL PAY

The cash retainer for nonemployee directors should be sufficient for all of the expected duties of the director. However, an additional retainer should be paid when there are internal investigations or other extraordinary services required of directors. Retainers can be differentiated among nonemployee directors to recognize the additional burden imposed upon directors who are chairs of committees. Given the heavy responsibilities of the audit committees, it is not unusual to have a larger cash retainer paid to the chair of that committee. Similar pressure is currently being exerted on the chair of the compensation committee and consideration should be given to a larger retainer to the chair of that committee.

According to the NACD Report, differential pay for a particular committee, based upon the demands on the director of the committee or the position, has become a majority practice among the "Top 200" companies. After the passage of the Sarbanes-Oxley Act of 2002, an increased amount was paid to audit committee members over their counterparts on other committees, such as the compensation and corporate governance/nominating committees. According to the NASD Report, audit committee members for the "Top 200" companies received nearly double the pay of compensation committee members. With the adoption by the SEC in 2006 of heightened executive and director compensation disclosure requirements, it is expected that this differential may decrease because of the increased burdens on compensation committee members.

MINIMUM EQUITY REQUIREMENTS

BEST PRACTICE

Directors should generally have a substantial equity ownership in the company on whose board they serve, but should be given a reasonable amount of time to accumulate that equity.

There is general agreement that, as a best practice, directors should have substantial equity ownership in the company on whose board they serve. However, there is no universal agreement as to what is "substantial" and whether there should be exceptions for persons of modest net worth, such as academics and former government officials or retired military officers. In addition, there is always a danger that a director with too much equity ownership may reject risky strategies for the company because of the personal risk to their portfolio, even though such strategies may be in the long-term interest of the company.

The Council of Institutional Investors suggests equity ownership by nonemployee directors of at least 3 to 5 times their annual compensation. However, the Council recognizes that not all directors have the financial means to immediately satisfy this goal and recommends a reasonable time period to achieve this objective.

The Council also suggests that companies should adopt holding requirements for a significant majority of equity-based compensation until the nonemployee director leaves the board. They suggest, for example, that 80% of equity compensation grants be retained by the director until retirement from the board. The Council would also prohibit directors from engaging in any hedging transactions that were otherwise permitted by SEC rules so that the directors remain at risk. The purpose of these provisions is to align the interest of the directors and the long-term shareholders.

The NACD Report recommends that the board should establish "substantial target for stock ownership for each director and a time period during which this target is to be met." Some companies have set the stock amount at five times the director's retainer or total cash compensation. The NACD Report suggests that, to insure a director's financial neutrality in a hostile takeover situation, about ten times the value of the director's total compensation may be needed. However, the NACD Report also suggests that exceptions should be made for academics and former government officials who may not have the net worth to justify this level of equity ownership.

If a portion of the director retainer is paid in equity, a substantial amount of equity can be accumulated over a number of years of service as a director. The use of phantom stock, which is paid in actual stock upon termination of the directorship, is a common method of accumulating equity for directors.

DIRECTOR COMPENSATION PROCEDURE AND PROCESS

BEST PRACTICE

Director compensation should be established by independent directors utilizing the services of independent compensation consultants, should be reviewed annually, and should be fully disclosed to shareholders.

The establishment of director compensation by directors involves a conflict of interest. To attempt to mitigate the conflict of interest, a committee consisting solely of independent directors should establish director compensation. Typically, this is the compensation committee of the board of directors. However, other committees composed solely of independent directors may undertake this task, such as the corporate governance committee. According to the Council of Institutional Investors, any compensation arrangement should be approved by all independent directors (whether or not on the committee) and should align the interests of directors with the long-term interests of shareholders.

The NACD Report strongly recommends the full disclosure to shareholders of the process of establishing director compensation and all elements of director compensation. SEC disclosure rules require such disclosure for public companies. Still, companies that are not subject to SEC rules should also consider making such disclosures to shareholders.

Because of the inherent conflict of interests involved in establishing director compensation, a thorough record should be created by the compensation committee (or other appropriate committee) that reflects their consideration of each component of director compensation and its value. Each component of director compensation should be annually reviewed and valued.

Similarly, compensation committees (or other appropriate committees) should utilize independent compensation consultants to assist them in establishing appropriate levels of director compensation. The use of independent compensation consultants on which the committee reasonably relies provides legal protection against charges by shareholders of conflict of interest or other breaches of fiduciary duties.

Finally, both SEC rules and good corporate governance requires a discussion of the philosophy of establishing director compensation and the process used by the compensation committee or other applicable committee.

BEST PRACTICE

Consider establishing a fair and objective methodology for determining nonemployee director compensation and disclose such methodology to shareholders.

Some companies have established an objective formula for determining nonemployee director compensation. An objective methodology, if it is fair, helps to avoid the appearance of a conflict of interest.

For example, PNM Resources, Inc., a gas and electric utility company, has created an objective formula for establishing nonemployee director compensation that uses the same peer group to benchmark director compensation as is utilized to benchmark executive compensation. PNM Resources, Inc. states as follows in its proxy statement: "In order to recommend a reasonable compensation package that will attract and retain highly qualified nonemployee directors, the [Governance and Public Policy Committee of the board] selects, weighs, and reviews each element of director compensation on an annual basis to recommend a total compensation amount that will approximate the 50th percentile of non-employee director compensation for directors of comparable utility and energy companies in the list of the Company's compensation Peer Group as identified on page 22 of this proxy statement."[3]

The disadvantage of an objective formula is that it does not take into account special circumstances, such as any unusual amount necessary to attract an outstanding person to the board of directors. In addition, any formula will have to be tempered with the additional director fees which may become payable in connection with special investigations, hostile takeovers, and mergers.

Notwithstanding these disadvantages, there are good arguments for using a fair and objective formula, subject to these special circumstances.

SHAREHOLDER APPROVAL

Most commentators do not believe that it is practical to give shareholders a vote on director compensation. The NACD Report states that it is "unworkable" to give shareholders such a vote. Shareholders always have the opportunity to vote against the reelection of any director whose compensation is unreasonable.

The Council of Institutional Investors strongly supports a shareholder approval of both equity-based plans for directors as well as material amendments to those plans. Stock market listing rules generally require such approvals with limited exceptions. The Council recommends a conservative interpretation of what is a "material" amendment.

PERQUISITES, REPRICING AND EXCHANGE PROGRAMS, CHANGE IN CONTROL, AND SEVERANCE PAYMENTS

The Council of Institutional Investors opposes any perquisites other than reimbursement to directors for meeting-related expenses of the board and

---

[3]PNM Resources, Inc. Schedule 14A filed on April 12, 2007, p. 15.

its committees. This would also include charitable award programs for directors, which the Council suggests should be made by the directors from their own funds. However, the Council would not oppose as perquisites "infrequent token gifts of modest value."

One suspects that the Council would not look favorably upon the following disclosure in the FedEx Corp. proxy statement filed August 14, 2006:

> "FedEx invited Board members' spouses to travel with the directors to attend a Board meeting held in Shanghai during fiscal 2006. In connection with this meeting, FedEx paid spousal air travel expenses for Philip Greer ($12,552), Dr. Shirley A. Jackson ($12,155) and Charles T. Manatt ($1,981)."[4]

Likewise, the Council opposes option repricing or exchange programs and change in control and severance payments, presumably because of potential conflicts of interest.

Finally, the Council does not object to allowing directors to defer cash retainers by adopting a deferred compensation plan that mirrors those offered to employees in broad-based plans. However, the Council would oppose any form of retirement benefits for directors.

The NACD Report opposes benefit programs for outside directors because of the risk of undermining director independence. Benefit programs include director retirement plans, grants to charity, director legacy donations, and free products and services. The NACD Report acknowledges that some of these plans are tax effective and "nice to have." However, these generous benefit programs could, according to the NACD Report, create incentives to avoid challenging management, especially when a term of director service is required before the benefits vest.

DISGORGEMENT

The Council of Institutional Investors believes in requiring directors to disgorge compensation in the event of malfeasance or other breach of fiduciary duty involving the director. This is similar to the "clawback" clauses discussed earlier in executive employment contracts.

We next turn to best practices for the executive in negotiating his or her own compensation package.

---

[4]FedEx Schedule 14A filed on August 14, 2006, p. 19.

CHAPTER 12

Negotiating for the Executive

The purpose of this chapter is to describe best practices for CEOs and other executives who are negotiating employment or severance contracts, including new candidates for CEO positions. This chapter, which is from the viewpoint of the executive, should be read in conjunction with Chapter 7 that deals with negotiating employment and severance contracts from the company's prospective.

Before discussing best practices, it is important to understand what an employment contract is and what it is not. Some executives have the view that if they negotiate a five-year contract they are guaranteed a job for five years. Nothing can be further from the truth. The company is legally able to fire the CEO any time the company wishes (subject to minor exceptions in the case of protected classes under the antidiscrimination laws). The CEO may have a right to sue the company for damages for breach of his or her employment contract, but normally would have no right to retain the position. Even a legal action by the executive for damages resulting from the breach of contract is subject to the legal duty to mitigate damages. Unless the duty to mitigate damages has been disclaimed in the employment contract, the executive will be required by the mitigation duty to use his or her best efforts to find another job and to have the earnings from that position reduce the executive's damage claim.

From the executive's viewpoint, a five-year employment contract without a disclaimer of the legal duty of mitigation only protects the executive to the extent the executive cannot find a new job at the same or greater salary for the period subsequent to the termination. That is why experienced attorneys for executives will always insist upon a disclaimer of the duty of mitigation or similar language in any employment agreement.

CEO Turnover

A paper by Professors Kaplan and Minton[1] in July 2006 concluded that there was a significant decrease in the tenure of CEOs since 1998, based upon a sample of large U.S. companies. CEO turnover increased to 16.5% since 1998, implying an average CEO turnover of just over six years. This contrasts sharply with a CEO turnover of 10% per year in the 1970s and 1980s and 11% in the 1990s. The paper concluded that the turnover was significantly related to three components of firm performance:

1. Performance relative to industry.
2. Industry performance relative to the overall market.
3. The performance of the overall stock market.

New Candidates for CEO or Other Executive Positions

BEST PRACTICE

Create an attractive but defendable resume of your past activities, experiences, and skills.

There is a tendency by potential CEOs and their professional resume writers to unduly embellish their resumes. While a little embellishment is expected, the executive candidate should be concerned by excessive exaggeration of his or her accomplishments, particularly prior schooling. The executive should assume that the resume will be extensively checked and rechecked. Ultimately, the verbal interviews with the hiring committee can be of equal, if not of greater, importance than the written resume.

---

[1]"How has CEO Turnover Changed? Increasingly Performance Sensitive Boards and Increasingly Uneasy CEOs," by Steven N. Kaplan and Bernadette A Minton, First Draft: March 2006, This Draft: July 2006.

BEST PRACTICE

Executives should proactively develop their own ideas for a fair, competitive, and performance-based compensation package and, in appropriate cases, seek the help of a compensation consultant to create such a package.

Executives should attempt to proactively develop their own ideas as to a fair, competitive, and performance-based compensation program for themselves. The use of a compensation consultant would be helpful in developing a reasonable compensation program. At an appropriate time, the executive should be prepared to share his or her ideas with the compensation committee as part of the negotiation process.

Executives must realize that they will have to deal with these same directors during their tenure with the company and should avoid beginning the relationship on a sour note. A proactive approach containing reasonable performance-based compensation proposals is the best way to commence the relationship.

BEST PRACTICE

Hire an attorney specializing in executive employment contracts to represent you or at least review the final document before signing it. If the amount involved justifies it, consider hiring your own compensation consultant to assist you in the negotiation process.

When negotiating any contract, it is important to hire the best qualified professionals to represent you. There are attorneys who specialize in employment contracts and you should consider hiring one, for no other reason than to review the terms of the final agreement. A compensation consultant can be very helpful, not only in developing a reasonable compensation package (as suggested above) but also in the negotiating process. In certain cases, the company will reimburse the expense of these professionals if it is part of your negotiations.

Your agreements should be carefully reviewed for compliance with Section 409A of the Internal Revenue Code. See Chapter 13. If Section 409A is violated, you could be liable to pay up to a maximum of 55% (plus interest retroactive to the vesting date) federal tax on the deferred compensation which violated Section 409A (and up to 85% for California residents). Care should be taken to insert a fixed schedule of severance payments in any employment agreement to comply with Section 409A.

When negotiating with a prospective employer, it is useful for you to take a more passive position and to have your attorney take the lead in advocating your views, thereby playing "good cop/bad cop." However, if that does not work, you should be prepared to share your views frankly and directly with the members of the hiring committee. Ultimately, you will have to work with the people on the hiring committee and it is important that you understand what kind of relationship you can expect in the future.

BEST PRACTICE

Any employment agreement should clearly specify your position and authority and to whom you are to report.

If you expect to be both president and chief executive officer of the company, make certain that you are named both CEO and president in the employment agreement. If you are just named the president of the company in the employment, the company may have the right to hire a CEO to whom you will report. Your exact duties and authority should be spelled out, including to whom you are to report.

BEST PRACTICE

The employment agreement should clearly specify the location of your principal office. If you do not expect to move your existing home, you should specify a limit on the number of miles at which your principal office can be located in relation to your existing home.

If you do not specify a location of your principal office in your employment agreement, the company can move its principal office anywhere in the world and you will have to follow. You may find yourself working in Fairbanks, Alaska, which may not be a disadvantage if you like living with caribou.

BEST PRACTICE

Your employment agreement should give you at least pro rata credit for any bonus due for the year in which your employment is terminated by the company or you terminate your employment for good reason.

Some employment agreements provide for no bonus unless the executive has been continuously employed by the company until the end of the fiscal year for which the bonus is due. It is fair to ask for a pro ration of the bonus if your employment is terminated without cause before the end of the fiscal year or if you terminate your employment for good reason before the end of the fiscal year. If your bargaining power is sufficient, you may insist upon a full bonus if the termination by the company without cause (or your termination for good reason) occurs after six months of the fiscal year on the theory that most of the bonus was then earned.

BEST PRACTICE

Your employment agreement should permit you to voluntarily terminate your employment for "good reason" and still receive the same benefits as if you had been terminated "without cause."

Modern employment agreements with CEOs permit the CEO to voluntarily terminate the agreement for "good reason" and receive the same benefits as if the CEO's employment had been terminated by the company "without cause." Although "good reason" is defined differently in various agreements, final regulations issued by the IRS under Section 409A[2] of the Internal Revenue Code have extensively defined "good reason" and it is expected that this definition may well become standard in employment agreements.

The definition of "good reason" in the IRS final regulations under Section 409A is as follows:

> "For these purposes, a good reason condition may consist of one or more of the following conditions arising without the consent of the service provider: (1) a material diminution in the service provider's base compensation; (2) a material diminution in the service provider's author- ity, duties, or responsibilities; (3) a material diminution in the authority, duties, or responsibilities of the supervisor to whom the service provider is required to report, including a requirement that a service provider report to a corporate officer or employee instead of reporting directly to the board of directors of a corporation (or similar entity with respect to an entity other than a corporation); (4) a material diminution in the budget over which the service provider retains authority; (5) a material change in geographic location at which the service provider must per- form the services; or (6) any other action or inaction that constitutes a material breach of the terms of an applicable employment agreement."

BEST PRACTICE

The definition of "cause" for involuntary termination of the CEO should be narrowed to the extent possible and appropriate cure periods permitted.

The employment agreements typically permit a CEO to be involuntarily terminated for "cause" and thereby deprived of any severance payments and stock options. The term "cause" should therefore be narrowly defined, since the adverse effects on the executive are so drastic. In addition, there should be cure periods in the agreement whereby the executive must be notified of the existence of the potential "cause" and afforded an opportunity

---

[2] §1.409A-1(n)(2)(ii) of IRS Regulations.

to remedy the potential "cause." For example, if "cause" includes failure to follow directions of the board of directors, the CEO should be given the opportunity to receive a written warning of such failure and the opportunity to cure such failure in a reasonable time period.

BEST PRACTICE

Confidentiality, non-solicitation, and non-competition provisions should be narrowly tailored to what is reasonably required to protect the company's interest.

It is typical in employment agreements to have provisions which prevent the CEO from reviewing confidential information of the company, from soliciting customers or employees after termination of the executive (with or without "cause"), and from provisions restricting competition by the CEO after termination (with or without "cause"). The CEO's attorney must be prepared to limit these clauses to what is really required by the company's interest as opposed to overly broad language drafted by the company's counsel.

BEST PRACTICE

The employment agreement should disclaim any duty by the executive to mitigate the damages of the company following a breach by the company of the employment agreement.

As noted earlier, the common law requires the executive, after a breach by the company of an employment agreement, to mitigate the damages of the company. This may include seeking another position quickly so that the earnings from this new position can be used to reduce the amount owed by the company to the executive. In the event of a breach by the company of the employment agreement, the company should not be in the position of requiring the executive to quickly seek other employment. To prevent the executive from being met by this argument, the employment agreement must clearly disclaim any duty by the executive to mitigate damages following a breach by the company of that agreement.

BEST PRACTICE

Executives should fully understand the terms of any equity incentive offered to them and should seek the advice of counsel for this purpose.

Equity incentives can be extremely complicated. Executives should seek the advice of competent counsel to fully understand the terms of the equity incentives. Appendix F of this book contains a simplified explanation of incentive and non-incentive stock options.

BEST PRACTICE

If the executive of a public company is subject to the so-called "six month rule" under Section 409A which prevents payments of severance pay for six months after termination, the employment agreement should require the company to pay the maximum amount of severance permissible under Section 409A during such six month period.

As discussed more fully in Chapter 13, a "specified employee" of a public company cannot receive "distributions" of "deferred compensation" (which includes severance pay) before the date that is six months after the date of separation from service (or if earlier, the date of death of the executive). A "specified employee" is an employee of a corporation of which any stock is publicly traded on an established securities market and who is an officer of the company having annual compensation greater than a specified amount ($145,000 in 2007), a 5% owner of the company, or a 1% owner having annual compensation of more than $150,000. The number of employees who could be deemed to be specified employees is limited to no more than 50.

However, there is an exemption from Section 409A which does permit payments during the first six months after separation which we have called the "two times exemption." This exemption permits up to a maximum of $450,000 (for 2007) to be paid in that six month period in the event of an involuntary termination or a termination for "good reason."

Employment Agreements with Private Equity Buyers of CEO's Business

Many entrepreneurs sell their businesses to private equity buyers and simultaneously enter into an employment agreement to operate the business. These CEO entrepreneurs usually have better bargaining positions with their new private equity employer than the typical CEO candidate. This is due to the fact that the private equity buyer at least initially usually needs the CEO entrepreneur to operate the business and the CEO entrepreneur is not competing with other CEO candidates. Such employment agreements are typically signed as part of the closing documents in connection with the sale of the CEO entrepreneur's business.

Appendix C is a typical employment agreement with the entity controlled after the closing by the private equity buyer. In this particular agreement, the CEO has retained a portion of the equity of the new business owned by the private equity buyer. In other separate agreements with the private equity buyer, the CEO entrepreneur entered into "put" and "call" agreements with the entity controlled by the private equity buyer for the purchase of the remainder of the stock of the CEO entrepreneur not acquired at the initial closing, with the purchase price depending upon the future earnings or EBITDA of the entity controlled by the private equity buyer. This type of earn-out is typical in private equity transactions.

Since the purchase price of the remaining stock owned by the CEO entrepreneur depends upon the future earnings or EBITDA of the entity employing the CEO entrepreneur, the following protections are suggested as best practices for the CEO entrepreneur.

BEST PRACTICE

CEO entrepreneurs should attempt to obtain an agreement from the private equity buyer that if the CEO is terminated "without cause" or terminates for "good reason" prior to completion of the earn-out period, the entire remaining maximum purchase price is due and payable since the CEO entrepreneur is prevented from achieving the earn-out.

If the purchase price (once such purchase price has been earned) for the remaining stock owned by the entrepreneur is to be paid in installments by the entity controlled by the private equity buyer, the CEO should attempt to prevent any management fees from being paid to the private equity buyer until the full purchase price has been paid.

Our final chapter on Section 409A of the Internal Revenue Code should be of equal importance to both executives and their companies.

CHAPTER 13

Executive Compensation and Section 409A of the Internal Revenue Code*

BEST PRACTICE

All forms of compensation payable to an executive must be reviewed for compliance with Section 409A of the Internal Revenue Code because failure to comply with Section 409A may cause the executive to pay federal income and additional taxes at a rate as high as 55% (plus interest retroactive to the vesting date).

There are nine important points to remember about the very complicated provisions of Section 409A of the Internal Revenue Code of 1986 ("Code") and the approximately 400 pages of preamble and final regulations under Section 409A issued by the Treasury and the Internal Revenue Service:[1]

- Section 409A impacts the structure of compensation paid to executives of private, not-for-profit, and public companies, employees, directors, and certain independent contractors (referred to as a "service provider" or "service providers").

---

*This chapter was co-authored by Wilhelm L. Gruszecki, Esq., Blank Rome LLP.
[1]Federal Register/Vol. 72, No. 73, April 17, 2007.

- If Section 409A applies and a failure to comply occurs in form or operation, the service provider who is affected will be required to pay a 20% federal additional tax in addition to a federal income tax that could be at a maximum rate of 35% in 2007, for a total of 55% (plus interest retroactive to the vesting date). If the service provider is a California resident, the combined federal and state income and additional tax rate will be a whopping 85% (before the effect of federal tax deductions for state taxes).

- Section 409A applies to a compensatory arrangement described in Section 409A as a "nonqualified deferred compensation plan." A nonqualified deferred compensation plan includes any form of agreement, method, program or other arrangement (collectively referred to as "plan") that provides for "deferred compensation." The term does not include certain types of plans, such as a qualified retirement plan, most types of welfare plans, or an incentive stock option under Code Section 422 or a tax-qualified employee stock purchase plan under Code Section 423. Generally, nontaxable benefits are not subject to Section 409A.

- A plan provides for "deferred compensation" if, under the relevant facts, (a) the service provider has a "legally binding right" during a taxable year to compensation, including cash, reimbursements, or in-kind services, that is or may be payable in a later taxable year and (b) the payment is not otherwise excepted from the definition of deferred compensation. If the compensation may be reduced unilaterally or eliminated by the recipient of his or her services after the services creating the right to the compensation have been performed, the service provider does not have a legally binding right to the compensation. However, if the compensation may be reduced or eliminated by operation of the objective terms of the plan, such as the application of a nondiscretionary, objective provision creating a substantial risk of forfeiture, the service provider is, nevertheless, considered to have a legally binding right to the compensation. Whether a plan provides for "deferred compensation" is generally determined at the time that the service provider obtains a legally binding right to the compensation.

- A bonus plan, employment agreement, severance arrangement, equity based compensation (such as a stock option, stock appreciation right,

SCENARIO 13.1

The CEO of a company has an agreement that provides that the CEO will be entitled to a $500,000 retention bonus if the CEO does not voluntarily terminate employment until two years have elapsed. The CEO has a legally binding right to the retention bonus upon execution of the agreement, even though it is subject to the performance of substantial services because it contains a nondiscretionary, objective provision creating a substantial risk of forfeiture applicable to the retention bonus. The retention bonus is payable within two years after the second anniversary of the start of employment. Assuming that the plan does not treat each payment as a "separate payment" for purposes of Section 409A, the short-term deferral exception discussed below would not be applicable and, in the absence of a specified time or fixed schedule for payment of the retention bonus, the retention bonus payments could be subject to the 55% (plus interest retroactive to the vesting date) maximum federal income and additional tax.

or phantom stock right), change in control agreement, traditional nonqualified deferred compensation, Code Section 457(f) plan, or split dollar agreement could be a nonqualified deferred compensation plan.

• If a plan fails to comply with Section 409A, the company that paid the deferred compensation might have liability for not complying with its tax reporting and withholding obligations, even though the primary tax burden would fall on the service provider.

• When analyzing the possible impact of Section 409A, first look for an exclusion from the coverage of Section 409A. For example, an exclusion referred to as "short term deferral" and other exclusions in the context of separation pay and stock-based compensation provide useful planning opportunities.

• If Section 409A applies because none of the exclusions are applicable, a nonqualified deferred compensation plan could be designed to comply with Section 409A provided that the appropriate terms are included in writing when required, which generally is at the time that the legally binding right arises. Designing a plan to comply with

Section 409A typically requires that the deferred compensation may not be distributed earlier than the occurrence of certain "payment triggers" and complying with the six-month rule for distributions to certain executives of public companies, as discussed below.

- Section 409A is generally effective for amounts earned and vested after December 31, 2004 and could apply to amounts earned and vested prior to that date if the plan under which the deferral was made is materially modified after October 3, 2004. The final regulations are effective January 1, 2009[2]. All nonqualified deferred compensation plans must be in writing and made compliant with Section 409A on or before December 31, 2008.[3]

This chapter is intended only to highlight a few important topics and areas of concern under Section 409A for executives and is not intended as a complete or exhaustive explanation of Section 409A, the final regulations under Section 409A, or the interim guidance issued under Section 409A, including the numerous transition rules. Refer to other more comprehensive works on Section 409A for more information.

BACKGROUND

Section 409A was added to the Code by Section 885 of the American Jobs Creation Act of 2004.[4] Section 409A impacts compensation provided through a nonqualified deferred compensation plan—a plan that provides for deferred compensation.

First, unless certain requirements are met, some of which are discussed below, all amounts deferred under a nonqualified deferred compensation plan for all taxable years are currently includible in the gross income of the service provider to the extent not subject to a substantial risk of forfeiture and not previously included in such gross income. Further, the amount required to be included in gross income is subject to an additional federal tax of 20%. These additional amounts may cause deferred compensation to be potentially taxed at a rate of (55%) (35% for ordinary

---

[2]The Treasury/IRS has established and retains discretion to reset this deadline.
[3]Prior to January 1, 2009, IRS Notice 2005-1 establishes the baseline for compliance with Section 409A.
[4]Public Law 108-357 (118 Stat. 1418).

income, based on rates in effect in 2007, plus 20%). In addition, interest is added at the federal underpayment rate plus 1% on the underpayments that would have occurred had the deferred compensation been includable in the gross income of the service provider for the taxable year in which first deferred or, if later, the first taxable year in which such deferred compensation is not subject to a substantial risk of forfeiture.[5]

In determining the consequences of noncompliance with Section 409A, if one type of nonqualified deferred compensation plan is noncompliant, all nonqualified deferred compensation plans of the same type are aggregated and deemed to be noncompliant also. The final regulations describe numerous types of plans for aggregation purposes. Examples of some of the categories include: an account balance plan that permits employee deferrals; an account balance plan with no elective deferrals; a nonaccount balance plan such as a SERP; and a separation pay plan.

Section 409A requires compliance, in both form and operation, with the rules that govern the following aspects of deferred compensation under a nonqualified deferred compensation plan: permissible payment events; when and how deferred compensation must be paid; changing the time when deferred compensation may be paid (including plan terminations and prohibitions on accelerated payments); and the time and manner in which an election to defer compensation must be made. Generally, Section 409A applies to compensation earned and vested on or after January 1, 2005. Also, Section 409A is effective with respect to amounts earned and vested in taxable years beginning before January 1, 2005 if the plan under which the deferred compensation is made is materially modified after October 3, 2004.[6]

---

[5]Section 409A also includes rules applicable to certain trusts or similar arrangements associated with nonqualified deferred compensation where such arrangements are located outside the United States or are restricted to the provision of benefits in connection with a decline in the financial health of the sponsor.

[6]In accordance with the requirements of Section 409A, the IRS published interim guidance, proposed regulations and on April 10, 2007, final regulations under Section 409A and, as of November 1, 2007, additional interim guidance. The final regulations discuss in substantial detail arrangements that are and are not subject to Section 409A and how a nonqualified deferred compensation plan must be designed and operated to comply with Section 409A.

Plans That Do Not Provide For the Deferral of Compensation

To address the challenges that Section 409A poses, the first approach is to find an exception from the coverage of Section 409A. Two of the most useful exceptions include a "short-term deferral" and "separation pay due to involuntary separation" (also colloquially called the "two times exception"). Each state that compensation paid pursuant to their terms does not provide for deferred compensation.

Short-Term Deferral

The short-term deferral exception provides a useful option to avoid Section 409A for payments of compensation that are typically made within a short period after being vested even though paid after the taxable year in which the legally binding right arises. A deferral of compensation does not occur under a plan with respect to any payment that is not a "deferred payment", provided that the service provider actually or constructively receives the payment on or before the last day of the "applicable 2½ month period," the plan is not subject to Section 409A.

A payment is a "deferred payment" if the payment will or *may* occur later than the applicable 2½ month period even if payment is actually made before the end of the applicable 2½ month period. The applicable 2½ month period is the period ending on the later of: (1) the 15th day of the third month following the end of the service provider's first taxable year in which the right to payment is no longer subject to a "substantial risk of forfeiture" or (2) the 15th day of the third month following the end of the service recipient's first taxable year in which the right to payment is no longer subject to a substantial risk of forfeiture. The final regulations provide some relief if a payment occurs later than the applicable 2½ month period because of prescribed reasons. If a service provider's and service recipient's taxable years are different, then the applicable 2½ month period ends on the 15th day of the third month after the last of the taxable years to end. For example, if a service provider has a calendar tax year and the service recipient has a fiscal tax year that ends on January 31, and the service recipient's right to a payment ceased to be subject to a substantial risk of forfeiture on December 15, the 2½ month deadline would be the following April 15th.

The short-term deferral applies separately to each payment. A payment refers to each separately identified amount to which a service provider is entitled on a determination date. An amount is separately identified only if the amount may be objectively determined under a nondiscretionary formula. The entitlement to a series of installment payments that is not a life annuity is treated as the entitlement to a single payment, unless the plan provides that the right to a series of installment payments is to be treated as a right to a series of separate payments. See Scenario 13.1.

Understanding what constitutes a "substantial risk of forfeiture" is important in applying the short term deferral. A substantial risk of forfeiture is present if entitlement to compensation is conditioned on either: (1) the performance of substantial future services (the service provider must work in order to become vested) or (2) the occurrence of a condition related to the purpose of the compensation. A condition related to a purpose of the compensation must relate to the service provider's performance for the service recipient or the service recipient's business activities or organizational goals. These types of conditions are utilized in the context of bonus plans or change in control payments. Further, the possibility of forfeiture must be substantial.

If a service provider's entitlement to payment is conditioned upon involuntary separation from service without cause, the right to the payment is conditioned upon a substantial risk of forfeiture provided that the possibility of forfeiture is substantial. A payment that is never conditioned

---

SCENARIO 13.2

Jane is an executive vice president of a software company that has a calendar-year tax year. Her annual salary is $300,000. Her severance agreement provides that she is entitled to $600,000 if she is terminated without cause, payable in a lump sum within 30 calendar days of her separation from service. Jane is terminated without cause in 2008. Because all separation payments will be paid before March 15 of the year following separation, those payments fall within the "short-term deferral" exception and are not deferred compensation for purposes of Section 409A.

BEST PRACTICE

If a service provider intends to rely on the short-term deferral exception, consider specifying a payment date before the end of the applicable 2½ month period. Specifying a payment date will permit the plan to comply with Section 409A in the event that payment is made after the deadline and the payment occurs before the end of the year in which the deadline occurred or, if later, the 15th day of the 3rd calendar month following the specified date, provided the service provider is not permitted, directly or indirectly, to specify the taxable year in which the amount is paid.

upon any substantial risk of forfeiture is treated as not being subject to a substantial risk of forfeiture at the time that the service provider is given the legally binding right to the payment and, therefore, the "short-term deferral" exception is not applicable at the time of payment.

Separation Pay Due to Involuntary Separation from Service

Severance pay and benefits are typically provided by most companies. The application of Section 409A or an exception to Section 409A must be considered with regard to each separation agreement or policy.

The separation pay due to involuntary separation from service provides a useful exception that may be used to avoid the restrictive requirements of Section 409A, including the six-month payment delay rule that Section 409A imposes on a "specified employee" of a publicly traded company and prohibitions on acceleration, discussed later in this chapter. If a separation pay arrangement provides for a payment only upon an involuntary separation from service, the arrangement will not provide for deferred compensation, and thus not be subject to Section 409A, to the extent that the separation pay, or portion of the separation pay, meets the following two requirements: (1) the separation pay (excluding certain reimbursements) does not exceed two times the lesser of (a) the sum of the service provider's annualized compensation (normal salary rate) based upon the annual rate of pay for services provided to the service recipient for the taxable year of the service provider in which the service provider has a separation from service, as adjusted by certain increases, and (b) the maximum amount that may be taken into account under a qualified plan under Code Section 401(a)(17) for the year in which the separation from service occurred (in 2007, the 401(a)(17) limit is $225,000) and (2) the plan provides that the separation pay must be paid no later than the last day of the second taxable year of the service provider following the taxable year of the service provider in which the involuntary separation from service occurred.

SCENARIO 13.3

The annual salary of Jim, an executive, is $275,000. His severance agreement provides one basis for payment, namely, if he is terminated without cause, Jim is entitled to $550,000, payable not later than two years after termination, which represents two times his annual salary. Jim is terminated without cause by the company in 2007. Because payments may be paid after March 15 of the year following separation, the "short-term deferral" exception does not apply. Under the involuntary separation exception, up to $450,000 can be exempted and will not be subject to Section 409A requirements. The $100,000 balance could be subject to the 55% (plus interest retroactive to the vesting date) maximum federal income and additional tax because there is no fixed schedule of severance payments, as discussed below. If Jim is a specified employee of a public company, any amount that is not excepted from the application of Section 409A cannot be paid until the expiration of six months following his termination (or, if earlier, the date of Jim's death).

The term involuntary separation from service includes a voluntary separation by a service provider under certain limited and bona fide conditions referred to as "good reason." Generally, these conditions will be set forth in the employment agreement or plan that provides for the separation pay. Good reason must be defined to require conduct by the service recipient that results in a material negative change to the service provider, such as the duties to be performed, the conditions under which the duties will be performed, or the compensation to be received for performing the services.

Other factors that are taken into account include the extent to which the payments for separation from service for good reason are the same amount and in the same form of payment as if the separation was initiated by the service recipient, and whether the service provider is required to give (1) notice of the existence of the condition that would result in treatment as a separation from service for good reason and (2) a reasonable opportunity to cure. The final regulations include a safe harbor that provides terms that may be used to secure certainty that a service provider's voluntary termination constitutes an involuntary separation from service for purposes of Section 409A. The safe harbor requires, among other conditions, that the service provider must provide notice of the existence of the good reason condition within ninety (90) days of its initial existence and the service recipient must be provided a period of at least 30 days during which to remedy the condition and not be required to pay the amount.

Other exceptions from Section 409A in the context of voluntary or involuntary separation include nonexcludable reimbursements for expenses that could be deducted under Code Section 162 or 167, reasonable out-placement expenses, and reasonable moving expenses, provided that the exception does not apply beyond the last day of the second taxable year of the service provider following the taxable year of the service provider in which the separation from service occurred. Reimbursement of medical expenses incurred and paid by the service provider, but not reimbursed otherwise by a person other than the service recipient and allowable as a deduction, is excepted to the extent that the right to reimbursement does not extend beyond the period that the service provider would have been entitled to COBRA. If not otherwise excluded, an amount payable under an involuntary separation pay plan is excepted if the amount does not exceed the amount that could be contributed to a 401(k) plan with regard to a calendar year (in 2007, this amount is $15,500).

NONQUALIFIED DEFERRED COMPENSATION PLAN — PLANS THAT PROVIDE FOR DEFERRED COMPENSATION

A plan that provides for deferred compensation and is not excluded from Section 409A coverage, (a "nonqualified deferred compensation plan") must be designed to comply with and administered in accordance with the provisions of Section 409A to avoid the adverse federal tax consequences that could result from noncompliance. Among other requirements, the nonqualified deferred compensation plan must provide that any deferred compensation payable under its terms may not be paid earlier than a "payment trigger," including:

- A separation from service
- The service provider becoming disabled
- The service provider's death ·
- A change in the ownership or effective control of the corporation, or in the ownership of a substantial portion of the assets of the corporation
- The occurrence of an unforeseeable emergency
- A specified time (or pursuant to a fixed schedule) specified under the plan at the time the compensation is deferred.

The first five of the above payment triggers are referred to in this chapter as the "event payment triggers."

SPECIAL RULE APPLICABLE TO SPECIFIED EMPLOYEES

The separation from service event payment trigger includes a special rule that applies to a service provider who is a "specified employee" as of the date of separation. No payment may be made to a specified employee before the date that is six-months after the date of the separation from service (or if earlier than the end of the six month period, the date of the specified employee's death). The delayed payments may be accumulated and paid on the first day of the seventh month following the date of the separation from service or paid after the expiration of the six-month period that applies to the payment. However, the six-month delay does not apply to certain reimbursement, outplacement service and reimbursement for medical expenses as discussed above in the context of an involuntary or voluntary separation from service.

A specified employee is an employee of a corporation of which any stock is publicly traded on an established securities market or otherwise, including a foreign securities market, and who is an officer of the company having annual compensation greater than a specified amount (in 2007,

$145,000), a 5% owner of the company, or a 1% owner having annual compensation of more than $150,000. No more than 50 employees can be officers who qualify as specified employees. The final regulations address certain issues with regard to the determination of who is a specified employee. Generally, unless otherwise elected, December 31 is the specified employee determination date and April 1 is the date as of which those identified as a specified employee on the determination date will be considered as a specified employee for the 12-month period beginning on that date.

SCENARIO 13.4

The CEO of a public company is awarded a supplemental executive retirement pension (SERP) in 2008. The company will pay the CEO a monthly benefit for life under the SERP beginning on the first day of the month following the CEO's retirement after attaining age 62. In 2010, the CEO attains age 62 and retires. The CEO is a "specified employee" as defined in Section 409A at the time of the separation from service. The SERP is a nonqualified deferred compensation plan and fails to comply with Section 409A because the benefit cannot start for six months after the CEO's retirement (or, if earlier, the date of the CEO's death).

CHANGE-IN-CONTROL EVENTS

The final regulations treat any one of three events that affect the ownership of a corporation or its assets as an event payment trigger provided that the corporation is: (1) the corporation for whom the service provider works at the time of the event; (2) the corporation or corporations that are liable for the payment of the deferred compensation as long as the deferred compensation relates to the services performed for that corporation, or there is a bona fide business purpose for the corporation's obligation to pay the deferred compensation; or (3) a corporation that is a "majority shareholder" (owns both more than 50% of the total fair market value and total voting power of the corporation) of a corporation identified in clauses (1) or (2) or any corporation in a chain of corporations in which each corporation is a majority shareholder of another corporation in the chain, ending in a corporation identified in clauses (1) or (2) (any of which is referred to in this chapter as the "Event Corporation").

These events include: (1) a change in ownership of a corporation, (2) a change in effective control of a corporation, and (3) a change in the ownership of a substantial portion of the assets of a corporation. The substantive terms that form these events are similar to those that apply under Code Section 280G "Golden Parachute Payments." However, the events described in the final regulations are in some ways narrower and in other ways broader than the events described under Code Section 280G. Some events that trigger the golden parachute rules will not trigger permissible payouts under Section 409A, and vice versa. These distinctions might be confusing to an executive or director who might assume that a change in control is a change in control for all purposes.

For example, it is possible that a director or executive would become subject to the additional tax under the golden parachute rules upon consummation of a transaction but not be permitted to receive a distribution of deferred compensation under a plan that the director or executive understood permitted a distribution on a change-in-control.[7]

CHANGE IN THE OWNERSHIP OF A CORPORATION

This event focuses on voting power or value and occurs when the threshold is met. A change in the ownership of a corporation occurs on the date that one person or more than one person acting as a group acquires stock

---

[7]To determine whether a change in control event has occurred, Section 318(a) of the Code, (describing attribution of stock to family members, from partnerships, estates, trusts, and corporations, to partnerships, estates, trusts and corporations and with regard to options) applies. Stock underlying a vested option is considered owned by the individual who holds the vested option (and the stock underlying an unvested option is not considered owned by the individual who holds the unvested option). However, if a vested option is exercisable for stock that is not substantially vested (as defined in Treas. Reg. Section 1.83-3(b) and (j)), the stock underlying the option is not treated as owned by the individual who holds the option.

that combined with stock previously owned constitutes more than 50% of the total fair market value or total voting power of the stock of the corporation (a larger percentage could be used if desired). This threshold is the same under the golden parachute rules. This event occurs when there is a transfer of stock of a corporation (or issuance of stock of a corporation) and stock in such corporation remains outstanding after the transaction.

There is an exception if any one person, or more than one person acting as a group, is considered to effectively control a corporation (ownership of stock of the corporation possessing 30% or more of the total voting power of the stock of such corporation) and the same person or persons acquire additional control of the corporation.

CHANGE IN THE EFFECTIVE CONTROL OF A CORPORATION

This event focuses on voting power or certain changes in the composition of a board of directors. A change in the effective control of a corporation occurs on the date that either one person, or more than one person acting as a group acquires (or has acquired during the 12-month period ending on the date of the most recent acquisition by such person or persons) ownership of stock of the corporation possessing 30% or more of the total voting power of the stock of such corporation. It may also occur if a majority of members of the corporation's board of directors is replaced during any 12-month period by directors whose appointment or election is not endorsed by a majority of the members of the corporation's board of directors before the date of the appointment or election, provided that for this purpose, the term corporation refers solely to an Event Corporation for which no other corporation is a "majority shareholder."

A change in the effective control of a corporation also may occur in any transaction in which either of the two corporations involved in the transaction has a change in the ownership of a corporation or a change in the ownership of a substantial portion of a corporation's assets. If any one person, or more than one person acting as a group, is considered to effectively control a corporation, the acquisition of additional control of the corporation by the same person or persons is not a change in the effective control of a corporation.

SCENARIO 13.5

An executive of a public company is awarded a phantom stock right that is vested upon grant and is payable in stock of the public company upon the earlier separation from employment or upon a change in control. Change in control is defined to mean when any one person or more than one person acting as a group acquires ownership of stock of the corporation possessing 25% of the total voting power of the stock of that public company. This change in control provision does not satisfy Section 409A that requires more than 30% test rather than a more than 25% test for a change in the effective control of a corporation. The phantom stock plan is not compliant with Section 409A.

CHANGE IN OWNERSHIP OF A SUBSTANTIAL PORTION OF A CORPORATION'S ASSETS

A change in ownership of a substantial portion of the assets occurs on the date that a person or more than one person acting as a group acquires (or has acquired during the 12-month period ending on the date of the most recent acquisition by such person or persons) assets from the corporation having a total gross fair market value equal to 40% or more of the total gross fair market value of all of the corporation's assets. A larger percentage could be used if desired. Again, the Section 409A rule is narrower than the golden parachute rule; an acquisition of 33-1/3% of a corporation's assets can trigger golden parachute treatment.

No change in the ownership of a substantial portion of a corporation's assets occurs: if there is a transfer to an entity that is controlled by the shareholders of the transferring corporation immediately after the transfer. A transfer of assets by a corporation is not treated as a change in the ownership of such assets if the assets are transferred to (1) a shareholder of the corporation (immediately before the asset transfer) in exchange for or with respect to its stock; (2) an entity, 50% or more of the total value or voting power of which is owned, directly or indirectly, by the corporation; (3) a person, or more than one person acting as a group, that owns, directly or indirectly, 50% or more of the total value or voting power of all the outstanding stock of the corporation; or (4) an entity, at least 50% of the total value or voting power of which is owned directly or indirectly, by a person described in clause (3).

STRUCTURING THE PAYMENTS UPON AN EVENT PAYMENT TRIGGER

In addition to specifying a payment trigger, a nonqualified deferred compensation plan must specify when the payment will be made. Several options are available. The plan could state that payment will be made on the date of the event payment trigger, another payment date that is objectively determinable and nondiscretionary at the time that the event occurs (the 30th day after the event payment trigger); or according to a schedule that is objectively determinable and nondiscretionary based on the date that the event payment trigger occurs. Payment may be made in a designated taxable year of the service provider that is objectively determinable and nondiscretionary at the time the event payment trigger occurs or during a designated period objectively determinable and nondiscretionary at the time that the event payment trigger occurs. However, the designated period must both begin and end within one taxable year of the service provider or the designated period cannot be more than 90 days and the service provider cannot have the right to designate the taxable year of the payment.

A plan may provide for the payment upon the earliest or latest of one of the event payment triggers or specified time. Generally, only one time and form of payment may be specified for an event payment trigger.

If a payment is not made when otherwise specified, some latitude is provided under the final regulations. Generally, a payment is treated as made upon the date specified in the plan if the payment is made on such date or a later date within the same taxable year of the service provider, or if later, the 15th day of the third calendar month following the date specified, provided that the service provider is not permitted to specify the taxable year of the payment. If the amount of a payment is not administratively practical due to events beyond the control of the service provider, the payment will be treated as made upon the date specified if the payment is made during the first taxable year of the service provider in which the calculation of the amount of the payment is administratively practicable.

Specified Time or Fixed Schedule

If a specified time or a fixed schedule is designated as a payment trigger, objectively determinable amounts must be payable at a date or dates that are nondiscretionary and objectively determinable at the time that the compensation is deferred. An amount is objectively determinable if the amount is specifically identified or the amount may be determined at the time payment is due pursuant to an objective, nondiscretionary formula specified at the time that the amount is deferred. Alternatively, a specified taxable year of the service provider may be designated at the time that the amount is deferred and that is objectively determinable, or a designation at the time an amount is deferred of a defined period or periods within the service provider's taxable year or years provided that no defined period begins within one taxable year and ends within another taxable year.

Generally, a nonqualified deferred compensation plan may not be amended to accelerate the time or schedule of payment. An impermissible acceleration does not occur if a payment is made in accordance with a plan provision or an election as to the time or form of payment in effect at the outset of the nonqualified deferred compensation plan pursuant to which payment is required on an accelerated schedule as a result of an intervening event payment trigger. Certain exceptions to this general rule are provided, including specific rules regarding when a nonqualified deferred compensation plan may be terminated and deferred compensation paid.

Equity-Based Compensation

BEST PRACTICE

Compensation committees should secure appropriate tax advice with regard to structuring or amending equity-based compensation plans that may be subject to Section 409A.

Incentive stock options and tax qualified employee stock purchase plans adopted under Section 423 of the Code are not subject to Section 409A.

An important safe harbor is provided for certain nonqualified stock options and stock appreciation rights (SARs). Generally, an option to purchase a service recipient stock will not provide for a deferral of compensation if: the exercise price may never be less than fair market value of the underlying stock on the date that the option is granted and the number of shares subject to the option is fixed on the original date of grant of the option; the transfer or exercise of the option is subject to taxation under Code Section 83 and its regulations; and the option does not include any feature for the deferral of compensation other than the deferral of recognition of income until the later of (i) the exercise or disposition of the option and (ii) the time the stock acquired pursuant to the exercise of the option first became substantially vested. Similar rules apply in the context of SARs. Any change in the terms of a nonqualified stock option or SARs must consider whether the change could cause Section 409A to apply. Certain extensions of the right to exercise are permitted without risk of becoming subject to Section 409A, provided that the extension does not exceed the earlier of the latest date upon which the stock right could have expired by its original terms or if shorter, 10 years from the date of original grant.

Subjecting an executive to a total federal tax of 55% (plus interest retroactive to the vesting date) or more is not a great performance motivator. Many companies attempt to disclaim any liability to the executive for the failure of their executive compensation plans to comply with Section 409A. However, such disclaimers of liability to the executive ignore the adverse effect on the executive's morale and also on the company from defective executive compensation plans whose primary beneficiary becomes the federal government (or potentially a state that also imposes a tax as a result of a failure to comply with Section 409A).

The complexity of Section 409A requires that the compensation committee secure appropriate tax advice with regard to the impact of Section 409A. The question of what constitutes a "nonqualified deferred compensation plan" within the scope of Section 409A is a complex question and requires an expert in the area. For example, certain provisions in an employment agreement could unknowingly create noncompliance with Section 409A. Section 409A is not limited to corporate employers. It applies to any "service recipient," including partnerships and entities receiving services from certain independent contractors.

SECTION 409A COMPLIANCE

> **BEST PRACTICE**
>
> Include the material terms of any potential deferred compensation plan in writing as of the adoption of the plan.

To protect a service provider from the additional taxes resulting from failure to comply with Section 409A of the Code, it is a best practice to set forth the material terms of the plan in writing as of the date of adoption. The material terms include the amount (or the method or formula for determining the amount) of deferred compensation to be provided under the plan and the time and form of payment. Incorporation by reference of a specific term appears to be permitted. A general clause that incorporates needed terms in order to make a plan Section 409A compliant is not permitted. If required, a plan must include the special rule applicable to specified employees.

> **BEST PRACTICE**
>
> Insert savings clauses in employment or severance agreements to help insure compliance with Section 409A.

To protect the executive from the additional taxes resulting from failure to comply with Section 409A of the Code, it is a best practice to place a clause similar to the following into employment contracts with executives:

"Section 409A Compliance

"To the extent applicable, this Agreement shall be interpreted in accordance with Section 409A of the Internal Revenue Code of 1986, as amended ("Section 409A"), and Department of Treasury regulations and other interpretive guidance issued thereunder, including without limitation any such regulations or other guidance that may be issued after the date hereof ("409A Guidance"). Notwithstanding any provision of the Agreement to the contrary, (i) if, at the time of the Executive's termination of employment with the Company, the Executive is a "specified employee" as defined in 409A Guidance and the deferral of the commencement of any payments or benefits otherwise payable hereunder as a result of such termination of employment is necessary in order to prevent any accelerated or additional tax under 409A Guidance, then the Company will defer the commencement of the payment of any such payments or benefits hereunder (without any reduction in such payments or benefits ultimately paid or provided to the Executive) until the date that is six months following the Executive's termination of employment with the Company (or the earliest date as is permitted under Section 409A) and (ii) if any other payments of money or other benefits due to the Executive hereunder could cause the application of an accelerated or additional tax under Section 409A, the Company may (a) adopt such amendments to the Agreement, including amendments with retroactive effect, that the Company determines necessary or appropriate to preserve the intended tax treatment of the benefits provided by the Agreement and/or (b) take such other actions as the Company determines necessary or appropriate to comply with the requirements of 409A Guidance; provided, however, that the Company shall consult with the Executive in good faith regarding the implementation of this Section."

It should be noted that the final IRS regulations provide that, for purposes of determining the terms of a plan, "general provisions of the plan that purport to nullify noncompliant plan terms, or to supply any specific plan terms..., are disregarded." Therefore, it is not clear whether the savings language quoted above will be legally effective. However, it is still worthwhile including this savings provision in employment or severance agreements.

Compensation Committee Charter

ROLE

The role of the Compensation Committee ("Committee") of the Board of Directors ("Board") is to discharge the Board's responsibilities relating to compensation of the Company's executive officers and to oversee and advise the Board on the adoption of policies that govern the Company's compensation and benefit programs. The term "executive officers," as used herein, shall refer to all persons designated as "officers" for purposes of Section 16 of the Securities Exchange Act of 1934 and the rules and regulations thereunder.

MEMBERSHIP

The membership of the Committee consists of at least three directors, each of whom shall (a) meet the independence requirements established by the Board and applicable laws, rules, regulations, and listing requirements, (b) be a "nonemployee director" within the meaning of Rule 16b-3 under the Securities Exchange Act of 1934, and (c) be an "outside director" within the meaning of Section 162(m) of the Internal Revenue Code. The Board appoints the members of the Committee and the chairperson. The Board may remove any member from the Committee at any time with or without cause. A member shall promptly notify the Committee and the Board if the member no longer meets applicable independence requirements and such member shall be removed from the

Committee unless the Board determines that an exception to the independence requirements is available.

OPERATIONS

The Committee meets at least four times a year. Additional meetings may occur as the Committee or its chair deems advisable. The Committee will meet periodically in executive session without Company management present. The Committee will cause to be kept adequate minutes of its proceedings, and will report on its actions and activities at the next regular meeting of the Board. Committee members will be furnished with copies of the minutes of each meeting and any action taken by unanimous consent. The Committee is governed by the same rules regarding meetings (including meetings by conference telephone or similar communications equipment), action without meetings, notice, waiver of notice, and quorum and voting requirements as are applicable to the Board. The Committee is authorized to adopt its own rules of procedure not inconsistent with (a) any provision of this Charter, (b) any provision of the Bylaws of the Company, or (c) the laws of the state of incorporation of the Company. The Committee may request that any directors, officers, or employees of the Company, or other persons whose advice and counsel are sought by the Committee, attend any meeting of the Committee and provide such pertinent information as the Committee requests.

AUTHORITY

The Committee will have the resources and authority necessary to discharge its duties and responsibilities. The Committee has sole authority to retain and terminate outside counsel, compensation consultants, or other experts or consultants, as it deems appropriate, including sole authority to approve the fees and other retention terms for such persons. Any communications between the Committee and legal counsel in the course of obtaining legal advice will be considered privileged communications of the Company. In discharging its responsibilities and duties, the Committee is empowered to investigate any matter brought to its attention that it determines to be within the scope of its authority with full access to all books, records, facilities, and personnel of the Company.

Except as otherwise delegated by the Board or the Committee, the Committee will act on behalf of the Board. The Committee will serve as the "Committee" established to administer equity-based and other employee benefit plans, which are required to be administered by the Board or a Committee of the Board and as such will discharge any responsibilities imposed on the Committee under those plans, including making and authorizing grants, in accordance with the terms of those plans. The Committee may delegate to one or more executive officers the authority to make grants of stock options and other equity awards to eligible individuals who are not executive officers. Any executive officer to whom the Committee grants such authority shall regularly report to the Committee grants so made. The Committee may revoke any such delegation of authority at any time.

The Committee may form and delegate authority to subcommittees and may delegate authority to one or more designated members of the Committee to perform certain of its duties on its behalf including, to the extent permitted by applicable law, the delegation to a subcommittee of the authority to grant equity awards.

RESPONSIBILITIES

The principal responsibilities and functions of the Compensation Committee are as follows:

Develop policies, processes, and procedures for considering and determining the compensation and benefits of executive officers (including the Company's policy with respect to Section 162(m) of the Internal Revenue Code), and annually review and reassess the adequacy of such policies, processes, and procedures.

Assist the Board in establishing corporate goals and objectives (both long-term and short-term) for the executive officers, which need not be the same for each executive officer, and determine what the Company's compensation programs are designed to reward.

Review the adequacy of the Company's executive compensation programs to ensure (a) the attraction and retention of executive officers, (b) the motivation of executive officers to achieve the Company's business objectives, and (c) the alignment of the interests of the executive officers with the long-term interests of the Company's shareholders.

Review trends in executive compensation, oversee the development of new compensation plans, and, when necessary, approve the revisions of existing plans.

Oversee an evaluation of the performance of the executive officers (including an evaluation of the executive officer's performance against the corporate goals and objectives for each executive officer), and approve the annual compensation, including salary, bonus, equity compensation, other incentive compensation, and benefits for each executive officer.

Review and approve employment, severance, and change in control agreements, and any amendments or renewals thereof, with existing and prospective executive officers.

Review and discuss with the Board plans for executive officer development and corporate succession plans for the chief executive officer and other executive officers.

Review and make recommendations concerning long-term incentive compensation plans, including the use of equity-based plans.

Administer equity-based and other employee benefit plans that are required to be administered by the Board or a Committee of the Board, and appoint and remove plan administrators for the Company's other employee benefit plans that require an administrator.

Periodically review the compensation paid to nonemployee directors and make recommendations to the Board for any adjustments; however, no member of the Committee will act to fix his or her own compensation except for uniform compensation to directors for their services as a director.

Review periodic reports from management on matters relating to the Company's compensation practices.

SEC Reports and Other Functions

Review and discuss with the Company's management the Compensation Discussion and Analysis ("CD&A") required by SEC Regulation S-K, Item 402, to be included in the Company's annual proxy statement or Form 10-K.

Based on such review and discussion, determine whether to recommend to the Board that the CD&A be included in the Company's annual proxy statement or Form 10-K and oversee the preparation of the Compensation Committee Report described in SEC Regulation S-K Item 407 for inclusion in such documents.

Perform any other functions required by applicable laws, rules, regulations, or listing requirements.

CHARTER REVIEW AND ANNUAL SELF-EVALUATION

Annually review and make recommendations about changes to the charter of the Committee.

Annually obtain or perform an evaluation of the Committee's composition (including the independence of its members) and performance, and make applicable recommendations to the Board.

Corporate and Securities Update: SEC Adopts Sweeping Overhaul of its Executive Compensation Disclosure Requirements (September 2006 and revised December 2006)

O n July 26, 2006, the Securities and Exchange Commission (SEC) adopted a sweeping overhaul of its rules governing the disclosure of executive and director compensation, related party transactions, director independence and other corporate governance matters, as well as security ownership of officers and directors. These changes reflect the SEC's most far-reaching executive compensation disclosure reforms in nearly 14 years. The amended rules affect disclosure in proxy statements, annual reports and registration statements, as well as the current reporting of compensation arrangements. The amended rules also require that most of this disclosure be provided in plain English in order to make it easier to understand.

---

*Reproduced with the consent of Blank Rome LLP, © 2006.

On December 22, 2006, the SEC adopted, as interim final rules, revisions to the Summary Compensation Table and Director Compensation Table disclosure with respect to stock awards and option awards to provide disclosure of the compensation cost of awards over the requisite service period, as described in Financial Accounting Standards Board Standards No. 123 (revised 2004) *Share-Based Payment* (FAS 123R). FAS 123R defines a requisite service period as the period or periods over which an employee is required to provide service in exchange for a share-based payment. The amendments also revised the Grants of Plan-Based Awards Table and the Director Compensation Table.

Compliance with the amended rules is required in:

- Form 10-Ks for fiscal years ending after December 15, 2006
- Proxy statements and registration statements requiring executive compensation disclosure for fiscal years ending on or after December 15, 2006; and
- Form 8-Ks for triggering events occurring on or after November 7, 2006

Executive and Director Compensation

The amended rules refine and clarify the currently required tabular disclosure to improve the information provided in the tables. This tabular disclosure includes all elements of compensation and a column for total compensation. This disclosure is combined with additional narrative discussions to provide clearer and more complete disclosure regarding executive compensation and related policies and procedures.

Compensation Discussion and Analysis Section

The amended rules require a new section entitled "Compensation Discussion and Analysis" to address, using principles-based rather than rules-based disclosure principles, the objectives and implementation of executive compensation programs and focus on the most important factors underlying each company's compensation policies and decisions.

This new section will provide an overview that explains the material elements of compensation for the named executive officers and addresses, among other things, the following:

What are the objectives of the company's compensation programs?

What is the compensation program designed to reward?

What is each element of compensation?

Why does the company choose to pay each element?

How does the company determine the amount (and, where applicable, the formula) for each element?

How does each element and the company's decisions regarding that element fit into the company's overall compensation objectives and affect decisions regarding other elements?

This section would be considered "filed" with the SEC and, by inclusion or incorporation by reference in a company's Form 10-K, be subject to the officer certifications required by that form.

A slimmed-down Compensation Committee Report is required. The Compensation Committee Report must include a statement as to whether the compensation committee has reviewed and discussed the Compensation Discussion and Analysis section with management and, based on this review and discussion, recommended that it be included in the company's annual report on Form 10-K and proxy statement. However, the Compensation Committee Report will be deemed furnished but not filed with the SEC.

The Performance Graph has been retained, but is no longer coupled with executive compensation disclosure. The Performance Graph is to be included with disclosure regarding the market price of the company's common equity and related stockholder matters. The Performance Graph is to be required only in annual reports to security holders that accompany or precede proxy statements relating to annual meetings at which directors are to be elected. The Performance Graph will be deemed furnished but not filed with the SEC.

For companies that are small business issuers, neither the Compensation Discussion and Analysis section, nor the Compensation Committee Report nor the Performance Graph will be required.

Tabular and Narrative Disclosure

In addition to the "Compensation Discussion and Analysis" section, the executive compensation disclosure will be organized into three broad categories:

1. Compensation over the last three years;
2. Holdings of outstanding equity-related interests received as compensation that are the source of future gains; and
3. Retirement plans, deferred compensation, and other postemployment payments and benefits.

The Summary Compensation Table (see Exhibit B.1) is the principal disclosure method for executive compensation, detailing compensation for each named executive officer over the last three years under a number of categories of compensation. The Summary Compensation Table is required to be accompanied by narrative disclosure and a Grants of Plan-Based Awards Table (see Exhibit B.2) that explains the compensation information presented in the table. The Summary Compensation Table is to include, in addition to columns for salary and bonus:

- A dollar value of all equity-based awards, shown in separate columns for stock and stock options, measured at grant date fair value, computed in accordance with Statement of Financial Accounting Standards No. 123 (revised 2004), Share-Based Payment ("FAS 123R") with footnote disclosure of all assumptions utilized in the valuation by reference to the footnotes in the financials;
- A column reporting the amount of compensation under nonequity incentive plans;
- A column reporting the annual change in the actuarial present value of accumulated pension benefits and above-market or preferential earnings on nonqualified deferred compensation, so that these amounts can be deducted from total compensation for purposes of determining the named executive officers;
- A column showing the aggregate amount of all other compensation not reported in the other columns of the table, including the amount of perquisites and other personal benefits (perquisites must be included in the table and identified by type unless the aggregate amount of all perquisites is less than $10,000 (with footnote disclosure of the value

SUMMARY COMPENSATION TABLE

Name and Principal Position (a)	Year (b)	Salary ($) (c)	Bonus ($) (d)	Stock Awards ($) (e)	Option Awards ($) (f)	Non-Equity Incentive Plan Compensation ($) (g)	Change in Pension Value and Nonqualified Deferred Compensation Earnings ($) (h)	All Other Compensation ($) (i)	Total ($) (j)
PEO									
PFO									
A									
B									
C									

and valuation methodology of any perquisite exceeding the greater of $25,000 or 10% of all perquisites for a named executive officer), and additional interpretive guidance has been provided for determining what is a perquisite); and

- A column disclosing total compensation.

As to the all other compensation category, the SEC has provided a two-step test to determine whether an item is a perquisite or other personal benefit. First, an item is not a perquisite or personal benefit if it is integrally and directly related to the performance of an executive's duties, meaning that the executive needs the item to do his or her job. Examples of these are business travel expenses and the cost of computers and other technology if integral to the executive's duties. If an item is not integrally and directly related to the performance of duties, then the item is a perquisite if (1) it confers a direct or indirect benefit that has a personal aspect, regardless of whether it may be provided for some business reason, and (2) it is not generally available on a non-discriminatory basis to all employees. Examples of these perquisites include personal financial or tax advice, personal travel using company transportation, personal use of company property, relocation assistance, security at a personal residence and discounts on products or services not made available to employees generally.

The SEC has added a Grants of Plan-Based Awards Table (see Exhibit B.2) as a supplement to the Summary Compensation Table. This new table requires, among other things, disclosure of the terms of both equity-based and nonequity based grants made during the last completed fiscal year on a grant-by-grant basis, including the amount of estimated future payouts, the threshold, target and maximum amounts of such grants and the grant date fair value of awards computed in accordance with FAS 123R.

In addition to the tabular information required in the Summary Compensation Table and the Grants of Plan-Based Awards Table, the SEC requires narrative disclosure to give context to the tabular disclosure. The narrative description must include any additional material factors necessary for readers to understand the tabular information. The narrative disclosures are intended to provide specific context to the quantitative disclosure contained in these tables.

The SEC decided not to adopt at this time the controversial "Katie Couric" provision that would have required disclosure of up to three

EXHIBIT B.2 **GRANTS OF PLAN-BASED AWARDS TABLE**

Name (a)	Grant Date (b)	Estimated Future Payouts Under Non-Equity Incentive Plan Awards			Estimated Future Payouts Under Equity Incentive Plan Awards			All Other Stock Awards: Number of Shares of Stock or Units (#) (i)	All Other Option Awards: Number of Securities Underlying Options (#) (j)	Exercise or Base Price of Option Awards ($/Sh) (k)	Grant Date Fair Value of Stock and Option Awards (l)
		Threshold ($) (c)	Target ($) (d)	Maximum ($) (e)	Threshold (#) (f)	Target (#) (g)	Maximum (#) (h)				
PEO											
PFO											
A											
B											
C											

employees (without specifically naming them) who were not executive officers during the prior fiscal year, and whose total compensation exceeded that of any of the named executive officers. Instead, the SEC resubmitted for comment a provision that would require disclosure of total compensation for up to three non-executive officer employees (without naming them) whose total compensation exceeded that of any of the named executive officers, except that employees having no responsibility for significant policy decisions would be excluded. The SEC also asked for comment on restricting the application of the provision to large accelerated filers.

Disclosure regarding outstanding equity interests includes two revised tables:

- The Outstanding Equity Awards at Fiscal Year-End Table (see Exhibit B.3) discloses outstanding awards of options, units, restricted stock or other equity incentive compensation representing potential amounts that may be received in the future. The table requires disclosure of, among other things, the amount of securities underlying exercisable and unexercisable options, the exercise prices and the expiration dates for each outstanding option (rather than on an aggregate basis), the number and market value of shares of unearned or unvested stock, units, and equity incentive plan awards, and the market or payout value of such unearned or unvested awards; and
- The Option Exercises and Stock Vested Table (see Exhibit B.4) requires disclosure of the number of shares and amounts realized on option exercises and the number of shares and value of restricted stock that became vested, each during the last fiscal year.

Retirement plan, post-employment and change in control arrangements are to be disclosed through tables and a narrative discussion, as follows:

- The Pension Benefits Table (see Exhibit B.5) includes, for each named executive officer, and for each plan in which such named executive officer participates:
  - the number of years of credited service;
  - the actuarial present value of each named executive officer's accumulated benefit under each pension plan (computed using the same assumptions—except for the normal retirement age—as

EXHIBIT B.3   OUTSTANDING EQUITY AWARDS AT FISCAL YEAR-END TABLE

| | Option Awards | | | | | Stock Awards | | | |
| | Number of Securities Underlying Unexercised Options (#) Exercisable | Number of Securities Underlying Unexercised Options (#) Unexercisable | Equity Incentive Plan Awards: Number of Securities Underlying Unexercised Unearned Options (#) | Option Exercise Price ($) | Option Expiration Date | Number of Shares or Units of Stock That Have Not Vested (#) | Market Value of Shares or Units of Stock That Have Not Vested ($) | Equity Incentive Plan Awards: Number of Unearned Shares, Units or Other Rights That Have Not Vested (#) | Equity Incentive Plan Awards: Market or Payout Value of Unearned Shares, Units or Other Rights That Have Not Vested ($) |
Name (a)	(b)	(c)	(d)	(e)	(f)	(g)	(h)	(i)	(j)
PEO									
PFO									
A									
B									
C									

EXHIBIT B.4	OPTION EXERCISES AND STOCK VESTED TABLE

	Option Awards		Stock Awards	
	Number of Shares Acquired on Exercise (#)	Value Realized on Exercise ($)	Number of Shares Acquired on Vesting (#)	Value Realized on Vesting ($)
Name (a)	(b)	(c)	(d)	(e)
PEO				
PFO				
A				
B				
C				

EXHIBIT B.5	PENSION BENEFITS TABLE

Name (a)	Plan Name (b)	Number of Years Credited Service (#) (c)	Present Value of Accumulated Benefit ($) (d)	Payments During Last Fiscal Year ($) (e)
PEO				
PFO				
A				
B				
C				

used for financial reporting purposes under generally accepted accounting principles); and

  • the amount of any payments under the plan made during the last fiscal year.

• The Nonqualified Deferred Compensation Table (see Exhibit B.6) includes, with respect to nonqualified deferred compensation plans, disclosures of executive and company contributions, aggregate earnings (not just the above-market or preferential portion), withdrawals and the year-end balance.

• Each of these tables must be followed by a narrative description of material factors as necessary to make the tabular information understandable.

• The SEC has adopted significant changes to the narrative disclosure requirements regarding post-retirement and change in control provisions of executive compensation arrangements. These requirements now include, at a minimum, a discussion of:

  • The specific circumstances triggering post-retirement payments or benefits;

EXHIBIT B.6   NONQUALIFIED DEFERRED COMPENSATION

Name (a)	Executive Contributions in Last FY ($) (b)	Registrant Contributions in Last FY ($) (c)	Aggregate Earnings in Last FY ($) (d)	Aggregate Withdrawals/ Distributions ($) (e)	Aggregate Balance at Last FYE ($) (f)
PEO					
PFO					
A					
B					
C					

- The estimated amount of lump sum or annual payments that would be provided in each covered circumstance, including the duration and source of such payments;
- How the triggering payment and benefit levels are determined.
- Any material conditions or obligations applicable to the receipt of payments, such as compliance with non-compete, non-solicitation, non-disparagement or confidentiality covenants; and
- Any other material factors.

EXECUTIVE OFFICERS COVERED

The SEC has modified the rules governing which executive officers are covered by the tabular and narrative compensation disclosure rules, commonly referred to as the "named executive officers." These officers are now:

people who served as the principal executive officer and the principal financial officer at any time during the last fiscal year;

the three most highly compensated executive officers, other than the principal executive and financial officer(s); and

up to two individuals for whom disclosure would have been required but for the fact that they were no longer serving as executive officers at the end of the last completed fiscal year.

For small business issuers, the named executive officers include only the principal executive officer and the two other most highly compensated executive officers.

Also, the SEC has modified the threshold for determining the most highly compensated executive officers. Under the former rule, these officers included any person with total salary and bonus over $100,000. Under the new rules, all compensation will be included in making this determination, except for the sum of (1) the increase in pension values and (2) the amount of nonqualified deferred compensation above-market or preferential earnings, each as reported in the Summary Compensation Table. The SEC has also eliminated the ability to exclude an executive officer (other the chief executive officer) who received an unusually large amount of cash compensation that was not part of a recurring arrangement and was not likely to recur.

PHASE-IN OF YEARS COVERED

For the first year following implementation of the rules, companies need only include the tabular executive compensation information under the new rules for the most recent fiscal year. For the second year, companies will need to include two years of tabular executive compensation information under the new rules. Beginning with the third year and thereafter, companies (other than small business issuers) will need to include the full three years of tabular executive compensation information.

SPECIFIC DISCLOSURE REGARDING STOCK OPTION GRANTS

In light of the option backdating controversy, the SEC provided additional guidance regarding disclosure of company programs, plans, and practices relating to the granting of options, including in particular the timing of option grants in coordination with the release of material non-public information and the selection of exercise prices that differ from the underlying stock's price on the grant date. The amended rules will require the following new disclosures to be made regarding option granting practices:

- Tabular presentations of option grants including:
  - The grant date and grant date fair value determined under FAS 123R;
  - The closing market price on the grant date if it is greater than the exercise price of the award;
  - The date the compensation committee or full board of directors took action or was deemed to take action to grant the award if that date is different than the grant date; and
  - If the exercise price of an option grant is not the grant date closing market price per share, the amended rules require a description of the methodology for determining the exercise price.
- Given that additional disclosure is required for option awards not made at the closing price on the grant date, compensation committees should consider whether to grant option awards at a price which varies from the closing price on the grant date.

- The "Compensation Discussion and Analysis" section will also require enhanced narrative disclosure about the timing and pricing of option grants to executives, including, but not limited to:
  - if the company has had since the beginning of the last fiscal year, or intends to have during the current fiscal year, a program, plan or practice to select option grant dates for executive officers in coordination with the release of material, non-public information;
  - how the determination is made as to when to grant awards;
  - the reasons for selecting a particular grant date;
  - the reasons for selecting the terms of awards, including the number of shares of an award and the exercise price; and
  - the other applicable elements required to be discussed in this section with respect to other elements of executive compensation.
- With regard to the timing of stock options in particular, companies must answer questions such as:
  - How does any program, plan or practice to time option grants to executives fit in the context of the company's program, plan or practice, if any, with regard to option grants to employees more generally?
  - What was the role of the compensation committee in approving and administering such a program, plan or practice?
  - How did the board or compensation committee take such information into account when determining whether and in what amount to make those grants?
  - Did the compensation committee delegate any aspect of the actual administration of a program, plan or practice to any other persons?
  - What was the role of executive officers in the company's program, plan or practice of option timing?
  - Does the company set the grant date of its stock option grants to new executives in coordination with the release of material non-public information?
  - Does a company plan to time, or has it timed, its release of material nonpublic information for the purpose of affecting the value of executive compensation?
- While the SEC did not express a view as to whether a company may have valid reasons for timing stock option grants, it noted the

view of some commentators that timing practices may unfairly benefit executives and employees.

- Disclosure is also required where a company has not previously disclosed a program, plan or practice of timing option grants to executives, but has adopted such a program, plan or practice or has made one or more decisions since the beginning of the past fiscal year to time option grants.

- Similar disclosure standards apply if a company has a program, plan or practice of awarding options and setting the exercise price based on the stock's price on a date other than the actual grant date or if the company determines the exercise price of option grants by using formulas based on average prices (or lowest prices) of the company's stock in a period preceding, surrounding or following the grant date.

DIRECTOR COMPENSATION

Director compensation for the last fiscal year is required in a Director Compensation Table (see Exhibit B.7), which is similar in format to the Summary Compensation Table and requires the disclosure of fees earned or paid, stock and option awards, other non-equity compensation, changes in pension value, all other compensation (including disclosure of perquisites) and total compensation. This table is required to be accompanied by related narrative disclosure.

RELATED PERSON TRANSACTIONS, DIRECTOR INDEPENDENCE AND OTHER CORPORATE GOVERNANCE MATTERS

Related Person Transactions

The amended rules revise the related person transaction disclosures to, among other things:

- Increase the dollar threshold for transactions required to be disclosed from $60,000 to $120,000;

- Adopt a principles-based approach that generally requires the disclosure of any transaction since the beginning of the company's last fiscal year, or any currently proposed transaction, in which the

EXHIBIT B.7   DIRECTOR COMPENSATION TABLE

Name (a)	Fees Earned or Paid in Cash ($) (b)	Stock Awards ($) (c)	Option Awards ($) (d)	Non-Equity Incentive Plan Compensation ($) (e)	Change in Pension Value and Nonqualified Deferred Compensation Earnings (f)	All Other Compensation ($) (g)	Total ($) (h)
A							
B							
C							
D							
E							

company was or is to be a participant, in which the amount involved exceeds $120,000 and in which any "related person will have a direct or indirect material interest";

- Require disclosure of a company's policies and procedures for the review, approval or ratification of related person transactions and the identification of any related person transaction that was required to be reported where the company's polices and procedures did not require review, approval or ratification or where such policies and procedures were not followed;
- Require disclosure of compensation paid to executive officers who are not named executive officers unless the compensation was approved, or recommended to the board of directors for approval, by the compensation committee or group of independent directors performing a similar function; and
- Eliminate the distinction between indebtedness and other types of related person transactions and the requirements for disclosure of specific types of director relationships.

Director Independence and Corporate Governance Matters

A new Item 407 of Regulations S-K and S-B has been added which consolidates existing disclosure requirements regarding director independence and related corporate governance matters, in most cases without substantive change. The new Item 407 also updates disclosure requirements regarding director independence to reflect the SEC's current requirements and current listing standards. The disclosure under new Item 407 requires, among other things:

- Identification of each director who is independent (and of any audit, nominating and compensation committee members that are not independent) under the listing standards applicable to such company;
- A description, by specific category or type, of any transactions, relationships or arrangements not disclosed as a related person transaction that were considered by the board of directors when determining if applicable independence standards were satisfied; and

- Disclosures about the compensation committee, including its processes and procedures for the consideration of executive and director compensation, which is in addition to the Compensation Discussion and Analysis section described above.

Security Ownership of Named Executive Officers and Directors

The amended rules require disclosure regarding the number of the Company's shares pledged by named executive officers, directors and director nominees, and the inclusion of directors' qualifying shares in the total amount of securities owned.

Revisions to Form 8-K

Items 1.01 and 1.02—Entry into and Termination of a Material Definitive Agreement

The amended rules eliminate the requirement of filing a Form 8-K under Item 1.01 when the company enters into employment compensation arrangements identified in Item 601(b)(10)(iii)(A) and (B) of Regulation S-K.* Consistent with this change to Item 1.01, the termination of such agreements need not be disclosed on a Form 8-K under Item 1.02.

---

*Item 601(b)(10)(iii)(A) includes any management contract or any compensatory plan, contract or arrangement, including but not limited to plans relating to options, warrants or rights, pension, retirement or deferred compensation or bonus, incentive or profit sharing (or if not set forth in any formal document, a written description thereof) in which any director or any of the named executive officers of the registrant, as defined by Item 402(a)(3) of Regulation S-K, participates; and any other management contract or any other compensatory plan, contract, or arrangement in which any other executive officer of the registrant participates unless immaterial in amount or significance. Item 601(b)(10)(iii)(B) includes any compensatory plan, contract or arrangement adopted without the approval of security holders pursuant to which equity may be awarded, including, but not limited to, options, warrants or rights (or if not set forth in any formal document, a written description thereof), in which any employee (whether or not an executive officer of the registrant) participates unless immaterial in amount or significance.

Item 5.02 Departure of Directors or Certain Officers; Election of Directors; Appointment of Certain Officers; Compensatory Arrangements of Certain Officers

In addition to the information required under current Item 5.02 of Form 8-K, the amended rules require disclosure of material employment compensation arrangements involving named executed officers, that prior to the new amendments, would have been required under Item 1.01. For purposes of Item 5.02, the named executive officers are the persons for whom disclosure was required in the most recent filing with the SEC that required disclosure under Item 402(c) of Regulation S-K or Item 402(b) of Regulation S-B, as applicable. The amended rules expand Item 5.02 to include:

> information regarding retirement, resignation or termination, referred to as a "triggering event," of any named executive officer with respect to the previous fiscal year;

> a brief description of any material plan, contract or arrangement to which a covered officer or director is a party or in which he or she participates that is entered into or materially amended in connection with the triggering event, or any grant or award to a covered officer or director, or modification thereto, under any such plan, contract or arrangement in connection with any such event;

> a brief description of the terms and conditions of any material new compensatory plan, contract or arrangement, or new grant or award thereunder (whether or not written), as to which the principal executive officer, principal financial officer or any named executive officer may participate or is a party of, and any material amendment to any such compensatory plan, contract or arrangement (or any modification to a grant or award thereunder), except that grants or awards or modifications thereto will not be required to be disclosed if they are consistent with the terms of previously disclosed plans or arrangements and they are disclosed the next time the company is required to provide new disclosure under Item 402 of Regulation S-K; and

> disclosure of salary or bonus for the most recent fiscal year that was not available at the latest practicable date in connection with disclosure under Item 402 of Regulation S-K, including a new total compensation recalculation to reflect the new salary or bonus information.

The company is not required to provide information with respect to plans, contracts, and arrangements to the extent they do not discriminate in scope, terms, or operation, in favor of executive officers or directors of the registrant and that are available generally to all salaried employees.

Extension of Limited Safe Harbor under Exchange Act Section 10(b) and Rule 10b-5 to Item 5.02(e) of Form 8-K and Exclusion of Item 5.02(e) from Form S-3 Eligibility Requirements

The amended rules extend the safe harbors regarding Exchange Act Section 10(b) and Rule 10b-5 and Form S-3 eligibility in the event that a company fails to timely file reports required by Item 5.02(e) of Form 8-K. However, in amending the new rules, the SEC put the disclosure of salary or bonus for the most recent fiscal year that was not available at the latest practicable date (including a new total compensation recalculation to reflect the new salary or bonus information) in new Item 5.02(f) of Form 8-K, which is not included within the safe harbor as extended.

General Instruction D to Form 8-K

The amended rules provide that to the extent that Item 1.01 and one or more other items of the Form 8-K are applicable, Item 1.01 does not need to be listed so long as the substantive disclosure required by Item 1.01 is disclosed in the Form 8-K and the number and caption of the other applicable item(s) are provided.

PLAIN ENGLISH DISCLOSURE REQUIRED IN PROXY AND INFORMATION STATEMENTS

The new rules require most compensation disclosures (Items 402, 403, 404 and 407 of Regulation SK) in the proxy statement to be written in "clear, concise and understandable" language, commonly known as "plain English." Generally, plain English focuses on creating shorter and simpler sentences, the use of active rather than passive voice, decreased emphasis on industry jargon and defined terms, and breaking up long paragraphs into bulleted lists and shorter paragraphs.

REGISTERED INVESTMENT COMPANIES AND BUSINESS DEVELOPMENT COMPANIES

The amended rules modify certain disclosure requirements for registered investment companies and business development companies. Specifically, the amendments:

- Apply the executive compensation disclosure requirements for operating companies in their entirety to business development companies;
- Increase to $120,000 the current $60,000 threshold for disclosure of certain interests, transactions, and relationships of independent directors of registered investment companies, similar to the increase proposed for operating companies with respect to related party disclosure; and
- Reorganize the proxy rules applicable to investment companies to reflect organizational changes proposed for operating companies.

EFFECTIVE DATES

Compliance with these amended rules is required as follows:

- For Forms 8-K, compliance is required for triggering events that occur on or after November 7, 2006;
- For Forms 10-K and 10-KSB, compliance is required for fiscal years ending on or after December 15, 2006;
- For proxy and information statements covering public companies other than registered investment companies, compliance is required for any new proxy or information statements filed on or after December 15, 2006, that are required to include Item 402 and 404 disclosure for fiscal years ending on or after December 15, 2006;
- For Securities Act registration statements covering registrants, other than registered investment companies, and Exchange Act registration statements (including pre-effective and post-effective amendments, as applicable) compliance is required for registration statements filed with the SEC on or after December 15, 2006, that are required to include Item 402 and 404 disclosure for fiscal years ending on or after December 15, 2006;

- For initial registration statements and post-effective amendments that are annual updates to effective registration statements that are filed on Forms N-1A, N-2 and N-3 (except those filed by business development companies), compliance is required for registration statements and post-effective amendments that are filed with the SEC on or after December 15, 2006; and

- For proxy and information statements covering registered investment companies, compliance is required for any new proxy or information statement filed on or after December 15, 2006.

IMMEDIATE ACTION REQUIRED

The SEC estimates that it will take over 170 hours to implement these rule changes in the initial year (106 additional hours for small business issuers). As a result, it is important to commence preparation as soon as possible. In order to prepare for the effective date of the amended rules, companies should consider taking the following actions now:

- *Create a Record of Compensation Committee Activities.* Although the amended rules do not typically apply to proxy information and registration statements filed with the SEC before December 15, 2006, the Compensation Discussion and Analysis section applies to activities of the Compensation Committee in 2006. It is important that the Compensation create a credible record in 2006 which will have to be described in the Proxy Statement or Form 10-K filed in 2007.

- *Determine who will Prepare the Compensation Discussion and Analysis Section.* The Compensation Discussion and Analysis section will have to be prepared by someone who can answer all of the questions required to be answered in that section and is able to draft the section in "plain English." The company should designate someone immediately to act in this capacity and have them attend Compensation Committee and other meetings where compensation issues are discussed. Some compensation consultants have volunteered to prepare the Compensation Discussion and Analysis section. Some companies may elect to have inside or outside counsel do so or possibly the management person who prepares the SEC filings. Given the sensitive nature of the proceedings of the Compensation

Committee, having a company employee attend the meetings may not be desirable.

- *Determine Who are the Company's Named Executive Officers.* The method of determining the named executive officers requires the inclusion of stock option compensation valued by the FAS 123R methods. A large option grant, even though vesting over a three year period, is required to be valued as if it were fully vested on the date of grant and can have the effect of placing an executive among the top five executive officers for disclosure purposes. To avoid this result, option grants may have to be spaced over several years or given with a view toward avoiding unnecessary disclosure.

- *Track Perks and Other Personal Benefits.* In view of the lower threshold for perquisites and the broader definition of what is a perquisite, the person at the company who initially prepares the compensation charts should immediately begin identifying perquisites that must be disclosed.

- *Coordinate Form 8-K Filings.* Item 5.02(f) of Form 8-K provides that if salary or bonus of an executive officer cannot be calculated as of the most recent practicable date and is omitted from the summary compensation table, subsequent disclosure of such amounts when they become calculable is required in a Form 8-K. This requires close coordination between the Compensation Committee and the person in charge of filing Form 8-K reports in order to avoid missing the four-business-day filing requirement. Failure to file the Form 8-K pursuant to Item 5.02(f) will disqualify the company from using Form S-3 registration statements, in contrast to failing to file pursuant to new Item 5.02(e) which is not subject to a similar disqualification.

- *Identify Independent Directors.* New Item 407 of Regulation S-K requires companies to identify all directors who are "independent" and what standards are being used for that purpose and any transactions, relationships or arrangements that were considered in determining independence (if not otherwise disclosed). These independent standards will also apply to any person who served as a director during any part of the year, including for example a director who retired before the 2006 annual meeting of stockholders. Companies should immediately start reviewing former directors who served on the board during 2006 for independence purposes. All current directors should receive an annual questionnaire which attempts to elicit information concerning their relationships. The board should formally adopt a resolution relating to who is an independent director after considering all of the information on the questionnaire, including relationships not required to be disclosed under Item 404.

- *Begin to Draft the Executive Compensation Disclosures in "Plain English."* Because the annual meeting proxy statements of many companies have not typically been written in plain English, it might be helpful to begin thinking now about converting the compensation sections, as well as the entire proxy statement, into plain English format. Companies should plan now to allow extra time in the proxy statement drafting schedule in 2007 to focus on plain English issues.

Employment Agreement*

T HIS EMPLOYMENT AGREEMENT ("Agreement"), is made this 1st day of January 2007, by and between XYZ Company, a Delaware limited liability company (the "Company"), and John Doe (the "Executive").

BACKGROUND

1. The Executive is the current Chief Executive Officer ("CEO") of the Company. The Executive is also a member of the Company.

2. Pursuant to the terms of a Purchase Agreement dated as of even date herewith (the "Purchase Agreement"), a portion of the Executive's equity in the Company is being purchased by investors, a portion of the Executive's equity is being redeemed by the Company and the Executive will retain a portion of his equity interests in the Company.

3. As a condition to closing the Purchase Agreement, the Executive and the Company are entering into this Agreement to memorialize the terms of the Executive's continued employment with the Company. The rights provided to the Executive as set forth in this Agreement provide the Executive with certain rights not afforded by his current arrangement with the Company and the Executive agrees and acknowledges that such rights constitute sufficient consideration for this Agreement to be a binding agreement between the parties hereto.

---

*All exhibits omitted except Exhibit C.1.

NOW, THEREFORE, in consideration of the premises, agreements and covenants contained herein, the parties, intending legally to be bound, hereby agree as follows:

AGREEMENT

1. <u>DEFINITIONS.</u> The following capitalized terms when used in this Agreement shall have the meaning set forth below.
    1.1. "Board" means the board of directors of the Company.
    1.2. "Commencement Date" has the meaning set forth in Section 3.
    1.3. "Company" means XYZ Company, a Delaware limited liability company.
    1.4. "Compensation Committee" means any committee determined by the Board of the Company that addresses executive compensation or, in the absence of such committee, the Board itself.
    1.5. "Contract Year" means each twelve (12) month period of the Executive's employment by the Company commencing on February ___ and ending upon February ___ during the Term.
    1.6. "D&O Policy" means a Directors and Officer Liability Insurance Policy to be carried by the Company for the benefit of the members of the Board.
    1.7. "Disability Period" means the time during which the Executive is Disabled.
    1.8. "Disabled" means the first to occur of:
        (a) The Executive being declared legally incompetent under the laws of the State of New Jersey, in which event the date the Executive becomes Disabled shall be deemed to be the date of such declaration.
        (b) The Company receiving a written opinion from a physician mutually acceptable to both the Company and Executive to the effect that the Executive has incurred a mental or physical condition that can reasonably be expected to prevent the Executive from carrying out the Executive's material duties for the Company for a period of at least six (6) months during any twelve (12) month period, in which event the date the Executive shall be deemed

Disabled to be the date of the physician's examination. The Executive shall cooperate with the Company and such physician in providing the necessary examination.

(c) The date upon which the Executive was first found to be disabled pursuant to any applicable disability policy.

1.9. "Index" means the Consumer Price Index, All Cities Average (1982-84=100), published by the Department of Labor, Bureau of Labor Statistics.

1.10. "Initial Contract Period" has the meaning set forth in Section 3.

1.11. "Renewal Contract Period" has the meaning set forth in Section 3.

1.12. "Severance Period" means: (i) for terminations occurring during the Initial Contract Period the lesser of (A) the eighteen (18) month period immediately following the Termination Date and (B) the period commencing on the Termination Date and ending on the last day of the Initial Contract Period; and (ii) for terminations occurring during any Renewal Contract Period, the period commencing on the Termination Date and ending on the last day of the Renewal Contract Period.

1.13. "Term" has the meaning set forth in Section 3.

1.14. "Termination Date" means the date on which the Executive ceases to be employed by the Company.

2. EMPLOYMENT

2.1. The Executive shall be employed by the Company as its Chief Executive Officer upon the terms and conditions set forth in this Agreement.

2.2. During the term of his employment hereunder, the Executive shall primarily perform his services at the Company's facilities in New York City, NY.

2.3. The Executive shall be provided reasonable office space and the amenities, including, but not limited to, secretarial and other clerical support, which ordinarily accompany employment reasonably comparable within the business community to the employment accepted by the Executive.

2.4. It is acknowledged and agreed that the Executive will be required to travel for various Company purposes, commensurate with the duties to be performed by the

Executive. To the extent that such travel is on commercial aircraft, the Executive shall be entitled to travel in business-class (or first-class where business-class travel is otherwise unavailable) on all air travel where the scheduled flight time is in excess of three hours. The Company shall provide the Executive with active annual membership in one airline travel club of Executive's choice.

3. <u>TERM.</u> Unless earlier terminated pursuant to the terms of Section 15, the initial term of this Agreement shall commence on the date hereof (the "Commencement Date") and shall continue until the third (3rd) anniversary of the Commencement Date (the "Initial Contract Period"). Unless earlier terminated pursuant to the terms of Section 15, the term of this Agreement shall be extended for up to three (3) additional one (1) year periods following the Initial Contract Period (each, a "Renewal Contract Period", collectively, the "Renewal Contract Periods") unless one party provides the other with notice of his or its intention not to renew this Agreement not less than ninety (90) days prior to the end of the Initial Contract Period or the then current Renewal Contract Period. The terms of this Agreement as in effect at the end of the Initial Contract Period or a Renewal Contract Period (as such may be amended or modified according to the terms of this Agreement) shall be in effect during any subsequent Renewal Contract Period, as applicable. The period encompassing the Initial Contract Period and all Renewal Contract Periods prior to termination shall be collectively referred to herein as the "Term".

4. <u>DUTIES.</u> The Executive shall serve the Company as its Chief Executive Officer. The Executive shall be responsible for building an effective senior management team, marketing, operations, business strategy, financing, human resources, the supervision of budget preparation, the formation of relationships with third parties, determining which markets the Company will serve and such other duties that are typically performed by chief executive officers of similarly sized companies as the Board may prescribe from time to time. The Executive shall report to the Board. The Executive agrees to devote his full business time and efforts to the diligent and faithful performance of his duties to the Company, provided

that it shall not be a violation of this Agreement for the Executive to (i) serve in any capacity with any professional, community, industry, civic, educational or charitable organization, (ii) serve as a director, trustee, or member of a committee of any organization involving no conflict of interest with the interests of the Company; (iii) deliver lectures, fulfill speaking engagements, and teach at educational institutions or business organizations; and (iv) manage his and his family's personal investments and legal affairs, so long as, in each case, such activities do not breach or violate the Executive's primary obligations to the Company, including, without limitation, the duty of loyalty, the duty of good faith and fair dealing, and the obligation not to take any opportunity of the Company, and do not adversely affect or impair, in any material respect, the Executive's ability to discharge his duties on behalf of the Company hereunder.

5. BASE SALARY.

    5.1. As consideration for the services rendered by the Executive to the Company, the Company shall pay the Executive an annual base salary which (i) for the Contract Year ending February _____, 2007 shall be equal to Four Hundred Thousand Dollars ($400,000), and (ii) for each Contract Year thereafter, the Base Salary shall be equal to the Base Salary for the preceding Contract Year multiplied by a fraction, (A) the numerator of which is the Index on December 31 immediately prior to the new Contract Year and (B) the denominator of which is the Index on December 31 of one year prior to the date in (A) above (if the Index ceases to be published at intervals other than monthly, the Company shall select another reasonable method of adjusting the Base Salary to reflect changes in the cost of living) ("Base Salary").

    5.2. All payments of Base Salary shall be made in accordance with the Company's normal payroll practices.

    5.3. The Compensation Committee shall meet at least once per annum to determine whether the Base Salary shall be adjusted and the amount of such adjustment; provided, however, that in no event shall the Base Salary be reduced below the Base Amount.

6. <u>BONUS.</u> The Executive shall participate in the Company's bonus plan. The Executive shall be eligible for an annual bonus target equal to 50% of his Base Salary for such calendar year ("Bonus"), the payment of which is contingent upon achieving predetermined Company financial performance targets and individual key performance objectives as established by the Compensation Committee and the Executive working together and ratified by the Board; *provided, however*, that for any calendar year, the financial performance targets used in setting the Executive's bonus shall be based upon the financial performance projections for the Company for that year (projections for 2006 are attached hereto as Exhibit C) and shall not require the achievement of more than a 35% increase in the Company's organic revenue growth as compared to the prior calendar year. In the event that such targets have been reached, the Company shall pay such Bonus to the Executive.

7. <u>WITHHOLDING AND TAXES</u>. The Company shall withhold all sums authorized by the Executive or required to be withheld by law or court decree, including (but not limited to) income taxes, employment taxes, and the Executive contributions to benefit plans sponsored by the Company. For such time as the Executive is a member of the Company, all compensation under this Agreement shall be treated as a "Guaranteed Payment" under Section 707 of the Internal Revenue Code.

8. <u>BENEFITS</u>. The Executive shall have access to all benefits that the Company offers to its senior management and shall have the opportunity to participate at the same levels of coverage and deductibles as other members of senior management. Specifically, such benefits currently include, but are not limited to:

   8.1. 100% coverage for an individual's medical/dental insurance.

   8.2. Customary $50,000 Life policy, of which the Executive's estate and or designees is/are the beneficiar(ies).

   8.3. Long Term Disability coverage for the Executive.

   8.4. Short Term Disability coverage for the Executive.

   8.5. The Executive shall be eligible to participate in the Company's 401(k) plan.

   8.6. The Company may adopt, change, or terminate any benefit plan set forth in this Section 8 provided that such adoption, change of termination applies to all senior management of the Company and the Company adopts or maintains benefits which are substantially similar to those benefits specified in Sections 8.1–8.5 above.

9. <u>Vacation, Holidays and Sick Leave.</u> During the Term, the Executive shall be entitled to paid vacation, holidays, and sick leave on the same basis and the same terms as in effect on the day prior to the Commencement Date. Notwithstanding the foregoing, the Executive shall be entitled to a minimum of four weeks of paid vacation per year during the Term and shall be able to carryover, without limitation, any unused vacation days from year to year. Upon termination of the Executive's employment, unused vacation days will be paid out to Executive on the date of termination.

10. <u>AUTOMOBILE.</u> The Company shall provide the Executive with an automobile suitable for the Executive's position that shall be comparable to the automobile that the Company provided to the Executive prior to the effect of this Agreement. The Company shall own such automobile and shall be responsible for all payments (including insurance) relating to such automobile. The Company shall reimburse the Executive for all repairs, maintenance and gas relating to such automobile.

11. <u>OTHER BENEFITS.</u> The Company shall provide the following additional benefits to the Executive:

   11.1. A subsidy for the Executive's current apartment and parking in New York City of up to 75% of the monthly cost, capped at $5,000 per month.

   11.2. A cell phone, palm pilot, or similar device and laptop computer for business use.

   11.3. Reasonable club membership annual dues (for a membership class or plan similar to the Executive's membership class or plan in effect immediately prior to the Commencement Date) shall be reimbursed to the Executive for the following:
   (a) NY Athletic Club
   (b) Union League (Philadelphia).

   11.4. The Executive shall be reimbursed for tickets to sporting events and other cultural events to the extent such tickets are used for Company business.

11.5. The Company will reimburse the Executive for the reasonable costs of equipping a home office (e.g., desktop or laptop computer with docking station, dedicated phone line, high-speed internet access, printer, copier, scanner and fax machine).

12. <u>BUSINESS EXPENSES.</u> The Executive is expected to incur ordinary, necessary, and reasonable expenses for the business of the Company. The Company shall reimburse the Executive for these expenses, subject to the Company's reimbursement policies including satisfactory documentation of expenses.

13. <u>D&O POLICY AND INDEMNIFICATION.</u> The Company shall, at all times that the Executive serves as a member of the Board or as an officer, carry D&O and E&O Policies (and a tail policy for claims made during any period that the Executive no longer serves as a director or officer) on such terms and with such exclusions, limitations and deductibles as shall be reasonably satisfactory to the Board of Directors and the Executive. The Company shall pay any and all premiums on such policy as and when the same shall become due and payable. The Company shall indemnify the Executive and advance expenses to the Executive, to the fullest extent permitted by law.

14. <u>CONFIDENTIALITY OBLIGATIONS.</u> The Executive shall execute the Nonsolicitation and Confidentiality Agreement applicable to the Executive's employment attached hereto as Exhibit "B" (the "Nonsolicitation and Confidentiality Agreement").

15. <u>TERMINATION.</u>

15.1. <u>Termination by the Company for Cause.</u> The Company may terminate the Executive's employment immediately (upon providing written notice to the Executive) for Cause. For purposes of this Agreement, "Cause" shall mean:

(a) The Executive willfully and materially injures the Company or its assets;

(b) The Executive is convicted of a felony, which in the reasonable judgment of the Board, reflects adversely on the Company; or

(c) The Executive breaches the terms of Section 4 of this Agreement and does not cure such breach within 15 business days of receiving notice of such breach or the

Executive breaches the terms of the Nonsolicitation and Confidentiality Agreement attached hereto and does not cure such breach within five business days of receiving notice of such breach.

No act or failure to act on the part of the Executive shall be considered "willful" unless it is done, or omitted to be done, by the Executive in bad faith or without reasonable belief that the Executive's action or omission was in the best interests of the Company. Any act or failure to act that is based upon authority given pursuant to a resolution duly adopted by the Board or the advice of other counsel for the Company shall be conclusively presumed to be done, or omitted to be done, by the Executive in good faith and in the best interests of the Company. No act or failure to act by the Executive shall be considered "Cause" unless the Company has given detailed written notice thereof to the Executive and, where remedial action is feasible, he has failed to remedy the act or omission within fifteen (15) business days after receiving such notice.

15.2. <u>Termination by the Company Without Cause.</u> Subject to the provisions set forth in Section 15.6, the Company may, at any time, upon delivery of notice to the Executive, terminate the Executive's employment hereunder without Cause.

15.3. <u>Termination by Executive for Good Reason.</u> The Executive may terminate his employment hereunder at any time for Good Reason only by giving at least 60 days' prior written notice to the Company. Upon delivery of such notice, the Company may terminate Executive's employment at any time (regardless of the date set forth in the Executive's notice). Such written notice shall contain a short explanation of the underlying facts and circumstances that constitute Good Reason. For purposes of this Agreement, "Good Reason" shall mean the occurrence of any of the following: (a) the nature and scope of the Executive's duties and authority or his responsibilities with Company are reduced to a level below that which he enjoys on the Commencement Date, (b) his compensation is reduced to a level below that provided in Section 5 of this Agreement, (c) the benefits provided to the Executive on the date of this Agreement pursuant to Sections 6 and Sections 8–13 of this Agreement are materially reduced, (d) the Executive's position or title with the Company is reduced from his current position or title, (e) the Company requires that the Executive's principal place of employment change to a location greater than forty (40) miles from the Company's facilities (determined as of the date of this Agreement) in New York City, or (f) the Executive being requested to take any action or to refrain from taking any action that would have the likelihood of causing the Executive to violate (i) any statute, regulation or rule, including those of any self-regulatory organization, applicable to the Company, or any federal, state or local licensing authority applicable to the Company or the Executive, or (ii) the Company's then existing Code of Ethics and Business Practices or any similar policy or document. "Good Reason" shall not include any of the foregoing to the extent such item relates to the termination or reduction of duties pursuant to mutual agreement, death or Disability of the Executive or Cause.

15.4. <u>Resignation by Executive.</u> The Executive may terminate his employment at any time without Good Reason only if he delivers to the Company not less than six (6) months prior written notice of such termination. Upon delivery of such notice, the Company may terminate the Executive's employment at any time (regardless of the date set forth in the Executive's notice) and such termination shall be deemed to be for "Cause".

15.5. <u>Termination due to Death or Disability.</u>

    (a) <u>Death.</u> The Executive's employment with the Company will terminate automatically and immediately upon the death of the Executive.

    (b) <u>Disability.</u> If the Executive is Disabled, the Company may terminate the Executive's employment by delivery of written notice to him or his trustee or guardian, provided he is still Disabled at the time the notice is sent.

15.6. Effect of Termination.

    (a) <u>Termination by the Company for Cause; Employee Resignation.</u> In the event that the Executive is terminated by the Company for Cause pursuant to Section 15.1 or the Executive terminates employment with the Company without Good Reason pursuant to Section 15.3, the Company shall pay the Executive (i) Base Salary through the Termination Date and (ii) all accrued and unpaid Bonuses through the Termination Date (which shall be prorated for the partial period prior to termination). Following termination for Cause or the Executive's termination from employment with the Company without Good Reason, the Company shall have no further obligations to the Executive or his estate, and the Executive shall have no further obligations to the Company with respect to his employment or this Agreement, except the obligations set forth above in this subsection (a), the obligations set forth in Sections 7, 16, 17, and 19 and the terms of the Nonsolicitation and Confidentiality Agreement shall remain in full force and effect.

    (b) <u>Termination by the Company without Cause.</u> In the event that the Company terminates the Executive's employment hereunder without Cause, the Company shall (i) pay to the Executive an amount equal to the Executive's Base Salary for the Severance Period, (ii) pay to the Executive the full Bonus amount available to the Executive for the calendar year in which he is terminated plus the lesser of (A) one half of the full Bonus amounts available to Executive for the calendar year in which he is terminated and (B) one half of the Bonus amount earned by the Executive for the calendar year preceding the calendar year in which he is terminated and (iii) continue all benefits set forth herein or, at the Company's option, reimburse the Executive for the cost of benefits that are substantially similar to the benefits set forth herein during the Severance Period. If, at any time during the Severance Period, the Executive receives similar benefits from an employer or otherwise, the Company's obligation to fund such benefits shall terminate. Notwithstanding the foregoing, the Executive shall have no obligation to mitigate damages in the event of a termination of employment (regardless of the reason). If Executive is terminated without Cause or if the Executive terminates his employment with the Company for Good Reason, the Company shall have no further obligations to the Executive or his estate and the Executive shall have no further obligations to the Company with respect to his employment or this Agreement, except that obligations set forth above in this subsection (b), the obligations set forth in Sections 7, 16, 17, 18, and 19 and the terms of the Nonsolicitation and Confidentiality Agreement shall remain in full force and effect.

(c) <u>Termination by Executive for Good Reason.</u> In the event that the Executive terminates his employment with the Company for Good Reason, the Executive shall be entitled to the same payments and benefits set forth in Section 15.6(b) hereof.

(d) <u>Termination due to Death of Executive.</u> In the event of the Executive's death, the Company shall pay to the Executive's estate all accrued but unpaid Base Salary and accrued but unpaid Bonus amounts through the Termination Date (which shall be pro-rated for a partial period) and the Company shall have no further obligations to the Executive or his estate, and the Executive and his estate shall have no further obligations to the Company with respect to his employment or this Agreement, except that obligations under Sections 7, 16, 17, and 19 shall remain in full force and effect.

(e) <u>Termination Due to Disability.</u> In the event that the Company terminates the Executive's employment due to a Disability, the Company shall continue to pay the Executive his Base Salary until the expiration of any applicable waiting period under any short term or long term disability policy applicable to the Executive. Following termination due to a Disability, the Company shall have no further obligations to the Executive or his estate, and the Executive shall have no further obligations to the Company with respect to his employment or this Agreement, except that obligations under Sections 7, 16, 17, and 19 hereof and the terms of the Nonsolicitation and Confidentiality Agreement shall remain in full force and effect.

16. <u>NOTICES.</u>

16.1. <u>How Sent.</u> All notices, requests, demands, acceptances, and other communications pursuant to this Agreement ("Notices") shall be in writing and either delivered personally or sent by telecopier or facsimile, overnight delivery, express mail, or certified mail, postage prepaid, return-receipt requested. Notices to the Company shall be delivered personally to its Chief Operating Officer or sent to his attention.

16.2. <u>Where Sent.</u> If sent by mail, a Notice shall be addressed (i) to the Company at _____ or (ii) to the Executive at the last known address shown on the records of the Company. Copies of all Notices shall be sent to _____ _____. If sent by telecopier or facsimile, a Notice shall be sent (x) to the Company at _____ _____ or (y) to the Executive at his telecopier number on file with the Company.

16.3. <u>When Effective.</u> A Notice delivered personally shall be deemed to have been delivered when personally delivered. A Notice sent by telecopier shall be deemed to have been delivered when transmitted, provided that the sender receives written acknowledgment of its receipt. A Notice sent by overnight delivery or express mail shall be deemed to have been delivered twenty-four (24) hours after having been sent. A Notice that is properly addressed and is sent by certified mail with postage fully prepaid will be deemed to have been delivered when it is deposited in the U.S. mail.

16.4. <u>Change in Addressees or Addresses.</u> Either party may designate substitute addressees, addresses or telecopier numbers for Notices and copies, and thereafter, Notices and copies are to be directed to those substitute addressees or addresses or telecopier numbers.

17. <u>COSTS OF LITIGATION.</u> If either party files suit to enforce its or his rights under this agreement, the prevailing party is entitled to recover from the other party all reasonable expenses incurred in preparing for and in trying the case, including, but not limited to, investigative costs, court costs and reasonable attorneys' fees. For this purpose the "prevailing party" is the plaintiff if (i) in a case where only damages are sought, 51% or more of the damages sought are awarded, (ii) in a case where only equitable relief is sought, the relief sought is granted (each application for equitable relief being considered for these purposes as a separate action) or (iii) in a case where both damages and equitable relief are sought, either fifty-one percent (51%) or more of the damages sought are awarded or the equitable relief sought is granted; otherwise, the defendant is the "prevailing party."

18. <u>SECURITY.</u>

   18.1. In order to secure the Company's obligations to the Executive under Section 15.6(b) or (c), the Company shall, if and when requested by the Executive, and provided that the cost does not exceed $10,000 per annum, cause a reputable bank reasonably acceptable to the Executive to issue a Letter of Credit, in the face amount of at least twice the Executive's Base Salary on the date of termination and in the form attached as Exhibit C.1 (Letter of Credit), to be issued to the Executive as a beneficiary. In lieu thereof, the parties may establish a mutually acceptable escrow arrangement. The Letter of Credit shall not expire sooner than one year and thirty (30) days after the date of its issuance. The Company shall maintain the Letter of Credit in effect at all times during the Term and any other period of time during which the Executive is entitled to any benefits under this Agreement.

   18.2. The Executive will not present a draft under the Letter of Credit for payment unless (i) he shall have first made written demand on the Company for direct payment of the amount sought and the Company has not made full payment in cash to the Executive as required by this Agreement within thirty (30) days after notice of the written demand or (ii) a renewed Letter of Credit is not provided to the Company at least thirty (30) days prior to the expiration date of the existing Letter of Credit. Executive shall not draw any funds under the Letter of Credit with respect to costs or expenses already reimbursed to him by the Company.

Exhibit C.1
Letter of Credit

Name and Address of Bank Issuing Irrevocable Letter of Credit

DATE: _____

        NON-NEGOTIABLE

        Expires:_____

        Irrevocable Letter of Credit No._____

        Amount: $_____

        To: John Doe

            _____

            _____

You are hereby irrevocably authorized to draw at sight on the undersigned, for the account of XYZ Company, up to an aggregate of [_____] ($[_____ ____]) by one or more drafts, payable to your order, each draft bearing the clause "Drawn under (Name of Undersigned) Letter of Credit No....................." and accompanied by the following Document (together with the required supporting attachment): A sworn statement executed by you, in the form attached hereto as Document No. 1 (the "Affidavit"), with the appropriate blanks completed and with a copy attached of the notice referred to in paragraph C of the Affidavit.

No draft will be honored (i) if the draft is not accompanied by the aforesaid Document (together with the required supporting attachment) or (ii) if the aggregate amount drawn by you, taking into consideration the subject draft, would exceed the face amount of this Letter of Credit.

No draft will be honored unless it is drawn and presented for payment on or after the date hereof and no later than the expiration date.

The undersigned hereby agrees that a draft drawn under this Letter of Credit and in compliance with the foregoing will be duly honored during the period stated above on due presentation to the undersigned in compliance with the terms of this Letter of Credit by you.

The amount of each draft must be noted on this Letter of Credit. The original of this Letter of Credit will be retained by the undersigned for the purpose of making such notations.

                Yours very truly,

                NAME OF ISSUING BANK

                By:_____

19. MISCELLANEOUS.

19.1. <u>Governing Law.</u> The laws of the State of Delaware applicable to contracts made to be performed in Delaware will govern the validity and construction of this Agreement.

19.2. <u>Dispute Resolution.</u>

(a) Except for any claims made for specific performance or injunctive relief, any and all disputes among the parties to this Agreement (defined for the purpose of this provision to include their respective officers, directors, managers, members, partners, shareholders, agents and/or other Affiliates) arising out of or in connection with the negotiation, execution, interpretation, performance or nonperformance of this Agreement and the transactions contemplated herein shall be solely and finally settled by arbitration, which shall be conducted in Wilmington, Delaware, by a single arbitrator selected by the parties. The arbitrator shall be a lawyer familiar with the transactions and agreements of the type contemplated in this Agreement who shall not have been previously employed by or affiliated with any of the parties hereto. If the parties fail to agree on the arbitrator within thirty (30) days of the date, one of them invokes this arbitration provision, either party may apply to the American Arbitration Association to make the appointment.

(b) Except for any claims made for specific performance or injunctive relief, the parties hereby renounce all recourse to litigation and agree that the award of the arbitrator shall be final and subject to no judicial review. The arbitrator shall conduct the proceedings pursuant to the Commercial Arbitration Rules of the American Arbitration Association, as now or hereafter amended (the "Rules").

(c) The arbitrator shall decide the issues submitted (i) in accordance with the provisions and commercial purposes of this Agreement, and (ii) with all substantive questions of Law determined under the Laws of the State of Delaware (without regard to its principles of conflicts of laws). The arbitrator shall promptly hear and determine (after giving the parties due notice and a reasonable opportunity to be heard) the issues submitted and shall render a written decision in writing within 60 days after the appointment of the arbitrator. No fees shall be paid to the arbitrator with respect to services rendered by the arbitrator after the elapse of six (6) months after the appointment of the arbitrator.

(d) The parties agree to facilitate the arbitration by (i) conducting arbitration hearings to the greatest extent possible on successive days, and (ii) observing strictly the time periods established by the Rules or by the arbitrator for submission of evidence or briefs.

(e) The parties shall share equally the fees and expenses of the arbitrator.

(f) Judgment on the award of the arbitrator may be entered in any court having jurisdiction.

(g) The parties hereto agree that the provisions of this Section 19.2 shall not be construed to prohibit any party from obtaining, in the proper case, specific performance or injunctive relief in any court of competent jurisdiction with respect to the enforcement of any covenant or agreement of another party to this Agreement as provided herein.

19.3. <u>Confidentiality.</u> Neither party shall disclose the contents of this Agreement or of any other contemporaneous agreement to any person, firm or entity, except the agents or representatives of the parties, or except as required by law.

19.4. <u>Word Forms.</u> Whenever used, the singular shall include the plural and vice versa. The use of any gender, tense, or conjugation shall include all genders, tenses and conjugations.

19.5. <u>Headings.</u> The Section headings have been included for convenience only, are not part of this Agreement, and are not to be used to interpret any provision hereof.

19.6. <u>Amendments, Etc.</u> This Agreement may be amended, supplemented, waived, terminated (except as specifically provided herein), or discharged only by a writing signed by the party against whom the modification is sought to be enforced.

19.7. <u>Binding Effect and Benefit.</u> This Agreement shall be binding upon and inure to the benefit of the parties, their successors, heirs, personal representatives and other legal representatives.

19.8. <u>Entire Agreement.</u> This Agreement constitutes the entire agreement between the parties.

19.9. <u>Separability.</u> The covenants contained in this Agreement are separable, and if any court of competent jurisdiction declares any of them to be invalid or unenforceable, that declaration of invalidity or unenforceability shall not affect the validity or enforceability of any of the other covenants, each of which shall remain in full force and effect.

19.10. <u>Specific Performance.</u> In the event of a breach of this Agreement, the nonbreaching party shall be entitled to equitable relief (including without limitation, the right to specific performance). The right to equitable relief shall not preclude any other rights or remedies that the Executive may have, all of which rights and remedies are cumulative.

19.11. <u>No Set-off or Recoupment.</u> The Company's obligation to make the payments provided for in this Agreement and otherwise to perform its obligations hereunder shall not be affected by any set-off, counter-claim, recoupment, defense, or other claim, right or action that the Company may have against the Executive or others.

19.12. <u>Background.</u> The Background is a part of this Agreement.

IN WITNESS WHEREOF, the parties have executed this Agreement on the day and year first above written.

ATTEST: XYZ COMPANY.

_____   By: _____
                                              Title:

WITNESS: EXECUTIVE:

_____   _____
                                           John Doe

LETTER OF CREDIT NO. _____

DOCUMENT NO. 1

Affidavit

STATE OF   )
) ss.
COUNTY OF   )

[_____], being duly sworn according to law, hereby deposes and says that:

A. The draft which this Affidavit accompanies (hereinafter called the "Draft") is for payment to the undersigned of monies owed the undersigned pursuant to that certain Agreement dated [_____], 2006 (the "Agreement") by and between XYZ Company (the "Company") and John Doe.

B. The amount of the Draft does not exceed the aggregate of the amounts specified in the Agreement which are owed to the undersigned by The Company for which the Letter of Credit is intended as security and which The Company has not already directly paid to the undersigned.

C. A true and correct copy of the written demand on The Company for direct payment of the amount sought in the Draft is attached hereto and Hanover has not made full payment in cash to the undersigned as required by the Agreement within thirty (30) days after said written notice was delivered to The Company.

Dated:_____

_____
Signature of Drawing Beneficiary

Subscribed and sworn to before me this _____ day of _____, 2006.

Notary Public in and for said County/State of _____.

_____
Notary Public

Public Company Equity Incentive Plan

THE PSC CORPORATION: 2007 EQUITY INCENTIVE PLAN*

PURPOSE

The Plan has been established to advance the interests of the Company and its stockholders by providing for the grant to Participants of Stock-based and other incentive Awards to (i) enhance the Company's ability to attract and retain current or prospective Employees, directors, and consultants who are in a position to make contributions to the success of the Company and its Affiliates and (ii) encourage Participants to take into account the long-term interests of the Company and its stockholders through ownership of shares of Stock.

DEFINED TERMS

Exhibit D.1, which is incorporated by reference, defines the terms used in the Plan and sets forth certain operational rules related to those terms.

ADMINISTRATION

The Administrator shall have the right to construe the Plan and the Awards issued pursuant to it, to correct defects and omissions and to reconcile inconsistencies to the extent that the Administrator deems it to be

---

*All exhibits omitted except Exhibit D.1, D.2, D.3 and D.4.

EXHIBIT D.1   DEFINITION OF TERMS

The following terms, when used in the Plan, will have the meanings and be subject to the provisions set forth below:

Administrator: The Committee, provided that so long as any class of the Company's common equity securities is required to be registered under Section 12 of the Securities Exchange Act of 1934, the Committee shall consist of two or more directors, all of whom are both "outside directors" within the meaning of Section 162(m) and (if such common equity securities are so registered, whether or not required to be) "non-employee directors" within the meaning of Rule 16b-3 promulgated under the Securities Exchange Act of 1934; and provided further, that, to the extent permitted by law, the Committee may delegate (i) to one or more of its members such of its duties, powers, and responsibilities as it may determine; (ii) to one or more officers of the Company the authority to allocate other Awards among such persons (other than the delegated officers of the Company) eligible to receive Awards under the Plan as such delegated officer or officers determine consistent with such delegation; *provided,* that with respect to any delegation described in this clause (ii) the Committee (or a properly delegated member or members of such Committee) shall have authorized the issuance of a specified number of shares of Stock under such Awards and shall have specified the consideration, if any, to be paid therefore; and (iii) to such Employees or other persons as it determines such ministerial tasks as it deems appropriate. In the event of any delegation described in the preceding sentence, the term "Administrator" shall include the person or persons so delegated to the extent of such delegation.

Affiliate: Any corporation or other entity owning, directly or indirectly, 50% or more of the outstanding Stock of the Company, or in which the Company or any such corporation or other entity owns, directly or indirectly, 50% or more of the outstanding capital stock (determined by aggregate voting rights) or other voting interests. Notwithstanding the foregoing, with respect to an ISO, the term "Affiliate," as used herein, shall refer only to the Company or a Parent Corporation or a Subsidiary Corporation.

Award: The agreement or other document evidencing any or a combination of the following:

(i) Stock Options
(ii) SARs
(iii) Restricted Stock (also called "Restricted Shares")
(iv) Unrestricted Stock
(v) Stock Units, including Restricted Stock Units
(vi) Performance Awards

Board: The Board of Directors of the Company.

Change in Control: An event or events, in which:

(A) any "person" as such term is used in Sections 13(d) and 14(d) of the Securities Exchange Act of 1934 (the "1934 Act") (other than (i) the Company, (ii) any subsidiary of the Company, (iii) any trustee or other fiduciary holding securities under an employee benefit plan of the Company or of any subsidiary of the Company, (iv) any company owned, directly or indirectly, by the stockholders of the Company in substantially the same proportions as their ownership of stock of the Company, or (v) any individual or entity which on the date of adoption of this Plan by the Board owned securities of the Company representing [25%] or more of the Company's then outstanding securities), is or becomes the "beneficial owner" (as defined in Section 13(d) of the 1934 Act), together with all affiliates and Associates (as such terms are used in Rule 12b-2 of the General Rules and Regulations under the 1934 Act) of such person, directly or indirectly, of securities of the Company representing more than [50%] of the combined voting power of the Company's then outstanding securities;

(B) the stockholders of the Company approve a merger or consolidation of the Company with any other company, other than (i) a merger or consolidation which would result in the voting securities of the Company outstanding immediately prior thereto continuing to represent (either by remaining outstanding or by being converted into voting securities of the surviving entity), in combination with the ownership of any trustee or other fiduciary holding securities under an employee benefit plan of the Company or any subsidiary of the Company, more than [50%] of the combined voting power of the voting securities of the Company or such surviving entity outstanding immediately after such merger or consolidation or (ii) a merger or consolidation effected to implement a recapitalization of the Company (or similar transaction) after which no "person" (with the method of determining "beneficial ownership" used in clause (A) of this definition) owns more than [50%] of the combined voting power of the securities of the Company or the surviving entity of such merger or consolidation;

(C) during any period of two consecutive years (not including any period prior to the execution of the Plan), individuals who at the beginning of such period constitute the Board, and any new director (other than a director designated by a person who has conducted or threatened a proxy contest, or has entered into an agreement with the Company to effect a transaction described in clause (A), (B) or (D) of this definition) whose election by the Board or nomination for election by the Company's stockholders was approved by a vote of at least two-thirds (2/3) of the directors then still in office, who either were directors at the beginning of the period or whose election or nomination for

(Continued)

election was previously so approved cease for any reason to constitute at least a majority thereof;

(D) the sale or other disposition by the Company of all or substantially all of the Company's assets; or

(E) the dissolution or complete liquidation of the Company.

Code: The U.S. Internal Revenue Code of 1986 as from time to time amended and in effect, or any successor statute as from time to time in effect.

Committee: The Committee appointed by the Board to administer this Plan.

Common Stock: See definition of "Stock."

Company: [The PSC].

Disability: shall mean permanent and total disability of an employee or director participating in the Plan as determined by the Administrator in accordance with uniform principles consistently applied, upon the basis of such evidence as the Administrator deems necessary and desirable. Notwithstanding the foregoing, with respect to an Award that is subject to Code Section 409A, no condition shall constitute a "Disability" for purposes of the Plan unless such condition also constitutes a disability as defined under Code Section 409A and, in the case of an ISO, Code Section 22(e)(3).

Employee: Any person (including an officer) who is employed by the Company or an Affiliate, whether full-time or part-time.

Employment: A Participant's employment with the Company or its Affiliates. Employment will be deemed to continue, unless the Administrator expressly provides otherwise, so long as the Participant is employed by, or otherwise is providing services in a capacity described in Section 5 to the Company or its Affiliates. If a Participant's employment is with an Affiliate and that entity ceases to be an Affiliate, the Participant's Employment will be deemed to have terminated when the entity ceases to be an Affiliate unless the Participant transfers Employment to the Company or its remaining Affiliates or the Administrator expressly determines otherwise. Notwithstanding the foregoing, with respect to an ISO, the term "Affiliate," as used herein, shall refer only to the Company or a Parent Corporation or a Subsidiary Corporation.

ISO: A Stock Option intended to be an "incentive stock option" within the meaning of Section 422 of the Code. Each option granted pursuant to the Plan will be treated as providing by its terms that it is to be a non-incentive stock option unless, as of the date of grant, it is expressly designated as an ISO.

Parent Corporation: The term "parent corporation" as used in any Stock Option granted pursuant to this Plan, shall (except as otherwise provided in the Award) have the meaning that is ascribed to that term when contained in Section 422(b) of the Code and the regulations thereunder, and the Company shall be deemed to be the grantor corporation for purposes of applying such meaning.

Participant: A person who is granted an Award under the Plan.

Performance Award: An Award subject to Performance Criteria. The Administrator in its discretion may grant Performance Awards that are intended to qualify for the performance-based compensation exception under Section 162(m) and Performance Awards that are not intended so to qualify.

Performance Criteria: Specified criteria, other than the mere continuation of Employment or the mere passage of time, the satisfaction of which is a condition for the grant, exercisability, vesting or full enjoyment of an Award. For purposes of Awards that are intended to qualify for the performance-based compensation exception under Section 162(m), a Performance Criterion will mean an objectively determinable measure of performance relating to any or any combination of the following (measured either absolutely or by reference to an index or indices and determined either on a consolidated basis or, as the context permits, on a divisional, subsidiary, line of business, project or geographical basis or in combinations thereof): sales; revenues; assets; costs; earnings before or after deduction for all or any portion of interest, taxes, depreciation, or amortization, whether or not on a continuing operations or an aggregate or per share basis; return on equity, investment, capital or assets; one or more operating ratios; borrowing levels, leverage ratios or credit rating; market share; capital expenditures; cash flow; stock price; stockholder return or stockholder value; sales of particular products or services; customer acquisition or retention; safety, health or environmental affairs performance; compliance; acquisitions and divestitures (in whole or in part); joint ventures and strategic alliances; spin-offs, split-ups and the like; reorganizations; or recapitalizations, restructurings, financings (issuance of debt or equity) or refinancings. A Performance Criterion and any targets with respect thereto determined by the Administrator need not be based upon an increase, a positive or improved result or avoidance of loss. To the extent consistent with the requirements for satisfying the performance-based compensation exception under Section 162(m), the Administrator may provide in the case of any Award intended to qualify for such exception that one or more of the Performance Criteria applicable to such Award will be adjusted in an objectively determinable manner to reflect events (for example, but without limitation, acquisitions or dispositions) occurring during the performance period that affect the applicable Performance Criterion or Criteria.

Plan: [The PSC 2007] Equity Incentive Plan as from time to time amended and in effect.

(Continued)

Restricted Stock: Stock subject to restrictions requiring that it be redelivered or offered for sale to the Company if specified conditions are not satisfied.

Restricted Stock Unit: A Stock Unit that is, or as to which the delivery of Stock or cash in lieu of Stock is, subject to the satisfaction of specified performance or other vesting conditions.

Section 162(m): Section 162(m) of the Code.

SAR: A right entitling the holder upon exercise to receive an amount (payable in shares of Stock of equivalent value or cash) equal to the excess of the fair market value of the shares of Stock subject to the right over the fair market value of such shares at the date of grant.

Stock: Common Stock of the Company, [par value $.001] per share.

Stock Option: An option entitling the holder to acquire shares of Stock upon payment of the exercise price.

Stock Unit: An unfunded and unsecured promise, denominated in shares of Stock, to deliver Stock or cash measured by the value of Stock in the future.

Subsidiary Corporation: The term "subsidiary corporation" as used in any Stock Option granted pursuant to this Plan, shall (except as otherwise provided in the Award) have the meaning that is ascribed to that term when contained in Section 422(b) of the Code and the regulations thereunder, and the Company shall be deemed to be the grantor corporation for purposes of applying such meaning.

Unrestricted Stock: Stock that is not subject to any restrictions under the terms of the Award.

necessary or desirable to effectuate the purposes of the Plan and the Awards issued pursuant to it, and such action shall be final, binding, and conclusive upon all parties concerned. The Administrator has discretionary authority, subject only to the express provisions of the Plan, to determine eligibility for and grant Awards; determine, modify or waive the terms and conditions of any Award; prescribe forms, rules, and procedures; and otherwise do all things necessary to carry out the purposes of the Plan. In the case of any Award intended to be eligible for the performance-based compensation exception under Section 162(m), the Administrator will exercise its discretion consistent with qualifying the Award for that exception. No Administrator shall be liable for any act or omission (whether or not negligent) taken or omitted in good faith, or for the exercise of an authority or discretion granted in connection with the Plan, or for the acts or omission of other members of the Committee or other individuals or entities comprising the Administrator.

LIMITS ON AWARDS UNDER THE PLAN

(a) Number of Shares

The maximum number of shares of Stock that may be issued under the Plan and under ISOs issued pursuant to the Plan shall not exceed, in the aggregate, [____] shares of Stock. If any Award expires or is terminated, surrendered, forfeited, or canceled without having been fully exercised or results in any Common Stock not being issued, the shares of Common Stock covered by such Award shall again be available for the grant of Awards under the Plan. With respect to the issuance of SARs that may be settled in stock, the number of shares available for Awards under the Plan will be reduced by the total number of SARs granted. SARs that may be settled in cash only will not reduce the number of shares available for award under the Plan. The limit set forth in this Section 4(a) shall be construed to comply with Section 422 of the Code and regulations thereunder. To the extent consistent with the requirements of Section 422 of the Code and regulations thereunder, and with other applicable legal requirements (including applicable stock exchange requirements), Stock issued under awards of an acquired company that are converted, replaced, or adjusted in connection with the acquisition will not reduce the number of shares available for Awards under the Plan.

(b) Type of Shares

Stock delivered by the Company under the Plan may be authorized but unissued Stock or previously issued Stock acquired by the Company. Except as determined by the Administrator, no fractional shares of Stock will be delivered under the Plan.

(c) Section 162(m) Limits

The maximum number of shares of Stock for which Stock Options may be granted to any person in any fiscal year and the maximum number of shares of Stock subject to SARs granted to any person in any fiscal year will each be [100%] of the aggregate number of Shares that may be issued under the Plan. The maximum number of shares subject to other Awards granted to any person in any fiscal year will be [___] shares of Stock. The foregoing provisions will be construed in a manner consistent with Section 162(m).

(d) Stock Dividends, Stock Splits, etc

In the event of any change in the outstanding shares of the Common Stock of the Company by reason of a stock dividend, stock split, combination of shares, recapitalization, merger, consolidation, transfer of assets, reorganization, conversion or what the Administrator deems in its sole discretion to be similar circumstances, the aggregate number and kind of shares that may be issued under this Plan (including, but not limited to, the provisions of Section 4(a) and Section 4(c) hereof) shall be appropriately adjusted in a manner determined in the sole discretion of the Administrator.

(e) Par Value

Notwithstanding anything herein to the contrary, if a Participant is required by applicable law to pay the par value of the Common Stock subject to an Award, such payment may be made in any form permitted by applicable law, including services performed or contracted to be performed, in the sole discretion of the Administrator.

ELIGIBILITY AND PARTICIPATION

The Administrator will select Participants from among those key current and prospective Employees, directors and consultants to the Company or its Affiliates who, in the opinion of the Administrator, are in a position to make a significant contribution to the success of the Company and its Affiliates. Eligibility for ISOs is limited to Employees of the Company or of a "Parent Corporation" or "Subsidiary Corporation" of the Company on the date of grant of the ISO.

Rules Applicable to Awards

(a) All Awards

(1) Award Provisions. The Administrator will determine the terms of all Awards, subject to the limitations provided herein. By accepting any Award granted hereunder, the Participant agrees to the terms of the Award and the Plan. Notwithstanding any provision of this Plan to the contrary, awards of an acquired company that are converted, replaced, or adjusted in connection with the acquisition may contain terms and conditions that are inconsistent with the terms and conditions specified herein, as determined by the Administrator. No Award shall be legally effective unless it is in writing and the document is signed by the Administrator.

(2) Term of Plan. No Awards may be made under this Plan ten (10) years after date of its adoption by the Board, but previously granted Awards may continue beyond that date in accordance with their terms.

(3) Transferability. An ISO may not be transferred except to the extent permitted by Section 422 of the Code. An Award other than an ISO may not be transferred except to the extent set forth in the Award.

(4) Dividend Equivalents, Etc. The Administrator may provide for the payment of amounts in lieu of cash dividends or other cash distributions with respect to an Award; however, no dividends or other distributions may be paid in connection with an Award of a Stock Option or SAR except to the extent such Stock Option or SAR has been properly exercised.

(5) Rights Limited. Nothing in the Plan will be construed as giving any person the right to continued employment or service with the Company or its Affiliates, or any rights as a stockholder except as to shares of Stock actually issued under the Plan. The loss of existing or potential profit in Awards will not constitute an element of damages in the event of termination of Employment for any reason, even if the termination is in violation of an obligation of the Company or Affiliate to the Participant.

(6) Section 162(m). This Section 6(a)(6) applies to any Performance Award intended to qualify as performance-based for the purposes of Section 162(m) other than a Stock Option or SAR. In the case of any Performance Award to which this Section 6(a)(6) applies, the Plan and such Award will be construed to the maximum extent permitted by law in a manner consistent with qualifying the Award for the performance-based compensation exception under Section 162(m). With respect to such Performance Awards, the Administrator will preestablish, in writing, one or more specific Performance Criteria no later than 90 days after the commencement of the period of service to which the performance relates (or at such earlier time as is required to qualify the Award as perform-ance-based under Section 162(m)). Prior to grant, vesting or payment of the Performance Award, as the case may be, the Administrator will cer-tify whether the applicable Performance Criteria have been attained and such determination will be final and conclusive. No Performance Award to which this Section 6(a)(6) applies may be granted after the first meet-ing of the stockholders of the Company held five (5) or more years after the date of approval of this Plan by the Stockholders of the Company until the listed performance measures set forth in the definition of "Per-formance Criteria" (as originally approved or as subsequently amended) have been resubmitted to and reapproved by the stockholders of the Company in accordance with the requirements of Section 162(m) of the Code, unless such grant is made contingent upon such approval.

(7) Section 409A of the Code.

(i) Awards under the Plan are intended either to be exempt from the rules of Section 409A of the Code or to satisfy those rules and shall be construed accordingly, except as otherwise determined by the Administra-tor. However, the Company shall not be liable to any Participant or other holder of an Award with respect to any Award-related adverse tax conse-quences arising under Section 409A or other provision of the Code.

(ii) If any provision of the Plan or an Award agreement contravenes any regulations or Treasury guidance promulgated under Code Section 409A or could cause an Award to be subject to the interest and penalties under Code Section 409A, such provision of the Plan or Award shall be deemed automatically modified to maintain, to the maximum extent practicable,

the original intent of the applicable provision without violating the provisions of Code Section 409A. Moreover, any discretionary authority that the Administrator may have pursuant to the Plan shall not be applicable to an Award that is subject to Code Section 409A to the extent such discretionary authority will contravene Section 409A or the regulations or guidance promulgated thereunder.

(iii)   Notwithstanding any provisions of this Plan or any Award granted hereunder to the contrary, no acceleration shall occur with respect to any Award to the extent such acceleration would cause the Plan or an Award granted hereunder to fail to comply with Code Section 409A.

(iv)   Notwithstanding any provisions of this Plan or any applicable Award agreement to the contrary, no payment shall be made with respect to any Award granted under this Plan to a "specified employee" (as such term is defined for purposes of Code Section 409A) prior to the six-month anniversary of the employee's separation of service to the extent such six-month delay in payment is required to comply with Code Section 409A.

(v)   In the case of an Award providing for the payment of deferred compensation subject to Section 409A of the Code, and assuming that no other exemption from Section 409A of the Code is applicable, any payment of such deferred compensation by reason of a Change in Control shall be made only if (A) satisfies the definition of Change in Control contained in the Award and, in addition, (B) the Change in Control is one described in subsection (a)(2)(A)(v) of Section 409A and the guidance thereunder, and shall be paid consistent with the requirements of Section 409A. The definitions of Change in Control, as contained in Section 409A of the Code, are summarized in the Change in Control Attachment to this Plan. If any deferred compensation that would otherwise be payable by reason of a Change in Control cannot be paid by reason of the immediately preceding sentence, it shall be paid as soon as practicable thereafter consistent with the requirements of Section 409A, as determined by the Administrator.

(8) For Cause Terminations.   Notwithstanding anything to the contrary contained in this Plan or in any Award, all Awards held by a Participant whose employment, directorship, consulting, service or other relationship with the Company or any Affiliate was terminated for "Cause" shall terminate immediately as of the date of such termination for "Cause", unless otherwise determined by the Administrator in its sole discretion. In addition, if a Participant's employment, directorship, consulting, service or other relationship with the Company or any Affiliate is terminated for "Cause", the Company shall be entitled, in its discretion, to recover all profits earned or realized by the Participant from all Awards then held or previously held by the Participant. A termination of a Participant's employment, directorship, consulting, service or other relationship with the Company or any Affiliate shall be for "Cause" if the Administrator determines that the Participant: (i) was guilty of fraud, gross negligence, or willful misconduct in the performance of his or her duties for the Company or any Affiliate, (ii) willfully and continually failed to perform substantially the Participant's duties with the Company or any Affiliate (other than any such failure resulting from incapacity due to Disability) after delivery of written demand for substantial performance to the Participant by the Board, the Administrator or the Chief Executive Officer that specifically identified the manner in which the Board, the Administrator or the Chief Executive Officer believed the Participant did not substantially perform his or her duties, (iii) breached or violated, in a material respect, any agreement between the Participant and the Company, or any Affiliate or any of the Company's or its Affiliates' codes of conduct or corporate policies, including policy statements regarding conflicts-of-interest, insider trading or confidentiality, (iv) committed a material act of dishonesty or breach of trust, (v) acted in a manner that was inimical or injurious, in a material respect, to the business or interests of the Company or any of its Affiliates, or (vi) was convicted of, or plead guilty or nolo contendere to, a felony or any other crime involving moral turpitude that subjects, or if generally known, would subject the Company or any of its Affiliates to public ridicule or embarrassment.

(b) Stock Options and SARs

(1) Duration of Stock Options and SARs. The latest date on which a Stock Option or a SAR may be exercised will be the tenth anniversary of the date the Stock Option (fifth anniversary in the case of an ISO granted to a ten percent shareholder within the meaning of Section 422(b)(6) of the Code) or SAR was granted, or such earlier date as may have been specified by the Administrator at the time the Stock Option or SAR was granted.

(2) Vesting. The Administrator shall fix the term during which each Stock Option or SAR may be exercised, but no Stock Option or SAR shall be exercisable after the tenth anniversary of its date of grant. A Stock Option and a SAR shall become exercisable as provided in the Award. Notwithstanding any other provision of the Plan, the Administrator may determine with respect to an Award that the date on which any outstanding Stock Option or SAR or any portion thereof is exercisable shall be advanced to an earlier date or dates designated by the Administrator in accordance with such terms and subject to such conditions, if any, as the Administrator shall specify.

(3) Time and Manner of Exercise. Unless the Administrator expressly provides otherwise, an Award requiring exercise by the holder will not be deemed to have been exercised until the Administrator receives a notice of exercise (in form acceptable to the Administrator) signed by the appropriate person and accompanied by any payment required under the Award. If the Award is exercised by any person other than the Participant, the Administrator may require satisfactory evidence that the person exercising the Award has the right to do so.

(4) Exercise Price. Unless otherwise determined by the Administrator, the exercise price (or in the case of a SAR, the base price above on which appreciation is to be measured) of each Award requiring exercise shall be 100% (in the case of an ISO granted to a ten-percent shareholder within the meaning of Section 422(b)(6) of the Code, 110%) of the fair market value of the Stock subject to the Award, determined as of the date of grant, or such higher amount as the Administrator may determine in connection with the grant. Notwithstanding the foregoing, a Stock Option (whether or not an ISO) may be issuing or assuming with an exercise price determined according to the provisions of Section 424(a) of the Code, if such issuance or assumption of such Option is pursuant to a transaction described in Section 424(a) of the Code. If and to the extent required by the corporation law of the state of incorporation by the Company, the exercise price paid for each share of Stock shall not be less than the par value per share of the Stock.

(5) Payment of Exercise Price. Where the exercise of an Award is to be accompanied by payment, the Administrator shall state in the Award the required or permitted forms of payment.

(6) Stock Option and SAR Forms. Unless otherwise determined by the Administrator and subject to the authority of the Administrator set forth in Section 3 hereof, an ISO granted pursuant to this Plan to an Employee shall be issued substantially in the form set forth in Exhibit D.2, which form is hereby incorporated by reference and made a part hereof, and shall contain substantially the terms and conditions set forth therein. Subject to the authority of the Administrator set forth in Section 3 hereof, a Stock Option which is not an ISO granted pursuant to this Plan to an Employee shall be issued substantially in the form set forth in Exhibit X (not shown), which form is hereby incorporated by reference and made a part hereof, and shall contain substantially the terms and conditions set forth therein. Subject to the authority of the Administrator set forth in Section 3 hereof, a SAR granted pursuant to this Plan to an Employee shall be issued substantially in the form set forth in Exhibit D.3 below, which form is hereby incorporated by reference and made a part hereof, and shall contain substantially the terms and conditions set forth therein. Subject to the authority of the Administrator set forth in Section 3 hereof, a Stock Option granted pursuant to this Plan to an individual or entity that is not an Employee shall be issued substantially in the form set forth in Exhibit X (not shown), which form is hereby incorporated by refer-ence and made a part hereof, and shall contain substantially the terms and conditions set forth therein. Subject to the authority of the Administrator set forth in Section 3 hereof, a SAR granted pursuant to this Plan to an individual or entity that is not an Employee shall be issued substantially in the form set forth in Exhibit D.4 below, which form is hereby incorpo-rated by reference and made a part hereof, and shall contain substantially the terms and conditions set forth therein. At the time of the grant of a Stock Option or a SAR, the Administrator may, in the Administrator's sole discretion, amend or supplement any of the terms or conditions contained in Exhibits hereof for any particular Participant, provided that with respect to an ISO, the Stock Option satisfies the requirements for an ISO set forth in the Code.

EXHIBIT D.2   INCENTIVE STOCK OPTION

[Employees of Public or Private Companies, except consider removing paragraph (e) for Public Companies and consider Rule 701 for Private Companies]

To:

Name

_____

Address

_____

Date of Grant: _____

You are hereby granted an option, effective as of the date hereof, to purchase _____ shares of common stock, no par value ("Common Stock"), of [PSC Corporation]., a [Pennsylvania] corporation (the "Company"), at a price of $ _____ per share pursuant to the Company's [2006] Equity Incentive Plan (the "Plan").

This option shall terminate and is not exercisable after ten years from the date of its grant (the "Scheduled Termination Date"), except if terminated earlier as hereafter provided.

Your option may first be exercised on and after one year from the date of grant, but not before that time. On and after one year and prior to two years from the date of grant, your option may be exercised for up to [25%] of the total number of shares subject to the option minus the number of shares previously purchased by exercise of the option (as adjusted for any change in the outstanding shares of the Common Stock of the Company by reason of a stock dividend, stock split, combination of shares, recapitalization, merger, consolidation, transfer of assets, reorganization, conversion or what the Administrator deems in its sole discretion to be similar circumstances). Each succeeding year thereafter your option may be exercised for up to an additional [25%] of the total number of shares subject to the option minus the number of shares previously purchased by exercise of the option (as adjusted for any change in the outstanding shares of the Common Stock of the Company by reason of a stock dividend, stock split, combination of shares, recapitalization, merger,

(Continued)

consolidation, transfer of assets, reorganization, conversion or what the Administrator deems in its sole discretion to be similar circumstances). Thus, this option is fully exercisable on and after three years after the date of grant, except if terminated earlier as provided herein.

In the event of a "Change in Control" (as defined in the Plan) of the Company, your option may, from and after the date (the "Acceleration Event") which is six months after the Change in Control, and notwithstanding the immediately preceding paragraph, be exercised for up to 100% of the total number of shares then subject to the option minus the number of shares previously purchased upon exercise of the option (as adjusted for any change in the outstanding shares of the Common Stock of the Company by reason of a stock dividend, stock split, combination of shares, recapitalization, merger, consolidation, transfer of assets, reorganization, conversion or what the Administrator deems in its sole discretion to be similar circumstances) and your vesting date will accelerate accordingly.

You may exercise your option by giving written notice to the Secretary of the Company on forms supplied by the Company at its then principal executive office, accompanied by payment of the option price for the total number of shares you specify that you wish to purchase. The payment may be in any of the following forms: (a) cash, which may be evidenced by a check and includes cash received from a stock brokerage firm in a so-called "cashless exercise"; (b) (unless prohibited by the Administrator) certificates representing shares of Common Stock of the Company, which will be valued by the Secretary of the Company at the fair market value per share of the Company's Common Stock (as determined in accordance with the Plan) on the date of delivery of such certificates to the Company, accompanied by an assignment of the stock to the Company; or (c) (unless prohibited by the Administrator) any combination of cash and Common Stock of the Company valued as provided in clause (b). The use of the so-called "attestation procedure") to exercise a stock option may be permitted by the Administrator. Any assignment of stock shall be in a form and substance satisfactory to the Secretary of the Company, including guarantees of signature(s) and payment of all transfer taxes if the Secretary deems such guarantees necessary or desirable.

Your option will, to the extent not previously exercised by you, terminate three months after the date on which your employment by the Company or a Company subsidiary corporation is terminated (whether such termination be voluntary or involuntary) other than by reason of Disability (as defined in the Plan) or death, in which case your option will terminate one year from the date of termination of employment due to Disability or death (but in no event later than the Scheduled Termination Date). After the date your employment is terminated, as aforesaid, you may exercise this option only for the number of shares which you had a right to purchase and did not purchase on the date your employment terminated. Provided you are willing to continue your employment for the Company or a successor after a Change in Control at the same compensation you enjoyed immediately prior to such Change in Control, if your employment is involuntarily terminated without cause after a Change in Control and prior to the Acceleration Event, you may exercise this option for the number of shares you would have had a right to purchase on the date of an Acceleration Event. If you are employed by a Company subsidiary corporation, your employment shall be deemed to have terminated on the date your employer ceases to be a Company subsidiary corporation, unless you are on that date transferred to the Company or another Company subsidiary corporation. Your employment shall not be deemed to have terminated if you are transferred from the Company to a Company subsidiary corporation, or vice versa, or from one Company subsidiary corporation to another Company subsidiary corporation.

If you die while employed by the Company or a Company subsidiary corporation, your executor or administrator, as the case may be, may, at any time within one year after the date of your death (but in no event later than the Scheduled Termination Date), exercise the option as to any shares which you had a right to purchase and did not purchase during your lifetime. If your employment with the Company or a Company parent or subsidiary corporation is terminated by reason of your Disability, you or your legal guardian or custodian may at any time within one year after the date of such termination (but in no event later than the Scheduled Termination Date), exercise the option as to any shares which you had a right to purchase and did not purchase prior to such termination. Your executor, administrator, guardian or custodian must present proof of his authority satisfactory to the Company prior to being allowed to exercise this option.

In the event of any change in the outstanding shares of the Common Stock of the Company by reason of a stock dividend, stock split, combination of shares, recapitalization, merger, consolidation, transfer of assets, reorganization, conversion or what the Administrator deems in its sole discretion to be similar circumstances, the number and kind of shares subject to this option and the option price of such shares shall be appropriately adjusted in a manner to be determined by the Administrator, whose decision shall be final, binding and conclusive in the absence of clear and convincing evidence of bad faith.

In the event of a liquidation or proposed liquidation of the Company, including (but not limited to) a transfer of assets followed by a liquidation of the

(Continued)

Company, or in the event of a Change in Control (as defined in the Plan) or proposed Change in Control, the Administrator shall have the right to require you to exercise this option upon thirty (30) days prior written notice to you. If at the time such written notice is given this option is not otherwise exercisable, the written notice will set forth your right to exercise this option even though it is not otherwise exercisable. In the event this option is not exercised by you within the thirty (30) day period set forth in such written notice, this option shall terminate on the last day of such thirty (30) day period, notwithstanding anything to the contrary contained in this option.

This option is not transferable otherwise than by will or the laws of descent and distribution, and is exercisable during your lifetime only by you, including, for this purpose, your legal guardian or custodian in the event of Disability. Until the option price has been paid in full pursuant to due exercise of this option and the purchased shares are delivered to you, you do not have any rights as a shareholder of the Company. The Company reserves the right not to deliver to you the shares purchased by virtue of the exercise of this option during any period of time in which the Company deems, in its sole discretion, that such delivery would violate a federal, state, local or securities exchange rule, regulation or law.

Notwithstanding anything to the contrary contained herein, this option is not exercisable until all the following events occur and during the following periods of time:

(a) Until the Plan pursuant to which this option is granted is approved by the shareholders of the Company in the manner required by any applicable provision of the Code (as defined in the Plan) and the regulations thereunder and any applicable securities exchange or listing rule or agreement;

(b) Until this option and the optioned shares are approved, registered and listed with such federal, state, local and foreign regulatory bodies or agencies and securities exchanges as the Company may deem necessary or desirable, or the Company deems such option or optioned shares to be exempted therefrom;

(c) During any period of time in which the Company deems that the exercisability of this option, the offer to sell the shares optioned hereunder, or the sale thereof, may violate a federal, state, local or foreign law, rule or regulation, or any applicable securities exchange or listing rule or agreement, or may cause the Company to be legally obligated to issue or sell more shares than the Company is legally entitled to issue or sell;

(d) Until you have paid or made suitable arrangements to pay (which may include payment through the surrender of Common Stock, unless prohibited by the Administrator) (i) all federal, state, local and foreign tax withholding required by the Company in connection with the option exercise and (ii) the employee's portion of other federal, state, local and foreign payroll and other taxes due in connection with the option exercise; or

(e) Until you have executed such shareholder agreements as shall be required by the Company. Such shareholder agreements may, at the Company's option, include (among other provisions) provisions requiring you to (i) enter into any "lock-up" agreements required by underwriters, (ii) enter into voting trust agreements, (iii) grant to the Company or its nominees an option to repurchase the stock, (iv) not sell, pledge or otherwise dispose of the stock without the consent of the Company, (v) maintain any tax elections made by the Company, (vi) grant rights of first refusal to the Company or its nominees with respect to the stock, and (vii) join in any sale of a majority or all of the outstanding stock of the Company.

The following two paragraphs shall be applicable if, on the date of exercise of this option, no registration statement and current prospectus under the Securities Act of 1933 covers the Common Stock to be purchased pursuant to such exercise, and shall continue to be applicable for so long as such registration has not occurred and such current prospectus is not available:

(a) You hereby agree, warrant and represent that you will acquire the Common Stock to be issued hereunder for your own account for investment purposes only, and not with a view to, or in connection with, any resale or other distribution of any of such shares, except as hereafter permitted. You further agree that you will not at any time make any offer, sale, transfer, pledge or other disposition of such Common Stock to be issued hereunder without an effective registration statement under the Securities Act of 1933, as amended, and under any applicable state securities laws or an opinion of counsel acceptable to the Company to the effect that the proposed transaction will be exempt from such registration. You agree to execute such instruments, representations, acknowledgments and agreements as the Company may, in its sole discretion, deem advisable to avoid any violation of federal, state, local or foreign law, rule or regulation, or any securities exchange rule or listing agreement.

(b) The certificates for the Common Stock to be issued to you hereunder shall bear the following legend:

> "The shares represented by this certificate have not been registered under the Securities Act of 1933, as amended, or under applicable state securities laws. The shares have been acquired for investment and may not be offered, sold, transferred, pledged or otherwise disposed of without an effective registration statement under the Securities Act of 1933, as amended, and under any applicable

(Continued)

state securities laws or an opinion of counsel acceptable to the Company that the proposed transaction will be exempt from such registration."

The foregoing legend shall be removed upon registration of the legended shares under the Securities Act of 1933, as amended, and under any applicable state laws, and the availability of a current prospectus, or upon receipt of any opinion of counsel acceptable to the Company that such registration and current prospectus are no longer required.

The sole purpose of the agreements, warranties, representations and legend set forth in the two immediately preceding paragraphs is to prevent violations of the Securities Act of 1933, as amended, and any applicable state securities laws.

It is the intention of the Company and you that this option shall, if possible, be an "Incentive Stock Option" as that term is used in Section 422(b) of the Code and the regulations thereunder. In the event this option is in any way inconsistent with the legal requirements of the Code or the regulations thereunder for an "Incentive Stock Option," this option shall be deemed automatically amended as of the date hereof to conform to such legal requirements, if such conformity may be achieved by amendment. To the extent that the number of shares subject to this option which are exercisable for the first time exceed the $100,000 limitation contained in Section 422(d) of the Code, this option will not be considered an Incentive Stock Option.

Nothing herein shall modify your status as an at-will employee of the Company or any of its Affiliates (as defined in the Plan). Further, nothing herein guarantees you employment for any specified period of time. This means that either you or the Company or any of its Affiliates may terminate your employment at any time for any reason, with or without cause, or for no reason. You recognize that, for instance, you may terminate your employment or the Company or any of its Affiliates may terminate your employment prior to the date on which your option becomes vested or exercisable.

You understand and agree that the existence of this option will not affect in any way the right or power of the Company or its shareholders to make or authorize any or all adjustments, recapitalizations, reorganizations, or other changes in the Company's capital structure or its business, or any merger or consolidation of the Company, or any issuance of bonds, debentures, preferred or other stocks with preference ahead of or convertible into, or otherwise affecting the common shares or the rights thereof, or the dissolution or liquidation of the Company, or any sale or transfer of all or any part of its assets or business, or any other corporate act or proceeding, whether of a similar character or otherwise.

Any notice you give to the Company must be in writing and either hand-delivered or mailed to the office of the General Counsel of the Company. If mailed, it should be addressed to the General Counsel of the Company at its then main headquarters. Any notice given to you will be addressed to you at your address as reflected on the personnel records of the Company. You and the Company may change the address for notice by like notice to the other. Notice will be deemed to have been duly delivered when hand-delivered or, if mailed, on the day such notice is postmarked.

Any dispute or disagreement between you and the Company with respect to any portion of this option (excluding Attachment A hereto) or its validity, construction, meaning, performance or your rights hereunder shall be settled by arbitration, at a location designated by the Company, in accordance with the Commercial Arbitration Rules of the American Arbitration Association or its successor, as amended from time to time. However, prior to submission to arbitration you will attempt to resolve any disputes or disagreements with the Company over this option amicably and informally, in good faith, for a period not to exceed two weeks. Thereafter, the dispute or disagreement will be submitted to arbitration. At any time prior to a decision from the arbitrator(s) being rendered, you and the Company may resolve the dispute by settlement. You and the Company shall equally share the costs charged by the American Arbitration Association or its successor, but you and the Company shall otherwise be solely responsible for your own respective counsel fees and expenses. The decision of the arbitrator(s) shall be made in writing, setting forth the award, the reasons for the decision and award and shall be binding and conclusive on you and the Company. Further, neither you nor the Company shall appeal any such award. Judgment of a court of competent jurisdiction may be entered upon the award and may be enforced as such in accordance with the provisions of the award.

This option shall be subject to the terms of the Plan in effect on the date this option is granted, which terms are hereby incorporated herein by reference and made a part hereof. In the event of any conflict between the terms of this option and the terms of the Plan in effect on the date of this option, the terms of the Plan shall govern. This option constitutes the entire understanding between the Company and you with respect to the subject matter hereof and no amendment, supplement or waiver of this option, in whole or in part, shall be binding upon the Company unless in writing and signed by the President of the Company. This option and the performances of the parties hereunder shall be construed in accordance with and governed by the laws of the Commonwealth of Pennsylvania.

In consideration of the grant to you of this option, you hereby agree to the confidentiality and non-interference provisions set forth in Attachment A hereto.

(Continued)

EXHIBIT D.2   (CONTINUED)

Please sign the copy of this option and return it to the Company's Secretary, thereby indicating your understanding of and agreement with its terms and conditions, **including Attachment A hereto.**

[PSC CORPORATION]

By: _____

ACKNOWLEDGMENT

I hereby acknowledge receipt of a copy of the Plan. I hereby represent that I have read and understood the terms and conditions of the Plan and of this option, **including Attachment A, hereto**. I hereby signify my understanding of, and my agreement with, the terms and conditions of the Plan and of this option, **including Attachment A, hereto**. I agree to accept as binding, conclusive, and final all decisions or interpretations of the Administrator concerning any questions arising under the Plan with respect to this option. I accept this option in full satisfaction of any previous written or verbal promise made to me by the Company or any of its Affiliates with respect to option or stock grants.

Date: _____   _____

Signature of Optionee

_____

Print Name

ATTACHMENT **A** TO STOCK OPTION

Confidentiality and Non-Interference.

(a)   You covenant and agree that, in consideration of the grant to you of this stock option, you will not, during your employment with the Company or at any time thereafter, except with the express prior written consent of the Company or pursuant to the lawful order of any judicial or administrative agency of government, directly or indirectly, disclose, communicate or divulge to any individual or entity, or use for the benefit of any individual or entity, any knowledge or information with respect to the conduct or details of the Company's business which you, acting reasonably, believe or should believe to be of a confidential nature and the disclosure of which not to be in the Company's interest.

(b)   You covenant and agree that, in consideration of the grant to you of this stock option, you will not, during your employment with the Company, except with the express prior written consent of the Company, directly or indirectly, whether as employee, owner, partner, member, consultant, agent, director, officer, shareholder or in any other capacity, engage in or assist any individual or entity to engage in any act or action which you, acting reasonably, believe or should believe would be harmful or inimical to the interests of the Company.

(c)   You covenant and agree that, in consideration of the grant to you of this stock option, you will not, for a period of two years after your employment with the Company ceases for any reason whatsoever (whether voluntary or not), except with the express prior written consent of the Company, directly or indirectly, whether as employee, owner, partner, member, consultant, agent, director, officer, shareholder or in any other capacity, for your own account or for the benefit of any individual or entity, (i) solicit any customer of the Company for business which would result in such customer terminating their relationship with the Company; or (ii) solicit or induce any individual or entity which is an employee of the Company to leave the Company or to otherwise terminate their relationship with the Company.

(d)   The parties agree that any breach by you of any of the covenants or agreements contained in this Attachment A will result in irreparable injury to the Company for which money damages could not adequately compensate the Company and therefore, in the event of any such breach, the Company shall be entitled (in addition to any other rights and remedies which it may have at law or in equity) to have an injunction issued by any competent court enjoining and restraining you and/or any other individual or entity involved therein from continuing such breach. The existence of any claim or cause of action which you may have against the Company or any other individual or entity shall not constitute a defense or bar to the enforcement of such covenants. If the Company

(Continued)

is obliged to resort to the courts for the enforcement of any of the covenants or agreements contained in this Attachment A, or if such covenants or agreements are otherwise the subject of litigation between the parties, and the Company prevails in such enforcement or litigation, then the term of such covenants and agreements shall be extended for a period of time equal to the period of such breach, which extension shall commence on the later of (a) the date on which the original (unextended) term of such covenants and agreements is scheduled to terminate or (b) the date of the final court order (without further right of appeal) enforcing such covenant or agreement.

(e)   If any portion of the covenants or agreements contained in this Attach-ment A, or the application hereof, is construed to be invalid or unenforceable, the other portions of such covenant(s) or agreement(s) or the application thereof shall not be affected and shall be given full force and effect without regard to the invalid or enforceable portions to the fullest extent possible. If any covenant or agreement in this Attachment A is held unenforceable because of the area covered, the duration thereof, or the scope thereof, then the court making such determination shall have the power to reduce the area and/or duration and/or limit the scope thereof, and the covenant or agreement shall then be enforceable in its reduced form.

(f)   For purposes of this Attachment A, the term "the Company" shall include the Company, any successor to the Company and all present and future direct and indirect subsidiaries and affiliates of the Company.

EXHIBIT D.3   **STOCK APPRECIATION RIGHT FOR OFFICERS AND OTHER KEY EMPLOYEES**

[EMPLOYEES OF PUBLIC OR PRIVATE COMPANIES, EXCEPT CONSIDER
REMOVING PARAGRAPH (E) FOR PUBLIC COMPANIES AND CONSIDER RULE
701 FOR PRIVATE COMPANIES]

To:

Name

_____

Address

_____

Date of Grant: _____

You are hereby granted a stock appreciation right ("SAR"), effective as of the date hereof, with respect to _____ shares of common stock, no par value ("Common Stock" OR "shares"), of [PSC Corporation], a [Pennsylvania] corporation (the "Company"), at an exercise base price of $ ____ per share pursuant to the Company's [2006] Equity Incentive Plan (the "Plan").

This SAR shall terminate and is not exercisable after ten years from the date of its grant (the "Scheduled Termination Date"), except if terminated earlier as hereafter provided.

Your SAR may first be exercised on and after one year from the date of grant, but not before that time. On and after one year and prior to two years from the date of grant, your SAR may be exercised for up to 25% of the total number of shares subject to the SAR minus the number of shares previously purchased by exercise of the SAR (as adjusted for any change in the outstanding shares of the Common Stock of the Company by reason of a stock dividend, stock split, combination of shares, recapitalization, merger, consolidation, transfer of assets, reorganization, conversion or what the Administrator deems in its sole discretion to be similar circumstances). Each succeeding year thereafter your SAR may be exercised for up to an additional 25% of the total number of shares subject to the SAR minus the number of shares previously purchased by exercise of the SAR (as adjusted for any change in the outstanding shares of the Common Stock of the Company by reason of a stock dividend, stock split, combination of shares, recapitalization, merger, consolidation, transfer of assets, reorganization, conversion or what the Administrator deems in its sole discretion to be

(Continued)

similar circumstances). Thus, this SAR is fully exercisable on and after four years after the date of grant, except if terminated earlier as provided herein.

In the event of a "Change in Control" (as defined in the Plan) of the Company, your SAR may, from and after the date (the "Acceleration Event") which is six months after the Change in Control, and notwithstanding the immediately preceding paragraph, be exercised for up to 100% of the total number of shares then subject to the SAR minus the number of shares previously purchased upon exercise of the SAR (as adjusted for any change in the outstanding shares of the Common Stock of the Company by reason of a stock dividend, stock split, combination of shares, recapitalization, merger, consolidation, transfer of assets, reorganization, conversion or what the Administrator deems in its sole discretion to be similar circumstances) and your vesting date will accelerate accordingly.

You may exercise your SAR by giving written notice to the Secretary of the Company on forms supplied by the Company at its then principal executive office, accompanied by a designation of the total number of shares with respect to which you are exercising your SAR. Upon proper exercise of your SAR, you will be entitled to receive, with respect to the shares for which you are exercising your SAR, that number of whole shares of common stock that is closest in Fair Market Value (but does not exceed) the excess (if any) of (i) the Fair Market Value of the common stock on the last trading date preceding the receipt by the Company of the written exercise notice (or if there is no trading in the common stock on such date, on the next preceding date on which there was trading) as reported in *The Wall Street Journal* (or other reporting service approved by the Administrator) over (ii) the exercise base price for each of the SAR. No fractional shares of common stock shall be issued; instead, cash shall be distributed equal in Fair Market Value to the value of a whole share of common stock multiplied by the such fraction. In the event that shares of common stock are not publicly traded at the time a determination of Fair Market Value is required to be made herein, the determination of Fair Market Value shall be made in good faith by the Administrator. The Administrator's determination of Fair Market Value shall be final, binding and conclusive in absence of clear and convincing evidence that such decision was not made in good faith.

Your SAR will, to the extent not previously exercised by you, terminate three months after the date on which your employment by the Company or a Company subsidiary corporation is terminated (whether such termination be voluntary or involuntary) other than by reason of Disability (as defined in the Plan) or death, in which case your SAR will terminate one year from the date of termination of employment due to Disability or death (but in no event later than the Scheduled Termination Date). After the date your employment is terminated, as aforesaid, you may exercise this SAR only for the number of shares which you had a right to acquire upon exercise of this SAR and did not so acquire on the date your employment terminated. Provided you are willing to continue your employment for the Company or a successor after a Change in Control at the same compensation you enjoyed immediately prior to such Change in Control, if your employment is involuntarily terminated without cause after a Change in Control and prior to the Acceleration Event, you may exercise this SAR for the number of shares you would have had a right to acquire upon exercise of this SAR on the date of an Acceleration Event. If you are employed by a Company subsidiary corporation, your employment shall be deemed to have terminated on the date your employer ceases to be a Company subsidiary corporation, unless you are on that date transferred to the Company or another Company subsidiary corporation. Your employment shall not be deemed to have terminated if you are transferred from the Company to a Company subsidiary corporation, or vice versa, or from one Company subsidiary corporation to another Company subsidiary corporation.

If you die while employed by the Company or a Company subsidiary corporation, your executor or administrator, as the case may be, may, at any time within one year after the date of your death (but in no event later than the Scheduled Termination Date), exercise the SAR as to any shares which you had a right to acquire upon exercise of this SAR and did not so acquire during your lifetime. If your employment with the Company or a Company parent or subsidiary corporation is terminated by reason of your Disability, you or your legal guardian or custodian may at any time within one year after the date of such termination (but in no event later than the Scheduled Termination Date), exercise the SAR as to any shares which you had a right to acquire upon exercise of this SAR and did not so acquire prior to such termination. Your executor, administrator, guardian or custodian must present proof of his authority satisfactory to the Company prior to being allowed to exercise this SAR.

In the event of any change in the outstanding shares of the Common Stock of the Company by reason of a stock dividend, stock split, combination of shares, recapitalization, merger, consolidation, transfer of assets, reorganization, conversion or what the Administrator deems in its sole discretion to be similar circumstances, the number and kind of shares subject to this SAR and the exercised base price of such shares shall be appropriately adjusted in a manner to be determined by the Administrator, whose decision shall be final, binding and conclusive in the absence of clear and convincing evidence of bad faith.

(Continued)

**In the event of a liquidation or proposed liquidation of the Company, includ-
ing (but not limited to) a transfer of assets followed by a liquidation of the
Company, or in the event of a Change in Control (as defined in the Plan) or proposed Change in Control, the Administrator shall have the right to require you
to exercise this SAR upon thirty (30) days prior written notice to you. If at the
time such written notice is given this SAR is not otherwise exercisable, the
written notice will set forth your right to exercise this SAR even though it is not
otherwise exercisable. In the event this SAR is not exercised by you within the
thirty (30) day period set forth in such written notice, this SAR shall terminate
on the last day of such thirty (30) day period, notwithstanding anything to the
contrary contained in this SAR.**

This SAR is not transferable otherwise than by will or the laws of descent
and distribution, and is exercisable during your lifetime only by you, including,
for this purpose, your legal guardian or custodian in the event of Disability.
Until the shares acquired upon exercise of this SAR are delivered to you, you do
not have any rights as a shareholder of the Company. The Company reserves
the right not to deliver to you the shares purchased by virtue of the exercise of
this SAR during any period of time in which the Company deems, in its sole
discretion, that such delivery would violate a federal, state, local or securities
exchange rule, regulation or law.

Notwithstanding anything to the contrary contained herein, this SAR is not
exercisable until all the following events occur and during the following periods
of time:

(a) Until the Plan pursuant to which this SAR is granted is approved by the
shareholders of the Company in the manner required by any applicable provision of the Code (as defined in the Plan) and the regulations thereunder and
any applicable securities exchange or listing rule or agreement;

(b) Until this SAR and the SAR shares are approved, registered and listed
with such federal, state, local and foreign regulatory bodies or agencies and
securities exchanges as the Company may deem necessary or desirable, or the
Company deems such SAR or SAR shares to be exempted therefrom;

(c) During any period of time in which the Company deems that the exercisability of this SAR, the offer to sell the shares which may be acquired under this
SAR, or the sale thereof, may violate a federal, state, local or foreign law, rule
or regulation, or any applicable securities exchange or listing rule or agreement, or may cause the Company to be legally obligated to issue or sell more
shares than the Company is legally entitled to issue or sell;

(d) Until you have paid or made suitable arrangements to pay (which may
include payment through the surrender of Common Stock, unless prohibited by

the Administrator) (i) all federal, state, local and foreign tax withholding required by the Company in connection with the SAR exercise and (ii) the employee's portion of other federal, state, local and foreign payroll and other taxes due in connection with the SAR exercise; or

(e) Until you have executed such shareholder agreements as shall be required by the Company. Such shareholder agreements may, at the Company's SAR, include (among other provisions) provisions requiring you to (i) enter into any "lock-up" agreements required by underwriters, (ii) enter into voting trust agreements, (iii) grant to the Company or its nominees a SAR to repurchase the stock, (iv) not sell, pledge or otherwise dispose of the stock without the consent of the Company, (v) maintain any tax elections made by the Company, (vi) grant rights of first refusal to the Company or its nominees with respect to the stock, and (vii) join in any sale of a majority or all of the outstanding stock of the Company.

The following two paragraphs shall be applicable if, on the date of exercise of this SAR, no registration statement and current prospectus under the Securities Act of 1933 covers the Common Stock to be purchased pursuant to such exercise, and shall continue to be applicable for so long as such registration has not occurred and such current prospectus is not available:

(a) You hereby agree, warrant and represent that you will acquire the Common Stock to be issued hereunder for your own account for investment purposes only, and not with a view to, or in connection with, any resale or other distribution of any of such shares, except as hereafter permitted. You further agree that you will not at any time make any offer, sale, transfer, pledge or other disposition of such Common Stock to be issued hereunder without an effective registration statement under the Securities Act of 1933, as amended, and under any applicable state securities laws or an opinion of counsel acceptable to the Company to the effect that the proposed transaction will be exempt from such registration. You agree to execute such instruments, representations, acknowledgments and agreements as the Company may, in its sole discretion, deem advisable to avoid any violation of federal, state, local or foreign law, rule or regulation, or any securities exchange rule or listing agreement.

(b) The certificates for the Common Stock to be issued to you hereunder shall bear the following legend:

> "The shares represented by this certificate have not been registered under the Securities Act of 1933, as amended, or under applicable state securities laws. The shares have been acquired for investment and may not be offered, sold, transferred, pledged or otherwise disposed of without an effective registration statement under the Securities Act of 1933, as amended, and under any applicable state securities laws or an opinion of counsel acceptable to the Company that the proposed transaction will be exempt from such registration."

(Continued)

The foregoing legend shall be removed upon registration of the legended shares under the Securities Act of 1933, as amended, and under any applicable state laws or upon receipt of any opinion of counsel acceptable to the Company that said registration is no longer required.

The sole purpose of the agreements, warranties, representations and legend set forth in the two immediately preceding paragraphs is to prevent violations of the Securities Act of 1933, as amended, and any applicable state securities laws.

Nothing herein shall modify your status as an at-will employee of the Company or any of its Affiliates (as defined in the Plan). Further, nothing herein guarantees you employment for any specified period of time. This means that either you or the Company or any of its Affiliates may terminate your employment at any time for any reason, with or without cause, or for no reason. You recognize that, for instance, you may terminate your employment or the Company or any of its Affiliates may terminate your employment prior to the date on which your SAR becomes vested or exercisable.

You understand and agree that the existence of this SAR will not affect in any way the right or power of the Company or its shareholders to make or authorize any or all adjustments, recapitalizations, reorganizations, or other changes in the Company's capital structure or its business, or any merger or consolidation of the Company, or any issuance of bonds, debentures, preferred or other stocks with preference ahead of or convertible into, or otherwise affecting the common shares or the rights thereof, or the dissolution or liquidation of the Company, or any sale or transfer of all or any part of its assets or business, or any other corporate act or proceeding, whether of a similar character or otherwise.

Any notice you give to the Company must be in writing and either hand-delivered or mailed to the office of the General Counsel of the Company. If mailed, it should be addressed to the General Counsel of the Company at its then main headquarters. Any notice given to you will be addressed to you at your address as reflected on the personnel records of the Company. You and the Company may change the address for notice by like notice to the other. Notice will be deemed to have been duly delivered when hand-delivered or, if mailed, on the day such notice is postmarked.

Any dispute or disagreement between you and the Company with respect to any portion of this SAR (excluding Attachment A hereto) or its validity, construction, meaning, performance or your rights hereunder shall be settled by arbitration, at a location designated by the Company, in accordance with the

Commercial Arbitration Rules of the American Arbitration Association or its successor, as amended from time to time. However, prior to submission to arbitration you will attempt to resolve any disputes or disagreements with the Company over this SAR amicably and informally, in good faith, for a period not to exceed two weeks. Thereafter, the dispute or disagreement will be submitted to arbitration. At any time prior to a decision from the arbitrator(s) being rendered, you and the Company may resolve the dispute by settlement. You and the Company shall equally share the costs charged by the American Arbitration Association or its successor, but you and the Company shall otherwise be solely responsible for your own respective counsel fees and expenses. The decision of the arbitrator(s) shall be made in writing, setting forth the award, the reasons for the decision and award and shall be binding and conclusive on you and the Company. Further, neither you nor the Company shall appeal any such award. Judgment of a court of competent jurisdiction may be entered upon the award and may be enforced as such in accordance with the provisions of the award.

This SAR shall be subject to the terms of the Plan in effect on the date this SAR is granted, which terms are hereby incorporated herein by reference and made a part hereof. In the event of any conflict between the terms of this SAR and the terms of the Plan in effect on the date of this SAR, the terms of the Plan shall govern. This SAR constitutes the entire understanding between the Company and you with respect to the subject matter hereof and no amendment, supplement or waiver of this SAR, in whole or in part, shall be binding upon the Company unless in writing and signed by the President of the Company. This SAR and the performances of the parties hereunder shall be construed in accordance with and governed by the laws of the Commonwealth of Pennsylvania.

In consideration of the grant to you of this SAR, you hereby agree to the confidentiality and non-interference provisions set forth in Attachment A hereto.

Please sign the copy of this SAR and return it to the Company's Secretary, thereby indicating your understanding of and agreement with its terms and conditions, **including Attachment A hereto.**

[PSC CORPORATION]

By:

_____

(Continued)

EXHIBIT D.3   (CONTINUED)

ACKNOWLEDGMENT

I hereby acknowledge receipt of a copy of the Plan. I hereby represent that I have read and understood the terms and conditions of the Plan and of this SAR, **including Attachment A, hereto**. I hereby signify my understanding of, and my agreement with, the terms and conditions of the Plan and of this SAR, **including Attachment A, hereto**. I agree to accept as final, binding and conclusive all decisions or interpretations of the Administrator concerning any questions arising under the Plan with respect to this SAR. I accept this SAR in full satisfaction of any previous written or verbal promise made to me by the Company or any of its Affiliates with respect to SAR or Stock grants.

Date: _____

_____
Signature of Participant

_____
Print Name

ATTACHMENT A TO STOCK APPRECIATION RIGHT

Confidentiality and Non-Interference.

(a) You covenant and agree that, in consideration of the grant to you of this SAR, you will not, during your employment with the Company or at any time thereafter, except with the express prior written consent of the Company or pursuant to the lawful order of any judicial or administrative agency of government, directly or indirectly, disclose, communicate or divulge to any individual or entity, or use for the benefit of any individual or entity, any knowledge or information with respect to the conduct or details of the Company's business which you, acting reasonably, believe or should believe to be of a confidential nature and the disclosure of which not to be in the Company's interest.

(b) You covenant and agree that, in consideration of the grant to you of this SAR, you will not, during your employment with the Company, except with the express prior written consent of the Company, directly or indirectly, whether as employee, owner, partner, member, consultant, agent, director, officer, shareholder or in any other capacity, engage in or assist any individual or entity to engage in any act or action which you, acting reasonably, believe or should believe would be harmful or inimical to the interests of the Company.

(c) You covenant and agree that, in consideration of the grant to you of this SAR, you will not, for a period of two years after your employment with the Company ceases for any reason whatsoever (whether voluntary or not), except with the express prior written consent of the Company, directly or indirectly, whether as employee, owner, partner, member, consultant, agent, director, officer, shareholder or in any other capacity, for your own account or for the benefit of any individual or entity, (i) solicit any customer of the Company for business which would result in such customer terminating their relationship with the Company; or (ii) solicit or induce any individual or entity which is an employee of the Company to leave the Company or to otherwise terminate their relationship with the Company.

(d) The parties agree that any breach by you of any of the covenants or agreements contained in this Attachment A will result in irreparable injury to the Company for which money damages could not adequately compensate the Company and therefore, in the event of any such breach, the Company shall be entitled (in addition to any other rights and remedies which it may have at law or in equity) to have an injunction issued by any competent court enjoining and restraining you and/or any other individual or entity involved therein from continuing such breach. The existence of any claim or cause of action which you may have against the Company or any other individual or entity shall not constitute a defense or bar to the enforcement of such covenants. If the Company

(Continued)

is obliged to resort to the courts for the enforcement of any of the covenants or agreements contained in this Attachment A, or if such covenants or agreements are otherwise the subject of litigation between the parties, and the Company prevails in such enforcement or litigation, then the term of such covenants and agreements shall be extended for a period of time equal to the period of such breach, which extension shall commence on the later of (a) the date on which the original (unextended) term of such covenants and agreements is scheduled to terminate or (b) the date of the final court order (without further right of appeal) enforcing such covenant or agreement.

(e) If any portion of the covenants or agreements contained in this Attachment A, or the application hereof, is construed to be invalid or unenforceable, the other portions of such covenant(s) or agreement(s) or the application thereof shall not be affected and shall be given full force and effect without regard to the invalid or enforceable portions to the fullest extent possible. If any covenant or agreement in this Attachment A is held unenforceable because of the area covered, the duration thereof, or the scope thereof, then the court making such determination shall have the power to reduce the area and/or duration and/or limit the scope thereof, and the covenant or agreement shall then be enforceable in its reduced form.

(f) for purposes of this Attachment A, the term "the Company" shall include the Company, any successor to the Company and all present and future direct and indirect subsidiaries and affiliates of the Company.

| EXHIBIT D.4 | **STOCK APPRECIATION RIGHT FOR DIRECTORS AND IMPORTANT CONSULTANTS** |

[Directors and Consultants of Public or Private Companies,
except consider removing paragraph (e) for Public Companies
and consider Rule 701 for Private Companies]

To:

Name

_____

Address

_____

Date of Grant: _____

You are hereby granted a stock appreciation right ("SAR"), effective as of the date hereof, with respect to _____ shares of common stock, no par value ("Common Stock" OR "shares"), of [PSC Corporation], a [Pennsylvania] corporation (the "Company"), at an exercise base price of $ _____ per share pursuant to the Company's [2006] Equity Incentive Plan (the "Plan").

This SAR shall terminate and is not exercisable after ten years from the date of its grant (the "Scheduled Termination Date"), except if terminated earlier as hereafter provided.

Your SAR may first be exercised on and after one year from the date of grant, but not before that time. On and after one year and prior to two years from the date of grant, your SAR may be exercised for up to 25% of the total number of shares subject to the SAR minus the number of shares previously purchased by exercise of the SAR (as adjusted for any change in the outstanding shares of the Common Stock of the Company by reason of a stock dividend, stock split, combination of shares, recapitalization, merger, consolidation, transfer of assets, reorganization, conversion or what the Administrator deems in its sole discretion to be similar circumstances). Each succeeding year thereafter your SAR may be exercised for up to an additional 25% of the total number of shares subject to the SAR minus the number of shares previously purchased by exercise of the SAR (as adjusted for any change in the outstanding shares of the Common Stock of the Company by reason of a stock dividend, stock split, combination of shares, recapitalization, merger, consolidation, transfer of assets, reorganization, conversion or what the Administrator deems in its sole discretion

(Continued)

to be similar circumstances). Thus, this SAR is fully exercisable on and after four years after the date of grant, except if terminated earlier as provided herein.

In the event of a "Change in Control" (as defined in the Plan) of the Company, your SAR may, from and after the date (the "Acceleration Event") which is six months after the Change in Control, and notwithstanding the immediately preceding paragraph, be exercised for up to 100% of the total number of shares then subject to the SAR minus the number of shares previously purchased upon exercise of the SAR (as adjusted for any change in the outstanding shares of the Common Stock of the Company by reason of a stock dividend, stock split, combination of shares, recapitalization, merger, consolidation, transfer of assets, reorganization, conversion or what the Administrator deems in its sole discretion to be similar circumstances) and your vesting date will accelerate accordingly.

You may exercise your SAR by giving written notice to the Secretary of the Company on forms supplied by the Company at its then principal executive office, accompanied by a designation of the total number of shares with respect to which you are exercising your SAR. Upon proper exercise of your SAR, you will be entitled to receive, with respect to the shares for which you are exercising your SAR, that number of whole shares of common stock that is closest in Fair Market Value (but does not exceed) the excess (if any) of (i) the Fair Market Value of the common stock on the last trading date preceding the receipt by the Company of the written exercise notice (or if there is no trading in the common stock on such date, on the next preceding date on which there was trading) as reported in *The Wall Street Journal* (or other reporting service approved by the Administrator) over (ii) the exercise base price for each of the SAR. No fractional shares of common stock shall be issued; instead, cash shall be distributed equal in Fair Market Value to the value of a whole share of common stock multiplied by the such fraction. In the event that shares of common stock are not publicly traded at the time a determination of Fair Market Value is required to be made herein, the determination of Fair Market Value shall be made in good faith by the Administrator. The Administrator's determination of Fair Market Value shall be final, binding and conclusive in absence of clear and convincing evidence that such decision was not made in good faith.

Your SAR will, to the extent not previously exercised by you, terminate three months after the date on which your directorship or consultancy by the Company or a Company subsidiary corporation is terminated (whether such termination be voluntary or involuntary) other than by reason of Disability (as defined in the Plan) or death, in which case your SAR will terminate one year from the date of termination of directorship or consultancy due to Disability or death (but in no event later than the Scheduled Termination Date). After the date your directorship or consultancy is terminated, as aforesaid, you may exercise this SAR only for the number of shares which you had a right to acquire upon exercise of this SAR and did not so acquire on the date your directorship or consultancy terminated. Provided you are willing to continue your director-ship or consultancy for the Company or a successor after a Change in Control at the same compensation you enjoyed immediately prior to such Change in Control, if your directorship or consultancy is involuntarily terminated without cause after a Change in Control and prior to the Acceleration Event, you may exercise this SAR for the number of shares you would have had a right to acquire upon exercise of this SAR on the date of an Acceleration Event. If you are a director or consultant of a Company subsidiary corporation, your director-ship or consultancy shall be deemed to have terminated on the date your employer ceases to be a Company subsidiary corporation, unless you are on that date transferred to the Company or another Company subsidiary corpora-tion. Your directorship or consultancy shall not be deemed to have terminated if you are transferred from the Company to a Company subsidiary corporation, or vice versa, or from one Company subsidiary corporation to another Com-pany subsidiary corporation.

If you die while a director or consultant of the Company or a Company sub-sidiary corporation, your executor or administrator, as the case may be, may, at any time within one year after the date of your death (but in no event later than the Scheduled Termination Date), exercise the SAR as to any shares which you had a right to acquire upon exercise of this SAR and did not so acquire during your lifetime. If your directorship or consultancy with the Company or a Com-pany parent or subsidiary corporation is terminated by reason of your Disability, you or your legal guardian or custodian may at any time within one year after the date of such termination (but in no event later than the Scheduled Termination Date), exercise the SAR as to any shares which you had a right to acquire upon exercise of this SAR and did not so acquire prior to such termination. Your exec-utor, administrator, guardian or custodian must present proof of his authority satisfactory to the Company prior to being allowed to exercise this SAR.

In the event of any change in the outstanding shares of the Common Stock of the Company by reason of a stock dividend, stock split, combination of shares, recapitalization, merger, consolidation, transfer of assets, reorganiza-tion, conversion or what the Administrator deems in its sole discretion to be similar circumstances, the number and kind of shares subject to this SAR and the exercised base price of such shares shall be appropriately adjusted in a

(Continued)

manner to be determined by the Administrator, whose decision shall be final, binding and conclusive in the absence of clear and convincing evidence of bad faith.

In the event of a liquidation or proposed liquidation of the Company, including (but not limited to) a transfer of assets followed by a liquidation of the Company, or in the event of a Change in Control (as defined in the Plan) or proposed Change in Control, the Administrator shall have the right to require you to exercise this SAR upon thirty (30) days prior written notice to you. If at the time such written notice is given this SAR is not otherwise exercisable, the written notice will set forth your right to exercise this SAR even though it is not otherwise exercisable. In the event this SAR is not exercised by you within the thirty (30) day period set forth in such written notice, this SAR shall terminate on the last day of such thirty (30) day period, notwithstanding anything to the contrary contained in this SAR.

This SAR is not transferable otherwise than by will or the laws of descent and distribution, and is exercisable during your lifetime only by you, including, for this purpose, your legal guardian or custodian in the event of Disability. Until the shares acquired upon exercise of this SAR are delivered to you, you do not have any rights as a shareholder of the Company. The Company reserves the right not to deliver to you the shares purchased by virtue of the exercise of this SAR during any period of time in which the Company deems, in its sole discretion, that such delivery would violate a federal, state, local or securities exchange rule, regulation or law.

Notwithstanding anything to the contrary contained herein, this SAR is not exercisable until all the following events occur and during the following periods of time:

(a) Until the Plan pursuant to which this SAR is granted is approved by the shareholders of the Company in the manner required by any applicable provision of the Code (as defined in the Plan) and the regulations thereunder and any applicable securities exchange or listing rule or agreement;

(b) Until this SAR and the SAR shares are approved, registered and listed with such federal, state, local and foreign regulatory bodies or agencies and securities exchanges as the Company may deem necessary or desirable, or the Company deems such SAR or SAR shares to be exempted therefrom;

(c) During any period of time in which the Company deems that the exercisability of this SAR, the offer to sell the shares which may be acquired under this SAR, or the sale thereof, may violate a federal, state, local or foreign law, rule or regulation, or any applicable securities exchange or listing rule or agreement, or may cause the Company to be legally obligated to issue or sell more shares than the Company is legally entitled to issue or sell;

(d) Until you have paid or made suitable arrangements to pay (which may include payment through the surrender of Common Stock, unless prohibited by the Administrator) (i) all federal, state, local and foreign tax withholding required by the Company in connection with the SAR exercise and (ii) the employee's portion of other federal, state, local and foreign payroll and other taxes due in connection with the SAR exercise; or

(e) Until you have executed such shareholder agreements as shall be required by the Company. Such shareholder agreements may, at the Company's SAR, include (among other provisions) provisions requiring you to (i) enter into any "lock-up" agreements required by underwriters, (ii) enter into voting trust agreements, (iii) grant to the Company or its nominees a SAR to repurchase the stock, (iv) not sell, pledge or otherwise dispose of the stock without the consent of the Company, (v) maintain any tax elections made by the Company, (vi) grant rights of first refusal to the Company or its nominees with respect to the stock, and (vii) join in any sale of a majority or all of the outstanding stock of the Company.

The following two paragraphs shall be applicable if, on the date of exercise of this SAR, no registration statement and current prospectus under the Securities Act of 1933 covers the Common Stock to be purchased pursuant to such exercise, and shall continue to be applicable for so long as such registration has not occurred and such current prospectus is not available:

(a) You hereby agree, warrant, and represent that you will acquire the Common Stock to be issued hereunder for your own account for investment purposes only, and not with a view to, or in connection with, any resale or other distribution of any of such shares, except as hereafter permitted. You further agree that you will not at any time make any offer, sale, transfer, pledge, or other disposition of such Common Stock to be issued hereunder without an effective registration statement under the Securities Act of 1933, as amended, and under any applicable state securities laws or an opinion of counsel acceptable to the Company to the effect that the proposed transaction will be exempt from such registration. You agree to execute such instruments, representations, acknowledgments, and agreements as the Company may, in its sole discretion, deem advisable to avoid any violation of federal, state, local or foreign law, rule or regulation, or any securities exchange rule or listing agreement.

(b) The certificates for the Common Stock to be issued to you hereunder shall bear the following legend:

> "The shares represented by this certificate have not been registered under the Securities Act of 1933, as amended, or under applicable state securities laws. The shares have been acquired for investment and may

(Continued)

not be offered, sold, transferred, pledged or otherwise disposed of without an effective registration statement under the Securities Act of 1933, as amended, and under any applicable state securities laws or an opinion of counsel acceptable to the Company that the proposed transaction will be exempt from such registration."

The foregoing legend shall be removed upon registration of the legended shares under the Securities Act of 1933, as amended, and under any applicable state laws or upon receipt of any opinion of counsel acceptable to the Company that said registration is no longer required.

The sole purpose of the agreements, warranties, representations and legend set forth in the two immediately preceding paragraphs is to prevent violations of the Securities Act of 1933, as amended, and any applicable state securities laws.

Nothing herein guarantees your term as a director of, or consultant to, the Company or any of its Affiliates (as defined in the Plan) for any specified period of time. This means that either you or the Company or any of its Affiliates may terminate your directorship or consultancy at any time for any reason, with or without cause, or for no reason. You recognize that, for instance, the Company or any of its Affiliates may terminate your directorship or consultancy with the Company or any of its Affiliates prior to the date on which your SAR becomes vested or exercisable.

You understand and agree that the existence of this SAR will not affect in any way the right or power of the Company or its shareholders to make or authorize any or all adjustments, recapitalizations, reorganizations, or other changes in the Company's capital structure or its business, or any merger or consolidation of the Company, or any issuance of bonds, debentures, preferred or other stocks with preference ahead of or convertible into, or otherwise affecting the common shares or the rights thereof, or the dissolution or liquidation of the Company, or any sale or transfer of all or any part of its assets or business, or any other corporate act or proceeding, whether of a similar character or otherwise.

Any notice you give to the Company must be in writing and either hand-delivered or mailed to the office of the General Counsel of the Company. If mailed, it should be addressed to the General Counsel of the Company at its then main headquarters. Any notice given to you will be addressed to you at your address as reflected on the records of the Company. You and the Company may change the address for notice by like notice to the other. Notice will be deemed to have been duly delivered when hand-delivered or, if mailed, on the day such notice is postmarked.

Any dispute or disagreement between you and the Company with respect to any portion of this SAR (excluding Attachment A hereto) or its validity, construction, meaning, performance or your rights hereunder shall be settled by arbitration, at a location designated by the Company, in accordance with the Commercial Arbitration Rules of the American Arbitration Association or its successor, as amended from time to time. However, prior to submission to arbitration you will attempt to resolve any disputes or disagreements with the Company over this SAR amicably and informally, in good faith, for a period not to exceed two weeks. Thereafter, the dispute or disagreement will be submitted to arbitration. At any time prior to a decision from the arbitrator(s) being rendered, you and the Company may resolve the dispute by settlement. You and the Company shall equally share the costs charged by the American Arbitration Association or its successor, but you and the Company shall otherwise be solely responsible for your own respective counsel fees and expenses. The decision of the arbitrator(s) shall be made in writing, setting forth the award, the reasons for the decision and award and shall be binding and conclusive on you and the Company. Further, neither you nor the Company shall appeal any such award. Judgment of a court of competent jurisdiction may be entered upon the award and may be enforced as such in accordance with the provisions of the award.

This SAR shall be subject to the terms of the Plan in effect on the date this SAR is granted, which terms are hereby incorporated herein by reference and made a part hereof. In the event of any conflict between the terms of this SAR and the terms of the Plan in effect on the date of this SAR, the terms of the Plan shall govern. This SAR constitutes the entire understanding between the Company and you with respect to the subject matter hereof and no amendment, supplement or waiver of this SAR, in whole or in part, shall be binding upon the Company unless in writing and signed by the President of the Company. This SAR and the performances of the parties hereunder shall be construed in accordance with and governed by the laws of the Commonwealth of Pennsylvania.

In consideration of the grant to you of this SAR, you hereby agree to the confidentiality and non-interference provisions set forth in Attachment A hereto.

Please sign the copy of this SAR and return it to the Company's Secretary, thereby indicating your understanding of and agreement with its terms and conditions, **including Attachment A hereto.**

[PSC CORPORATION]

By: _____

(Continued)

EXHIBIT D.4   (CONTINUED)

ACKNOWLEDGMENT

I hereby acknowledge receipt of a copy of the Plan. I hereby represent that I have read and understood the terms and conditions of the Plan and of this SAR, **including Attachment A, hereto**. I hereby signify my understanding of, and my agreement with, the terms and conditions of the Plan and of this SAR, **including Attachment A, hereto**. I agree to accept as final, binding and conclusive all decisions or interpretations of the Administrator concerning any questions arising under the Plan with respect to this SAR. I accept this SAR in full satisfaction of any previous written or verbal promise made to me by the Company or any of its Affiliates with respect to SAR or Stock grants.

Date: _____

_____
Signature of Participant

_____
Print Name

ATTACHMENT A TO STOCK APPRECIATION

Confidentiality and Non-Interference

(a) You covenant and agree that, in consideration of the grant to you of this SAR, you will not, during your term as a director of, or a consultant to, the Company or at any time thereafter, except with the express prior written consent of the Company or pursuant to the lawful order of any judicial or administrative agency of government, directly or indirectly, disclose, communicate or divulge to any individual or entity, or use for the benefit of any individual or entity, any knowledge or information with respect to the conduct or details of the Company's business which you, acting reasonably, believe or should believe to be of a confidential nature and the disclosure of which not to be in the Company's interest.

(b) You covenant and agree that, in consideration of the grant to you of this SAR, you will not, during your term as a director of, or a consultant to, the Company, except with the express prior written consent of the Company, directly or indirectly, whether as employee, owner, partner, member, consultant, agent, director, officer, shareholder or in any other capacity, engage in or assist any individual or entity to engage in any act or action which you, acting reasonably, believe or should believe would be harmful or inimical to the interests of the Company.

(c) You covenant and agree that, in consideration of the grant to you of this SAR, you will not, for a period of two years after your term as a director of, or a consultant to, the Company ceases for any reason whatsoever (whether voluntary or not), except with the express prior written consent of the Company, directly or indirectly, whether as employee, owner, partner, member, consultant, agent, director, officer, shareholder or in any other capacity, for your own account or for the benefit of any individual or entity, (i) solicit any customer of the Company for business which would result in such customer terminating their relationship with the Company; or (ii) solicit or induce any individual or entity which is an employee of the Company to leave the Company or to otherwise terminate their relationship with the Company.

(d) The parties agree that any breach by you of any of the covenants or agreements contained in this Attachment A will result in irreparable injury to the Company for which money damages could not adequately compensate the Company and therefore, in the event of any such breach, the Company shall be entitled (in addition to any other rights and remedies which it may have at law or in equity) to have an injunction issued by any competent court enjoining and restraining you and/or any other individual or entity involved therein from continuing such breach. The existence of any claim or cause of action which you

(Continued)

may have against the Company or any other individual or entity shall not constitute a defense or bar to the enforcement of such covenants. If the Company is obliged to resort to the courts for the enforcement of any of the covenants or agreements contained in this Attachment A, or if such covenants or agreements are otherwise the subject of litigation between the parties, and the Company prevails in such enforcement or litigation, then the term of such covenants and agreements shall be extended for a period of time equal to the period of such breach, which extension shall commence on the later of (a) the date on which the original (unextended) term of such covenants and agreements is scheduled to terminate or (b) the date of the final court order (without further right of appeal) enforcing such covenant or agreement.

(e) if any portion of the covenants or agreements contained in this Attachment A, or the application hereof, is construed to be invalid or unenforceable, the other portions of such covenant(s) or agreement(s) or the application thereof shall not be affected and shall be given full force and effect without regard to the invalid or enforceable portions to the fullest extent possible. If any covenant or agreement in this Attachment A is held unenforceable because of the area covered, the duration thereof, or the scope thereof, then the court making such determination shall have the power to reduce the area and/or duration and/or limit the scope thereof, and the covenant or agreement shall then be enforceable in its reduced form.

(f) for purposes of this Attachment A, the term "the Company" shall include the Company, any successor to the Company and all present and future direct and indirect subsidiaries and affiliates of the Company.

CHANGE IN CONTROL ATTACHMENT

Code Section 409A Change In Control Definitions

"Change in Control Event" means: (a) a **Change in the Ownership of a Corporation**; (b) a **Change in the Effective Control of a Corporation**; or (c) a **Change in the Ownership of a Substantial Portion of a Corporation's Assets**.

A **Change in the Ownership of a Corporation** occurs on the date that any one person, or more than one person acting as a group (as described below), acquires ownership of stock of the corporation that, together with stock held by such person or group, constitutes more than fifty percent (50%) of the total fair market value or total voting power of the stock of such corporation. However, if any one person, or more than one person acting as a group, is considered to own more than fifty percent (50%) of the total fair market value or total voting power of the stock of a corporation, the acquisition of additional stock by the same person or persons is not considered to cause a change in the ownership of the corporation (or to cause a Change in the Effective Control of a Corporation). An increase in the percentage of stock owned by any one person, or persons acting as a group, as a result of a transaction in which the corporation acquires its stock in exchange for property shall constitute an acquisition of stock for purposes of this definition. The event described herein shall occur when there is a transfer of stock of a corporation (or issuance of stock of a corporation) and stock in such corporation remains outstanding after the transaction. The event described herein shall not occur if any one person, or more than one person acting as a group, is considered to effectively control a corporation (ownership of stock of the corporation possessing 30% or more of the total voting power of the stock of such corporation) and the same person or persons acquire additional control of the corporation.

A **Change in the Effective Control of a Corporation** occurs on the date that either (a) any one person, or more than one person acting as a group (as described below) acquires (or has acquired during the 12-month period ending on the date of the most recent acquisition by such person or persons) ownership of stock of the corporation possessing thirty percent (30%) or more of the total voting power of the stock of such corporation; or (b) a majority of members of the corporation's board of directors is replaced during any 12-month period by directors whose appointment or election is not endorsed by a majority of the members of the corporation's board of directors before the date of the appointment or election, provided that for this purpose, the term corporation refers solely to a Relevant Corporation, for which no other corporation is a Majority Shareholder. A Change in the Effective Control of a Corporation also may occur in any transaction in which either of the two corporations involved in

(Continued)

the transaction has a Change in the Ownership of a Corporation or a Change in the Ownership of a Substantial Portion of a Corporation's Assets. If any one person, or more than one person acting as a group, is considered to effectively control a corporation as described herein, the acquisition of additional control of the corporation by the same person or persons does not constitute a Change in the Effective Control of a Corporation.

For purposes of **Change in the Ownership of a Corporation** and **Change in the Effective Control of a Corporation,** persons will not be considered to be acting as a group solely because they purchase stock of the corporation at the same time, or as a result of the same public offering. However, persons will be considered to be acting as a group if they are owners of a corporation that enters into a merger, consolidation, purchase or acquisition of stock, or similar business transaction with the corporation. If a person, including an entity, owns stock in both corporations that enter into a merger, consolidation, purchase or acquisition of stock, or similar transaction, such shareholder is considered to be acting as a group with other shareholders only with respect to the ownership in that corporation before the transaction giving rise to the change and not with respect to the ownership interest in the other corporation.

A **Change in the Ownership of a Substantial Portion of a Corporation's Assets** occurs on the date that any one person or more than one person acting as a group (as described below) acquires (or has acquired during the 12-month period ending on the date of the most recent acquisition by such person or persons) assets from the corporation that have a total gross fair market value equal to or more than forty percent (40%) of the total gross fair market value of all of the assets of the corporation immediately prior to such acquisition or acquisitions. For this purpose, gross fair market value means the value of the assets of the corporation, or the value of the assets being disposed of, determined without regard to any liabilities associated with such assets.

No **Change in the Ownership of a Substantial Portion of a Corporation's Assets** occurs: (a) if there is a transfer to an entity that is controlled by the shareholders of the transferring corporation immediately after the transfer or (b) if the assets are transferred to – (1) a shareholder of the corporation (immediately before the asset transfer) in exchange for or with respect to its stock; (2) an entity, fifty percent (50%) or more of the total value or voting power of which is owned, directly or indirectly, by the corporation; (3) a person, or more than one person acting as a group, that owns, directly or indirectly, fifty percent (50%) or more of the total value or voting power of all the outstanding stock of the corporation; or (4) an entity, at least fifty percent (50%) of the total value or voting power of which is owned directly or indirectly, by a person described in clause (c). Except as otherwise provided in this definition of **"Change in Control"**, a person's status is determined immediately after the transfer of the assets.

For purposes of a **Change in the Ownership of a Substantial Portion of a Corporation's Assets,** persons will not be considered to be acting as a group solely because they purchase assets of the corporation at the same time. However, persons will be considered to be acting as a group if they are owners of a corporation that enters into a merger, consolidation, purchase or acquisition of assets, or similar business transaction with the corporation. If a person, including an entity shareholder, owns stock in both corporations that enter into a merger, consolidation, purchase or acquisition of assets, or similar transaction, such shareholder is considered to be acting as a group with other shareholders in a corporation only to the extent of the ownership in that corporation before the transaction giving rise to the change and not with respect to the ownership interest in the other corporation.

To constitute any of the Change in Control Events as described herein as to the [service provider], the Change in Control Event must relate to one or more of the following ("Relevant Corporation"): (a) the corporation for whom the [service provider] is performing services at the time of the Change in Control Event; (b) the corporation that is liable for the payment of the deferred compensation (or all corporations liable for the payment if more than one corporation is liable) but only if either the deferred compensation is attributable to the performance of service by the service provider for such corporation (or corporations) or there is a bona fide business purpose for such corporation or corporations to be liable for such payment and, in either case, no significant purpose of making such corporation or corporations liable for such payment is the avoidance of federal income tax; or (c) a corporation that is a Majority Shareholder of a corporation identified in clause (a) or (b), or any corporation in a chain of corporations in which each corporation is a Majority Shareholder of another corporation in the chain, ending in a corporation identified in clause (a) or (b). Majority Shareholder means a shareholder owning more than fifty percent (50%) of the total fair market value <u>and</u> total voting power of such corporation.

To determine whether a Change in Control Event has occurred, Section 318(a) of the Internal Revenue Code of 1986, as amended (describing attribution of stock to family members, from partnerships, estates, trusts, and corporations, to partnerships, estates, trusts and corporations. and with regard to options) shall apply. Stock underlying a vested option is considered owned by the individual who holds the vested option (and the stock underlying an

(Continued)

unvested option is not considered owned by the individual who holds the unvested option). However, if a vested option is exercisable for stock that is not substantially vested (as defined in Treas. Reg. Section 1.83-3(b) and (j)), the stock underlying the option is not treated as owned by the individual who holds the option.

As defined herein, the meaning of Change in Control Event is intended to be coterminous with the meaning thereof set forth in Code Section 409A and the guidance issued thereunder and shall be construed in a manner consistent therewith.

In the event that the Relevant Entity is a partnership, **Change in the Ownership of a Corporation** and **Change in the Ownership of a Substantial Portion of a Corporation's Assets** shall apply by analogy to changes in the ownership of a partnership and changes in the ownership of a substantial portion of the assets of a partnership. Any reference to corporations, shareholders, and stock shall be treated as referring also to partnerships, partners, and partnership interests, respectively, and any reference to Majority Shareholder shall be treated as referring to a partner that (a) owns more than fifty percent (50%) of the capital and profits interests of such partnership and (b) alone or together with others is vested with the continuing exclusive authority to make the management decisions necessary to conduct the business for which the partnership was formed.

(7) Notification by Employees. Any Employee who disposes of shares acquired upon the exercise of an ISO either (i) within two years from the date of grant of such ISO or (ii) within one year after the transfer of such shares to the Employee shall notify the Company of such disposition and of the amount realized upon such disposition.

(c) Restricted Stock and Other Awards Not Requiring Exercise

(1) Consideration in General. In general, Awards that do not require exercise may be made in exchange for such lawful consideration, including services, as the Administrator determines. Any purchase price payable by a Participant to the Company for Stock under an Award not requiring exercise shall be paid in cash or check acceptable to the Administrator, through the delivery of shares of Stock that have been outstanding for at least six months (unless the Administrator approves a shorter period) and that have a fair market value equal to the purchase price, if and to the extent permitted by the Administrator, by delivery to the Company of a promissory note of the Participant, payable on such terms as are specified by the Administrator, or by any combination of the foregoing permissible forms of payment.

(2) Vesting.   Restricted Stock shall be granted subject to such restrictions on the full enjoyment of the shares as the Administrator shall specify; which restrictions may be based on the passage of time, satisfaction of Performance Criteria, or the occurrence of one or more events; and shall lapse separately or in combination upon such conditions and at such time or times, in installments or otherwise, as the Administrator shall specify.

(3) Restricted Stock Agreement Forms.   Unless otherwise determined by the Administrator and subject to the authority of the Administrator set forth in Section 3 hereof, Restricted Stock awarded pursuant to this Plan to an Employee which is intended to be time vested shall be issued substantially in the form set forth in Exhibit X (not shown), which form is hereby incorporated by reference and made a part hereof, and shall contain substantially the terms and conditions set forth therein. Subject to the authority of the Administrator set forth in Section 3 hereof, Restricted Stock awarded to an individual or entity who or which is not an Employee that is intended to be time vested shall be issued substantially in the form set forth in Exhibit X (not shown), which form is hereby incorporated by reference and made a part hereof, and shall contain substantially the terms and conditions set forth therein. At the time of the Award of Restricted Stock, the Administrator may, in the Administrator's sole discretion, amend or supplement any of the terms contained in Exhibit X (not shown) for any particular individual or entity receiving the Award.

AMENDMENT, SUPPLEMENT, WAIVER AND TERMINATION

The Board may at any time or times amend, supplement, or waive the Plan (or any of the provisions thereof) or any outstanding Award (or any of the provisions thereof) for any purpose that may at the time be permitted by law, and may at any time terminate the Plan as to any future grants of Awards; *provided*, that except as otherwise expressly provided in the Plan, the Board may not, without the Participant's consent, alter the terms of an Award so as to affect adversely the Participant's rights under the Award, unless the Administrator expressly reserved the right to do so at the time of the Award. Any amendments, supplement, waiver or termination to the Plan shall be conditioned upon stockholder approval only to the extent, if any, such approval is required by law (including the Code and applicable stock exchange or trading market requirements), as determined by the Administrator.

OTHER COMPENSATION ARRANGEMENTS

The existence of the Plan or the grant of any Award will not in any way affect the Company's right to award a Participant bonuses or other compensation in addition to Awards under the Plan.

WAIVER OF JURY TRIAL

By accepting an Award under the Plan, each Participant **waives any right to a trial by jury** in any action, proceeding or counterclaim concerning any rights under the Plan and any Award, or under any amendment, waiver, consent, instrument, document or other agreement delivered or which in the future may be delivered in connection therewith. By accepting an Award under the Plan, each Participant certifies that no officer, representative, or attorney of the Company has represented, expressly or otherwise, that the Company would not, in the event of any action, proceeding or counterclaim, seek to enforce the foregoing waiver.

MISCELLANEOUS

(a) No Shareholder Rights

The holder of an Award shall have no rights as a Company shareholder with respect thereto unless, and until the date as of which, shares of Stock are in fact issued upon exercise or in payment with respect to such Award.

(b) Securities Restrictions

No shares of Stock shall be issued, delivered or transferred upon exercise or in payment of any Award granted hereunder unless and until all legal requirements applicable to the issuance, delivery or transfer of such shares have been complied with to the satisfaction of the Administrator, and the Company, including, without limitation, compliance with the provisions of the Securities Act of 1933, the Securities Exchange Act of 1934 and the applicable requirements of the exchanges or trading markets on which the Company's Stock may, at the time, be listed. The Administrator and the Company shall have the right to condition any issuance of shares of Stock made to any Participant hereunder on such Participant's undertaking in writing to comply with such restrictions on his or her subsequent disposition of such shares as the Administrator and/or the Company shall deem necessary or advisable as a result of any applicable law, regulation or official interpretation thereof, and certificates representing such shares may be legended to reflect any such restrictions.

(c) Taxes

The Company shall have the right to deduct from all Awards hereunder paid in cash any federal, state, local, or foreign taxes required by law to be withheld with respect to such cash Awards. In the case of Awards to be distributed in Stock, the Company shall have the right to require, as a condition of such distribution, that the Participant or other person receiving such Stock either (i) pay to the Company at the time of distribution thereof the amount of any such taxes that the Company is required to withhold with respect to such Stock or (ii) make such other arrangements as the Company may authorize from time to time to provide for such withholding including, without limitation, having the number of the units of the Award cancelled or the number of the shares of Stock to be distributed reduced by an amount with a value equal to the value of such taxes required to be withheld.

(d) No Employment Right

No Employee, director, or consultant of the Company, or of any Affiliate of the Company, shall have any claim or right to be granted an Award under this Plan. Neither this Plan nor any action taken hereunder shall be construed as giving any Employee any right to be retained in the employ of the Company or any Affiliate or any director or consultant any right to continue as a director or consultant of the Company or any Affiliate.

(e) Stock to be Used

Distributions of shares of Stock upon exercise, in payment or in respect of Awards made under this Plan may be made either from shares of authorized but unissued Stock reserved for such purpose by the Board or from shares of authorized and issued Stock reacquired by the Company and held in its treasury, as from time to time determined by the Administrator. The obligation of the Company to make delivery of Awards in cash or Stock shall be subject to currency or other restrictions imposed by any government.

(f) Expenses of the Plan

The costs and expenses of administering this Plan shall be borne by the Company or its Affiliates and not charged to any Award or to any Participant.

(g) Plan Unfunded

This Plan shall be unfunded. The Company shall not be required to establish any special or separate fund or to make any other segregation of assets to assure the payment of any Award under this Plan and payment of awards shall be subordinate to the claims of the Company's general creditors.

(h) Corporate Action

Corporate action with respect to an Award to a Participant shall be deemed completed as of the date when the Administrator authorizes the Award, regardless of when the written documentation for the Award is actually delivered to, or acknowledged or agreed to by, the Participant.

(i) Governing Law

This Plan shall be governed by the laws of the state of incorporation of the Company and shall be construed for all purposes in accordance with the laws of such state.

Search Terms Typically Required to be Researched by Public Company in Option Backdating Investigations by the Securities and Exchange Commission

Search Terms

Adjust*	Authoriz* w/10 push*
Alter	Authoriz* w/10 pull*
Approv * w/10 option*	Authoriz* w/10 fix*
Approv* w/10 stock*	Back dat*
Approv* w/10 exercise*	Backdat*
Approv* w/10 sale*	Back-dat*
Approv* w/10 sell*	Cheat*
Approv* w/10 move*	Comp expense
Approv* w/10 change*	Comp meeting
Approv* w/10 alter*	Comp minutes
Approv* w/10 push*	Compensation expense
Approv* w/10 pull*	Compensation meeting
Approv* w/10 fix*	Compensation minutes
Audit*	Coverup
Authoriz* w/10 option*	Cover-up
Authoriz* w/10 stock*	Deceit

(Continued)

Search Terms

Authoriz* w/10 exercise*

Authoriz* w/10 sale*

Authoriz* w/10 sell*

Authoriz* w/10 move*

Authoriz* w/10 change*

Authoriz* w/10 alter*

Fix start date*

Forward dat*

Forward-date*

Fraud*

Full time

Full-time

Grant pric*

Grant* w/10 option*

Grant* w/10 stock*

Grant* w/10 exercise*

Grant* w/10 sale*

Grant* w/10 sell*

Grant* w/10 move*

Grant* w/10 change*

Grant* w/10 alter*

Grant* w/10 push*

Grant* w/10 pull*

Grant* w/10 fix*

Hide

Hire date

Illegal

Improper

In the money

Inapprop*

Inconsistent dat*

Investing*

Issu* w/10 option*

Issu* w/10 stock*

Issu* w/10 exercise*

Issu* w/10 sale*

Issu* w/10 sell*

Issu* w/10 change*

Out of the money

Deceive

Director w/10 hire* or new* or elect*

Don't tell

Fix offer

Fix part time

Fix price

Issu* w/10 move*

Issu* w/10 alter*

Issu* w/10 push*

Issu* w/10 pull*

Issu* w/10 fix*

Leave w/10 unpaid

LOA or ULOA

Misconduct

Misstat*

Mistake

Modified*

Modify*

New employee

New hire

New offer letter

New start dat*

Not ethical

Not legal

Offer letter

Officer w/10 hire* or new* or elect*

Option* AND date w/10 back*

Option* AND date w/10 mov*

Option* AND date w/10 chang*

Option* AND date w/10 pull*

Option* AND date w/10 push

Option* AND date w/10 alter*

Option* AND date w/10 fix*

Option* AND date w/10 low*

Option* AND price w/10 best*

Option* AND price w/10 low*

Option grant

Option pric*

Secret

Part-time

Post dat*

Post-dat*

Pre Dat*

Pre-dat*

Ratif* w/10 option*

Ratif* w/10 stock*

Ratif* w/10 exercise*

Ratif* w/10 sale*

Ratif* w/10 sell*

Ratif* w/10 move*

Ratif* w/10 change*

Ratif* w/10 alter*

Ratif* w/10 push*

Ratif* w/10 pull*

Ratif* w/10 fix*

Redo grant

Redo hire

Redo minute!

Redo offer

Redo part

Repric*

Retro*

Revise*

Scheme

Start date

Start-date

Stock grant*

Stock pric*

Stock* AND date w/10 back*

Stock* AND date w/10 mov*

Stock* AND date w/10 chang*

Stock* AND date w/10 pull*

Stock* AND date w/10 push

Stock* AND date w/10 alter*

Stock* AND date w/10 fix*

Stock* AND date w/10 low*

Stock* AND price w/10 best*

Stock* AND price w/10 low*

Substitut*

Uncomfortable

Under water

Underwater

Unethical

Vest immediately

Vesting pric*

Violat*

VP w/10 hire* or new* or elect*

Wrong

What an Employee Should Know About His or Her Stock Options

This Appendix is designed to be read by employees who have been awarded a stock option.

1. Q. What is an employee stock option?

   A. An employee stock option is a contractual right that is provided by a company to an employee to purchase, at the employee's option during the option term, one or more shares of the company's common stock at a fixed price that is generally equal to the fair market value of the stock at the time of the option grant. Your option form contains an option price at which the stock may be purchased, a time frame (typically up to ten years) during which the option may be exercised, the conditions to exercise and a vesting period. The option becomes valuable to the extent the fair market value of the stock in the company exceeds the option price per share as a result of the appreciation in the value of the stock during the option term.

2. Q. What is the advantage to an employee of a stock option?

   A. If the company's stock appreciates over time, the option holder can exercise the stock option at the lower fixed option price, thereby profiting from the excess of the fair market value of the stock over the option price.

3. Q. Are all stock options the same?

   A. In general, no two stock options are identical. You must carefully read the terms of your stock option to fully understand its terms. If you can afford a lawyer to help you, use a lawyer who is familiar with stock options and their tax consequences. Tax lawyers at large corporate law firms can best help you. If you cannot afford a lawyer, request the company's lawyers to explain the terms of your stock options to you.

4. Q. What is the most important provision of your stock option?

   A. The most important provision of your stock option is when it vests (i.e., when may you first exercise your option). Many options cannot be exercised immediately. The option may require you to continue to be employed by the company for a specified term of years before it can be exercised. For example, an option may be exercisable after one year with respect to 1/3 of the shares subject to the option, with an additional 1/3 being exercisable after each of the second and third years. Other options may require a certain event to occur, such as an initial public offering of the stock of the company or a change of control. Other options require you or the company to meet certain performance goals or profits (e.g., a 15% increase in sales before the option becomes exercisable).

5. Q. How do I exercise my stock option once it becomes exercisable?

   A. Once your option becomes exercisable, you may exercise it by paying cash (or a check) in the amount of the exercise price. Many options also permit you to pay all or a portion of the exercise price in other stock of the company. If your option permits you to use stock to pay the exercise price, the stock is typically valued at its fair market value at the time you surrender the stock certificates to pay the exercise price of the option.

6. Q. Are there any methods to exercise my option that do not require me to pay cash?

   A. Yes. Two common methods are pyramiding and cashless exercises.

7. Q.   What is pyramiding?

 A.   If you do not own any stock in your company, some options permit you to exercise your option for cash and then use that stock as the exercise price for additional stock acquired under your option. This is called "pyramiding."

For example, suppose you have an option to purchase stock at an exercise price of $5 per share and the fair market value of the stock has risen to $25 per share. If you paid $5, you could then acquire one share of stock. You could then surrender that one share of stock (worth $25) to the company in payment of the exercise price of 5 shares of stock. You could then surrender the 5 shares of stock (worth $125) to the company in payment of the exercise price of 25 shares of stock. This could be repeated until your option is fully exercised.

The downside of pyramiding is that if you acquire stock under an incentive stock option and use that stock within one year as the exercise price for other stock to be acquired under your ISO, you will have made a "disqualifying disposition" of the stock that you used as the exercise price, and will recognize ordinary income with respect to the surrendered stock. See question 30.

8. Q.   Can I pyramid my stock options without actually surrendering stock certificates?

 A.   The IRS has issued a private letter ruling that permits pyramiding without actually surrendering your stock certificates. The private letter ruling permits you to use a certification procedure instead of actually surrendering stock certificates. Under the private letter ruling, the shares you already own are called the Payment Shares. If the Payment Shares are held by a registered securities broker for you in "street name," you would provide the company with a notarized statement attesting to the number of shares owned that are intended to serve as Payment Shares. If you actually hold the certificates, you would provide the company with the certificate numbers. Upon receipt of the notarized statement for the Payment Shares from your broker, or upon confirmation of your ownership of the Payment Shares by the company's records, the company could treat the Payment Shares as being constructively exchanged and issue to you a new certificate for the net additional shares due to you, i.e. the number of shares subject to the option exercises less the number of Payment Shares. *Caution*: A private letter ruling issued to another taxpayer need not be honored by the IRS for your option exercise. The certification procedure is only available if the company permits it. The basis and holding period for the plans you acquire is described in Questions 29 and 30.

9. Q. Is there any reason why my company will not permit me to pyramid my option?

A. Many companies will not permit "pyramiding" under their option plans because they may suffer an accounting charge unless you have held the surrendered shares for at least 6 months.

10. Q. What is a cashless exercise?

A. Many public companies will permit cashless exercise. However, cashless exercise is typically not available for the exercise of stock options if the company is still private at the time of exercise.

A cashless exercise involves having a stock broker referred to you by the company sell the stock you acquire under the option simultaneously with your exercise of the option. Your profit, which equals the excess of the sale price over the exercise price (less a brokerage commission), is then remitted to you by the broker, who also pays the option exercise price to the company.

Thus, whether or not pyramiding is permitted under your option, you may never have to pay the cash exercise price if your company is publicly traded and permits cashless exercises.

11. Q. Once my option becomes exercisable, when should I in fact exercise my option?

A. The decision as to when to exercise the option and whether or not to sell the stock you acquire under your option is an investment decision. Sometimes by being too greedy you can lose the stock appreciation that has already been realized.

Your option allows you to profit from any appreciation in the stock for the full term of your option grant. Many employees who are entitled to exercise their stock options choose not to do so until close to the expiration date of their options in order to obtain the maximum benefit from their option. This permits them to have the benefit of the "free ride" on the stock for a longer term, i.e., you don't have to exercise the option to obtain the benefit of any appreciation in the value of the stock. However, if you need cash and wait too long to exercise the option and sell the stock, there might not be enough time for the stock to recover from a temporary decline in value.

12. Q. Is the receipt of my stock option subject to any federal income tax?

A. No. The grant of an option to you will generally not result in the receipt of any federal income for federal income tax purposes, although an exception may apply if the exercise price of the option is less than the fair market value of the stock on the date of grant. Although state and local income taxes generally do not apply to the grant of a stock option, you must check with your personal tax advisor to make certain that you are not in a state or local jurisdiction that taxes option grants.

13. Q. When my option becomes vested and becomes exercisable, am I subject to any federal income tax?

A. No. The earliest time you would normally be subjected to tax is upon actual exercise of your option, although an exception may apply if the exercise price of the option is less than the fair market value of the stock on the date of grant.

14. Q. What is an incentive stock option?

A. There are two types of options that you may have received:
   • incentive stock options (ISOs)
   • non–incentive stock options (non–ISOs) (non–ISOs are also called nonqualified or nonstatutory stock options)

   The difference between ISOs and non–ISOs are in the federal income tax consequences to you. Both ISOs and non–ISOs may be identical in all other respects, including the duration of the option, the exercisability provisions and the exercise price.

15. Q. How can I tell whether I have an ISO or a non-ISO?

    A. The easy way is to ask your employer.

    If your option states that it is not intended to be an incentive stock option, the Internal Revenue Code will honor that statement. If your option fails any of the tests for an ISO, it will be treated as a non-ISO regardless of what is stated in the option. For example, if your option has a term in excess of 10 years or an option exercise price that is below the fair market value on the grant date (with a minor exception), it will be treated as a non-ISO. There are a number of other tests for an ISO and flunking any of them will cause your option to be treated as a non-ISO.

16. Q. What are the federal income tax benefits of an ISO?

    A. If you received an ISO, there will be no ordinary income tax at the time of exercise. However, the exercise may trigger alternative minimum tax for certain employees. Therefore, you must consult your tax adviser before exercising an incentive stock option. Even if you are subject to alternative minimum tax, you can avoid paying that tax if you sell or make another disqualifying disposition of the stock before the last day of the year in which you exercise your stock option. However, if you do so, you will be taxed similarly to a non-ISO as described below.

    If you hold the stock acquired upon exercise of an ISO for at least one year from the exercise date, the appreciation above the exercise price when you do sell the stock will be considered long-term capital gains provided you satisfy two additional requirements:

    • You do not sell or make another disqualifying disposition of the stock for two years after the option grant date

    • You were an employee on the grant date and continued to be an employee when you exercised the option or you exercised the option not more than three months after your employment terminated (one year in the case of death or certain kinds of disability)

17. Q. What is the federal income tax benefit to me of having long-term capital gains on the stock appreciation?

A. Ordinary compensation income can be taxed up to a maximum rate of 35% for federal income tax purposes. However, long-term capital gains is only taxed at a maximum rate of 15%.[1]

18. Q. What happens if I exercise an incentive stock option but fail to hold the stock until one year after the exercise date and two years after the grant date?

A. If you have an incentive stock option, but fail to hold it until at least one year after the exercise date and two years after the grant date, you will be treated on sale or other "disqualifying disposition" as if you exercised a non-ISO, subject to one minor exception discussed below. The stock appreciation from the grant date will in general be taxed as ordinary compensation income.

19. Q. What is a disqualifying disposition?

A. A sale of stock acquired under an ISO within one year after exercise of the option or within two years after grant of the option is a disqualifying disposition and changes potential long-term capital gain into ordinary income.

However, other types of transfers may or may not be disqualifying dispositions:

- Death is not a disqualifying disposition.
- A transfer of ISO stock to your spouse – or to a former spouse in connection with a divorce – is not a disqualifying disposition.
- All gifts to non-spouses are disqualifying dispositions.
- A transfer of a stock certificate to a broker who will hold it in street name is not a disqualifying disposition.
- The IRS takes the position that a short sale of your company's stock while you hold ISO stock is a disqualifying disposition.
- Using ISO stock as collateral for a loan is not a disqualifying disposition.

---

[1] All tax rates are based upon those in effect at September 1, 2007.

20. Q.   If I make a disqualifying disposition of stock I acquired under my ISO, what are the federal income tax consequences?

   A.   If you make a sale or other disqualifying disposition within one year after the exercise of an ISO or within two years after the grant of an ISO, you will be considered to have realized ordinary income on the date of the sale or other disqualifying disposition. The IRS does not require federal income tax withholding in connection with a sale or another disqualifying disposition, but you may have to file a declaration of estimated tax. Consult your personal tax advisor.

   The amount of the income realized by you on the sale or other disqualifying disposition is computed as follows:

   • If you sell the shares for an amount less than your exercise price (a catastrophe!), you do not report any compensation income for federal income tax purposes and your loss is reported as a capital loss.

   • If you sold the shares for an amount above your exercise price, but not higher than the fair market value of the shares on the date of exercise, you report your gain as compensation income.

   • If you sell your shares at a price that is higher than the fair market value of your shares on the exercise date, you report two different items. The excess of the fair market value of your shares on the date of the ISO exercise over the exercise price is reported as ordinary compensation income. Any additional gain is reported as capital gain, which may be long-term or short-term depending on how long you held the stock.

   For example, suppose you exercise your ISO on January 1, 2007, at an exercise price of $5 per share and at that time the fair market value of the stock was $25 per share. You then sell the stock on February 1, 2007, for $27 per share. You would recognize ordinary compensation income of $20 per share on February 1, 2007 and a short term capital gain of $2 per share.

   If you made a disqualifying disposition on February 1, 2007, other than a sale (e.g., a gift to your child) within one year after ISO exercise or within two years after ISO grant, you have to report $20 per share as ordinary compensation income on February 1, 2007. This is true even if the value of the stock had gone down after the date you exercised your ISO. If the disqualifying disposition involves a sale to a related person other than your spouse, any gain that exceeds the $20 figure would be treated as short-term capital gain.

21. Q. Is there any limit on the amount of long-term capital gains I can receive from my ISO?

    A. Technically there is no limit. However, there is a $100,000 limit on the number of shares that will be treated as ISO shares each year in which your option is first exercisable. If your option exercise price multiplied by the number of shares subject to your option does not exceed $100,000, the limit is not applicable to you.

22. Q. If my stock option exceeds the $100,000 limit, how do I compute the maximum number of shares that will be treated as ISO shares?

    A. The number of option shares that will be treated as ISO shares is computed by dividing into $100,000 the option price per share for the shares that first become exercisable in any calendar year. For example, suppose you have an option for shares at an exercise price of $20 per share which becomes first exercisable as follows: 5000 shares in 2007; 8000 shares in 2008. The 5000 shares first exercisable in 2007 are all ISO shares since 5000 × $20 does not exceed $100,000. However, of the 8000 shares first exercisable in 2008, only 5000 will qualify as ISO shares; the remaining 3000 will not qualify since $100,000 divided by $20 per share equals 5000 shares.

    If your rate of first exercisability never exceeds $100,000 in any calendar year, all of your shares will be treated as ISO shares.

23. Q. Under what circumstances can I be subject to alternative minimum tax upon exercising an ISO?

    A. The exercise of an ISO may trigger federal and state alternative minimum tax. Alternative minimum tax is a separate tax from regular income tax and was intended by Congress to close loopholes in the regular tax system for the wealthy. Unfortunately, the federal alternative minimum tax is affecting more people who are not wealthy and who are obtaining profits from ISOs. There is no easy method of determining whether you will or will not be liable for these taxes without consulting a tax adviser who will perform a computation for you.

A simple method of avoiding AMT is to project, with the help of a tax professional, your taxable income for both regular and AMT taxes for the tax year before exercising your ISO. Use Form 1040 (regular tax) and Form 6251 (alternative minimum tax) to perform this calculation. Determine your regular tax (assume $40,000) and your alternative minimum tax (assume $30,000). Subtract the difference ($10,000) then divide the $10,000 by the AMT tax rate of 26% ($38,462) assuming 26% is your applicable AMT rate. Divide the $38,462 by the spread (assume $10) = 3,846 shares may be exercised without triggering the AMT.

Regular Tax (Form 1040)	$40,000
AMT (Form 6251)	$30,000
Difference	$10,000
Divide by AMT rate (26%)	$38,462
Divide by Spread per share	$10
Maximum Number of Shares that may be exercised without AMT	3,846

24. Q. If I am potentially subject to federal alternative minimum tax upon exercising an ISO, is there any way I can be certain that I will never have to pay the federal alternative minimum tax?

A. You can avoid paying any federal alternative minimum tax (AMT) by selling the ISO stock during the taxable year in which you exercised your ISO.

25. Q. What is the maximum federal alternative minimum tax rate and how does it work?

A. The maximum rate for federal alternative minimum tax is 28% (26% on the first $175,000 for married couples, $87,500 for married couples filing separately). If your ISO profit is small, the chances are that you will not be subject to alternative mini-mum tax because of the AMT exemption: $62,550 for joint filers, $42,500 for singles, and $31,275 for married couples fil-ing separately. However, this exemption is reduced by 25 cents for each dollar of AMT taxable income above $150,000 for couples ($112,500 for singles and $75,000 for married couples filing separately); filling out Form 6251 with the help of a tax professional is the only way to tell for certain. The payment of federal alternative minimum tax may permit you to obtain a credit in future years when you are not subject to this tax. Potentially, this credit applicable to future federal income taxes may permit you to eventually recover all of the federal alterna-tive minimum tax that you paid for the year in which you exercised your ISO. In addition, there are some benefits in computing your tax basis for the ISO stock for purposes of computing federal alternative minimum tax in the future.

The amount of your federal alternative minimum tax is also used in determining how much estimated federal income tax you have to declare and pay during the tax year.

26. Q. How are non-ISOs taxed?
   A. If your option is not an incentive stock option, you will be deemed to have received taxable compensatory income on the date you exercise your option in an amount equal to the excess of the fair market value of the stock on that date over the option exercise price. For example, if your option has an exer-cise price of $5 per share and the fair market value of the stock on the date of exercise is $25 per share, you will, upon exercis-ing your non-ISO, be deemed to have received $20 per share in compensation, taxable as ordinary income.

27. Q. Is federal income tax withholding required to be paid upon exercise of a non-ISO?
   A. Yes. The ordinary income realized by you upon exercise of a non-ISO is subject to federal income tax withholding, in amounts up to a maximum of 35%. In the previous example, you would be subject to federal tax withholding on the $20 per share com-pensation income of up to $5.60 per share (up to a maximum of

35% of $20). Therefore, in the previous example, you must be prepared to pay both the $5 exercise price and up to $5.60 in federal tax withholding. This is not a problem if you are permitted a "cashless" exercise, since the broker would pay the company both the $5 exercise price and the $5.60 withholding.

However, if your company is not public on the date of exercise or does not permit a cashless exercise price, you must be prepared to pay both the $5 exercise price plus the $5.60 tax withholding at the time of exercise.

28. Q.   Can federal income withholding be paid by surrendering my own stock?

A.   Some companies permit you to pay your exercise price and federal income tax withholding with other stock of the company, including stock you acquired on exercising your option. You must carefully check your option to see if this is permitted. Any stock you use to pay your federal income tax withholding may be subject to tax. Consult your tax adviser for more information. If you use stock acquired under an ISO to pay for your federal income tax withholding upon exercise of your non-ISO, this use is considered a disposition of your ISO stock and may constitute a "disqualifying disposition."

29. Q.   If I use stock to exercise my non-ISO, what are the federal income tax consequences?

A.   If you use other company stock to exercise your non-ISO, you are treated as having made a tax free exchange of old shares for an equal number of new shares (the "Tax Free Shares") and received additional shares (the "Extra Shares") for zero payment. The Tax Free Shares have the same basis and holding period as the shares you turned in. However, the fair market value of the Extra Shares are taxable as ordinary compensation income to you. They take a basis equal to the amount of income you realized and your holding period begins on your exercise date. If you use shares you owned from the previous exercise of an ISO, the exchange *will not* be treated as a disqualifying disposition of the ISO stock and the Tax Free Shares will continue to be ISO shares and must be held for the balance of the one year period after the exercise (or two years after grant). Example: You have a non–ISO to purchase 1000 shares at $5 per share (a total of $5000). You exercise the option by turning in 250 shares having a fair market value of $20 per share on the exercise date. You would receive 250 Tax Free Shares having the same basis and holding period as the shares you surrendered, plus 750 shares with a basis of $20 per share and a holding period that begins when you exercised the non-ISO. You would recognize income of $15,000, the value of the Extra Shares. The same result would apply even if you surrendered as the exercise price shares that you originally acquired under an ISO and held for less than one year.

30. Q. If I use stock to exercise my ISO, what are the federal income tax consequences?

A. The tax law treats the use of such ISO stock ("Immature Shares") as a disqualifying disposition of the ISO stock you used as the exercise price. The law does not reduce your reported income even though the old ISO stock has declined in value since the date of the prior ISO exercise. The shares you receive on exercise of the ISO are divided into the two groups: a number of shares equal to the number of surrendered shares (the "Tax Free Shares") and the additional shares (the "Extra Shares"). The Tax Free Shares have the same basis as the old ISO shares that had not satisfied their holding period that you surrendered, increased by the amount of income you reported because of the disqualifying disposition. The Tax Free Shares have the same holding period as the shares you turn in, but only for the purpose of determining whether any subsequent capital gain or loss or a sale is short term or long term. For purposes of determining whether you satisfied the one year after exercise (or two years after grant) holding period for the Tax Free Shares, your holding period begins on the exercise date.

The Extra Shares have a basis equal to any cash you paid on exercise and, if you paid no cash, your Extra Shares will probably have a zero basis. The Extra Shares are subject to the special holding periods applicable to ISO stock.

If you use old ISO stock that has satisfied the holding period (so-called "Mature Shares") or other shares, your federal income tax results are more favorable. No income is recognized on the exercise of the ISO for regular federal income tax purposes. The shares you receive are divided into two groups:

- the first group equals the number of shares you exchanged (the "Exchange Shares")
- the second group equals all extra shares (the "Extra Shares")

The Exchange Shares have the same federal income tax basis as the shares you turn in and the same holding period for purposes of determining whether a subsequent sale purchased long-term or short-term capital gain or loss. However, your holding period for the Exchange Shares for purposes of determining subsequent disqualifying dispositions starts on the exercise date on which the Exchange Shares were acquired.

The Extra Shares have a basis equal to any share you used to exercise the ISO and therefore your basis would probably be zero. The holding period for the Extra Shares starts on the exercise date for all purposes, including determining whether or not you made a disqualifying disposition.

This description is not intended to cover AMT consequences previously discussed.

31. Q. Is there any state and local income tax on the exercise of a stock option?

A. Before exercising your stock option, you must check applicable state and local taxes. Just because your exercise of an ISO is not subject to federal income tax, that does not mean that it is free of state or local income tax. For example, if you live in California you can expect to pay a hefty amount of state alternative minimum tax on top of any federal alternative minimum tax when you exercise an ISO.

If you are subject to both federal and state alternative minimum tax on the exercise of an ISO, proper timing of the payment of state taxes can reduce the amount of the federal alternative minimum tax you pay, or increase the amount of federal alternative minimum tax that qualifies for a credit.

You should consult a tax advisor before exercising your stock option.

32. Q. If I die, how long does my estate have to exercise my ISO and still obtain the federal income tax benefits of an ISO?

A. The Internal Revenue Code permits exercise of an ISO up to one year from the date of your death in order to obtain the federal income tax benefits of an ISO, but the option contract also needs to allow such an exercise. Most options do in fact also permit a one year period after death for the exercise to occur. However, you should carefully examine your own option form to make certain that the exercise period is not shorter than one year.

33. Q. If I am disabled and must leave employment, how long do I have to exercise my ISO and still obtain the federal income tax benefits of an ISO?

A. The Internal Revenue Code permits you to exercise your ISO up to one year after the date of your disability and still obtain the federal income tax benefits of an ISO, provided your disability meets the requirements of the Internal Revenue Code. In order to take advantage of the one year period, the Internal Revenue Code requires that your disability be "permanent and total." An individual is considered permanently and totally disabled if he or she is unable to engage in any substantial gainful activity by reason of any medically determinable physical or mental impairment that can be expected to result in death or that has lasted or can be expected to last for a continuous period of not less than 12 months. Your option should be checked to make sure that your employer is allowing you the full one year period permitted under the Internal Revenue Code.

34. Q. If I own ISO shares acquired on different dates, how can I be certain that I only sell the ISO shares that have satisfied the one year holding period?

A. If you do not specify which shares you are selling, the tax law treats you as if you had sold the earliest shares you bought. This may not be in your interest because your earliest shares might have a lower option exercise price (and hence larger long-term capital gains potential) than ISO shares which you acquired at a later time which have also satisfied the one year holding period.

To be certain that you are selling the ISO shares that will give you the best tax result, you must identify the specific certificates that you wish to sell, and if you do not have certificates, instruct your broker in writing as to the specific shares you wish to sell.

For example, suppose you purchased 100 ISO shares at $10.00 per share on January 1, 2007, and purchased another 100 ISO shares at $12.00 per share on January 1, 2008, and wish to sell 100 shares in 2009. It may be in your best tax interest to sell the shares that were purchased on January 1, 2008. These shares have a higher tax basis, namely $12.00 per share, then the shares purchased on January 1, 2007.

If you are using a broker to sell your shares, you should instruct your broker to sell the 100 shares that were acquired by you on January 1, 2008, and, if you possess the certificates, deliver the certificate representing those shares to the broker.

35. Q. Can I be required to declare and pay estimated federal and state income taxes in connection with my stock option?

A. Since the grant of a stock option to you does not normally subject you to any federal or state income tax, you do not have to be concerned about filing declarations or paying estimated tax on the grant date. This assumes that the exercise price of the option is not less than the fair market value on the stock on the grant date. However, if the exercise of your stock option or the subsequent sale or disqualifying disposition of the stock required under the option creates regular taxable income, capital gains or alternative minimum tax, you may be obligated to make a declaration of estimated tax and to pay that tax under both federal and state income tax laws.

If you fail to make a declaration and pay estimated taxes when due, the IRS can assess interest and penalties. You can avoid interest and penalties by increasing the income tax withholding on your salary or wages from your employer in an amount sufficient to cover any estimated taxes due for the relevant calendar year.

If you qualify for certain safe harbors provided by the Internal Revenue Code, you can void interest and penalties for failure to make declarations and pay estimated taxes. These safe harbors include the following:

- If your federal income taxes due are less than $1,000.
- If your estimated income tax payments, when added to your income tax withholding and credits equal 90% or more of your current year's tax liability.
- If your estimated income tax payments, when added to income tax withholding and credits, equals 100% of your prior year's income taxes. However, this safe harbor is not applicable if your adjusted gross income for the preceding taxable year exceeds $150,000, in which case the 100% rises to 110%.

36. Q. If I am terminated by my employer without cause, can I still exercise my option?

    A. Most option plans permit an employee who is terminated without cause to exercise their option for a period of time after the termination, typically three months. You must examine your specific option to determine whether it contains this right.

Some options also permit employees to exercise their option following termination of their employment for any reason, typically limited to a three-month period after termination. Again you must examine your specific option.

Some options will not be exercisable after the date you are terminated for cause by your employer. This provision sometimes leads to a race between the employer and the employee. If the employee submits his or her exercise notice, together with appropriate payment, before the actual time of termination, the employee would generally win the race. This might happen, for example, if the employee hears rumors that he or she is about to be fired and decides to exercise his or her option in advance.

37. Q. Can I sell the stock I acquire under my stock option immediately after I exercise my option?

    A. If the stock that you acquire under your option is publicly traded and if the stock is either registered by your employer under the

Securities Act of 1933 or exempt from such registration, you can sell your stock immediately after you exercise your option, provided there are no contractual restrictions on such resale contained in your stock option. Many stock options contain contractual restrictions on its resale. For example, if your company is engaged in a public offering at the time of your option exercise, the underwriter might require all optionees to enter into "lock-up agreements" that prevent the resale of the stock for a period of time, typically 6 months.

If the stock you acquire under your option is not publicly traded, there may be no one to repurchase the stock from you. Likewise, if your stock is not registered under the Securities Act of 1933 or exempt from such registration, you will not be able to resell the stock except in a private placement, which might include a resale to the company or one of its principal shareholders.

38. Q. If my company's stock is not publicly traded at the time I exercise my stock option, how can I profit by exercising my stock option?

A. Many private companies will agree to repurchase some or all the shares acquired under stock options to provide liquidity to the employee. Sometimes the principal shareholders will do so.

You should not exercise your stock option if your company's stock is not publicly traded without first determining what resale rights you will have. Many times the resale rights will be contained in a shareholders agreement that you are required to execute prior to exercising your stock option.

39. Q. If I am required to execute a shareholders agreement in order to exercise my stock option, what are the typical provisions contained in the shareholders agreement?

A. A typical shareholders agreement will contain the following provisions:

• A provision preventing you from selling or otherwise transferring your stock without consent and subject to rights of first refusal

- A provision preventing you from pledging your stock without consent
- A provision for repurchasing your stock in the event of your death
- A provision for repurchasing your stock in the event your employment terminates
- A provision requiring you to execute lock-up agreements with underwriters of public offerings of the company's stock
- A provision prohibiting you, after your employment terminates, from soliciting customers or employees of the company for a competitive business

There is no standard shareholders agreement and you must carefully review the exact terms of any shareholders agreement that you are requested to execute as a condition of exercising your stock option.

40. Q. What is a transferable stock option?

A. Some employers will issue options that are transferable during the lifetime of the employee. These options do not qualify as ISOs because they violate the requirement that ISOs can only be transferable by will or by the laws of descent and distribution after the employee's death.

The main reason that an employee would desire a transferable stock option is to use the stock option as a wealth transfer device to other family members, typically children or grandchildren, in order to reduce death taxes. If a stock option is transferred to a child in order to reduce death taxes, and the child exercises the option, the option profit is still taxed to the employee who received the option. Therefore, unless you have significant wealth apart from the option with which to pay the federal and state income taxes resulting from the option exercise by your child, you will not want a transferable option.

Index